LADIES MAN

LADIES MAN

An Autobiography

by Paul Henreid

with Julius Fast

St. Martin's Press
New York

Editor: Toni Lopopolo
Assistant Editor: Karen Johnsen
Managing Editor: Carol E.W. Edwards
Copyeditor: Erika Schmid

Library of Congress Cataloging in Publication Data

Henreid, Paul.
  Ladies man.

  "Filmography": p.
  Includes index.
  1. Henreid, Paul. 2. Actors—United States—Biography
  3. Moving-picture producers and directors—United States—
Biography. I. Fast, Julius, 1918-   II. Title.
PN2287.H427A34 1984   792'.028'0924 [B] 83-21134
ISBN 0-312-46384-7

Design by Lee Wade

First Edition
10 9 8 7 6 5 4 3 2 1

This book is dedicated to

Lisl
my very much loved wife
since 1936.

Ich liebe Dich so wie Du mich,
Vom Abend bis zum Morgen
Da war kein Tag wo Du und ich
Nicht teilten unsere Sorgen.
Auch waren sie für Dich und mich
Geteilt leicht zu ertragen:
Du tröstetest im Kummer mich,
Ich weint' in Deine Klagen.
Drum Gottes Segen über Dir,
Du meines Lebens Freude,
Gott schütze Dich, erhalt Dich mir,
Schütz and erhalt uns Beide!

Contents

A section of photographs follows page 118.

LADIES MAN

One *e*

◆

The Early Years

On my thirteenth birthday my friend Richard, speaking from the sophisticated maturity of fifteen, said, "You're a man now, Paul. You've come of age."

"You're certainly as big as a man," my other friend, Alexander, said with a touch of envy.

Richard frowned and put up one hand for silence. A leader in our school and a friend of mine in spite of the two years' difference in our ages, Richard had taken me aside with Alexander. "We are going to give you a real treat," he said, smiling benignly and putting one arm around my shoulders. "This afternoon we're taking you out for a surprise birthday present."

It was a Sunday afternoon, that January 10, 1921, a cold, wintry day in Vienna, the one day in the week our boarding school allowed its students to leave the grounds. So the three of us sallied forth onto the icy streets, my two friends, both sons of rich families, insisting that they would pay the way but at the same time refusing to answer any of my excited questions about where we were headed. It was, "You'll see." "This will be the treat of your life!" And, "The evening's on us."

We took a taxi to the center of town, and when we arrived at the address Richard gave I stared in excited wonder at the palatial rococo building. "Come on!" Richard paid the taxi and strode up to the door, with Alexander and me lagging a few steps behind. Richard, with cool assurance, knocked, and the door was opened by a liveried servant. Before I could catch my breath, the three of us were ushered into the parlor of Vienna's most elegant bordello.

"Gentlemen! Come in, come in." An older woman in a black gown with elbow-length white gloves, bare shoulders and a daring décolletage smiled at us rather hungrily. "Such handsome young gentlemen! Come in and sit down."

"Richard, where are we?" I gasped as we followed the woman into the next room, an elaborately ornate salon filled with well-dressed men and with women—young women, some half-naked, some completely naked, and a few with gauzy wrappers that seemed even more revealing than no clothes at all. We were immediately offered champagne and small sandwiches, and I accepted it all wonderingly.

"This is our birthday present to you, your first experience," Richard whispered. "Now act as if you know your way around."

"But I don't!" I said, my throat dry with a mixture of sheer terror and adolescent lust. I didn't dare stare at the girls, and yet I couldn't avoid them. They were everywhere, and each one was smiling at me, I thought.

"Perhaps you'd like to see some pictures first," the woman who had ushered us in suggested. "Just to arouse your interest. I know how jaded you young gentlemen are."

I looked at her quickly to see if she was making fun of us, but there was only a warm, maternal smile on her face. She led us into a darkened room where a flickering projector showed an Edwardian version of a blue movie. In its way it was very charming.

Two young girls with parasols wander through the Luxembourg Gardens, gardens filled with nude statutes of men, women and fauns. Suddenly one of the girls closes her parasol and, giggling, reaches it up to touch the penis of one of the lusty male nudes. The statue comes to life, leaps down from his pedestal, and leads the girl into the bushes. Then, discretely filmed through the leaves, the two have intercourse.

It literally stunned me. I had never seen anything like it. My total experience of pornography had been limited to a few whispered stories after lights-out at school and some well-thumbed picture postcards—and now this!

"Would you gentlemen like to select some of our lovely young ladies now?" the maternal madam suggested in a coaxing tone.

It was our moment of truth—and we all failed. For all the

sophisticated talk, Richard and Alexander had had no more experience than I. They had pooled their allowance to pay the madam for the evening, but now their courage failed. As the three of us came out of the dark room into the salon of eager ladies, we looked at one another in sheer terror. The women were everywhere, smiling at us, leaning against us, even caressing us suggestively. And we three? How did we react? We swallowed and, without another word, headed for the door. Alexander paid our bill—the refreshments were not on the house, as we had naively thought—and then we left the place at a run and kept running till we got to the school grounds.

My actual introduction to sex came a few years later. My aunt Grete's parents had a country estate in the southern part of Austria, and I was invited to spend a summer there. I was just fifteen, and I had a splendid vacation riding through the woods on horseback, playing tennis, and helping with the farm work.

My aunt had a young son and had hired a governess for him, a pretty blond Polish girl with whom I instantly fell in love. For most of the summer I admired her only from a distance, being too shy to talk to her, but every night she filled my sexual fantasies.

Then, one afternoon after lunch, I walked out to the edge of the woods, where I stretched out under a cherry tree and fell asleep. I woke up when a cherry hit my face and I looked up to see my Polish love smiling down from the tree and dropping cherries on me. From where I lay I could see her thighs, white and lovely, and between them the source of all my sleepless nights. She wore no panties.

Should I pretend to be asleep? But she must have seen me open my eyes, and she remained sitting up in the tree, making no attempt to cover herself. Finally I sat up, hoping I wouldn't betray my embarrassing eagerness.

"Won't you come down?" I asked, my voice breaking.

She climbed down and dropped onto the grass beside me. I tried to grab her in my arms, but she drew back, saying, "Gently, Pauli, gently." Then, with a great deal of patience on her part, we made love there on the grass under the cherry tree. It put a perfect touch to a perfect summer, repeated daily wherever and whenever we could, and I returned to school in the fall considering myself a man of the world.

The school I attended then, in the early nineteen twenties, was the Maria Theresianische Akademie, founded for the sons of the Austrian aristocracy by the empress Maria Theresia. It was a school intended as a pathway into the diplomatic service.

In one way, my brother and I qualified for entrance. We belonged to the Austrian aristocracy. My father, a banker, had been knighted for his services to the emperor, Franz Josef I, and my mother, though without a title herself, came from a titled family on her mother's side. But in a much more basic way neither my brother nor I belonged there. We simply could not afford the tuition.

My father had died in 1916, when I was eight years old, leaving a sizable fortune. My mother, wishing to be near her own parents, had moved to an apartment in Krems, a town on the Danube. Her parents owned a castle called Senftenberg, a magnificent old pile of a place. My grandmother, a regal lady, had an Austro-Daimler, a phaeton model, and I loved her madly, though to tell the truth I was never sure how much of my love for my grandmother was based on that car.

Grandma adored boiled beef and claimed that the only restaurant that could make it properly was in Vienna, so at least twice a month she and her woman friends would put on white dusters, goggles, hats and gloves and drive the phaeton into Vienna for their boiled-beef fix, and often, to my delight, she'd take me along.

I attended a grammar school in Krems then, and our family lived well. My mother, with no desire for business and no talent for it, left the management of her money to her brother-in-law Otto. Under my uncle Otto's mismanagement, and during the postwar inflation, her fortune was whittled down. The money my mother received grew less and less. With the government's final, extraordinary inflation, we three, my mother, my brother Robert, and I, were left practically penniless. The apartment in Krems became too expensive and we moved back to Vienna to share an apartment with an old friend of my mother.

Although my mother had been brought up in luxury and had

never had to concern herself with money during my father's lifetime, she decided, once she recovered from the shock of our condition, to go to work and support the family. "We will not be dependent on anyone's charity," she told us firmly. Unfortunately, although she was an attractive woman, well educated, experienced at entertaining royalty and running an elaborate estate, she had absolutely no job skills.

"It doesn't matter, children," she said cheerfully. "I'm willing to work."

Willing she was, but to work at what? One firm after another turned her down. No experience. Too old. We don't hire women. "But you mustn't worry," she assured us. "I will find something!"

And to our surprise she did. She found a job eminently suited to her ability. She went to work for the largest perfume manufacturer in Vienna, a sort of "hostess" in an elegant store in the city where most of the customers were old friends and she treated them as if they were guests in her own home, with charm and intimacy. The store was delighted with her, but although her salary was raised, it couldn't keep pace with Austria's runaway inflation, and the three of us struggled along at a subsistence level, dependent for any extras, in spite of my mother's resolve, on the charity of my uncles.

When my younger brother Robert and I were ready for the *Gymnasium* (high school), my mother decided it was time to call in some of the favors my father had done. "Your father was a generous man," she told us. "Now let's see if his generosity will be returned."

She went to the director of the Theresianische Akademie, a man indebted to my father, and with consummate nerve she asked if there were any scholarships for deserving young men, and if there were none, didn't he think it was an excellent idea to start two for my brother and me?

Very graciously Dr. von Matlachowski, the director, said, "Frau von Hernried, for your sons there will always be scholarships at the Theresianium!"

And so I started school, and my brother Robert started two years later, two scholarship students in among the wealthiest young aristocrats in Vienna. I must say, however, that in addition to being wealthy my schoolmates were extremely decent young men, and at no time was I made aware of my own poverty. The truth is, the students at the Theresianium were all social snobs, and the thing that mattered to them was background, not wealth. The "von" in our name came in very handy.

After World War I, when Austria became a democracy, the "von" was abolished from all legal documents, but it has persisted in common use to this day. An aristocracy is hard to eradicate.

Unfortunately, although I was readily accepted by the students, my schoolwork was another matter. At the end of my third year, I found myself failing in three subjects—Latin, Greek, and math— and I was told I'd have to repeat the whole year. My mother, who had gone to such trouble to get me the scholarship, was very disappointed in me.

"I just don't understand you," she said distractedly, and she called my uncle Otto over to talk to me "man to man." Otto was the oldest brother now that my father was dead, and he was the nominal head of the family. "Paul needs a father to set him straight," she told Uncle Otto.

"The boy needs more than a father," my uncle said in disgust after speaking to my teachers and reviewing my grades. "He's obviously an idiot and has no business in a school like this. He should be apprenticed to a carpenter or a shoemaker!"

My mother couldn't accept that, nor could my uncle Rudi, my father's second-youngest brother, a much more understanding and progressive man than Otto. "I think his problem is psychological," Uncle Rudi decided; "He probably has a will to fail." And he insisted that I go to see his good friend, Dr. Alfred Adler, the renowned Viennese psychiatrist.

Like all doctors in Vienna in those days, the famous Dr. Adler practiced in his own house, a very comfortable house that smelled of excellent food, of cooked meat and garlic. I liked Dr. Adler from the start. He was a roly-poly man, not too tall, but with a full beard. He wore a gray suit and across his vest hung a heavy gold chain. His immaculately white collar was stiff with starch, but there was nothing stiff in his manner.

"Sit down, sit down," he told me after I had been ushered into his office, and he came around his desk to sit next to me on a small settee. "Do you like coffee?"

I thought, this is more like it, and I nodded, and he rang a bell and a pretty young housemaid came in with a tray of coffee and Gugelhupf, a delicious Viennese coffee cake. "So you failed three subjects." Dr. Adler shook his head and, leaning close to me, said, "Don't worry. When I was your age I flunked math, too. Don't tell anyone, but believe me, math is nothing. Now tell me about yourself," he said, brushing some crumbs from his beard and ample belly. "Do you play soccer? Were you on the team at school?"

The questions were gentle, disarming, and yet, I realize now, very thorough. They covered my life at school and at home, my feelings about my mother and my dead father and even my dreams. I answered readily, completely comfortable with the interview, more concerned with the delicious Gugelhupf than with any probing questions.

Afterward Dr. Adler called my uncle Rudi and informed him that I was perfectly normal. "What the boy needs is some motivation," he told him. "Then, too, have you ever considered that Paul simply may not like Latin, Greek or math?" What you must do is motivate him to work harder at these studies. You can rest assured that he isn't a slow boy."

When Uncle Otto heard this diagnosis, he frowned and said, "If I had my way, I'd motivate him with a cane against his backside!"

But punishment wasn't necessary. Having to repeat the grade was punishment enough, and to my mother's pleasure I passed all three subjects. The work was difficult, but I graduated from the Theresianium with an excellent education, having passed the final exam, the "Matura," which meant that I was automatically admitted to the university.

"In ordinary times," my mother told me sadly, "you could take a year off now and travel, go on a world tour, but we are in no position to afford it. What would you like to do, Paul?"

"One of two things," I told her. "Either medicine or acting."
I had been introduced to acting by my German professor, Dr. Frank

Miklautz. Tall and ugly, Dr. Miklautz looked like an enormous owl, but he was a delightful and brilliant man. In addition to teaching German, he was in charge of dramatics, and something about me, my appearance or perhaps some latent ability, attracted his attention. He put me in every play he produced and introduced me to the work of Goethe and Schiller and planted an abiding love of the stage in my heart.

After my last year at the Theresianium I became a "theatre bum," saving up all my allowance and every spare cent I could borrow or cadge to attend the theatre or opera, usually sitting in the farthest gallery or standing in the rear. Indeed, in the years before I went to the Theatrical Academy I learned the scores to ten operas and the texts in four languages.

But acting as a career was not to be considered for anyone from a decent family. As my uncle Otto said angrily, "Acting and syphilis are on the same rung of the social ladder."

Uncle Rudi, more tolerant, also opposed the idea. "Suppose you find out that you haven't any talent for it and all you ever get is a walk-on, the man who comes on stage and says, 'The horse is saddled.' Do you want to spend your life doing that?" He shook his head. "Paul, do something where you can be assured of making a living, and then if you wish you can study acting on the side, go to the academy at night."

"Yes, I think a doctor would be much more sensible," my mother said gently. "After all, we've never had an actor in the family."

And so I started premedical studies at the university. With the last bit of our money, my mother bought a small apartment where we three could live. We couldn't afford servants, but we did manage a cleaning woman. My university life, however, lasted less than a year. Inflation continued and work became difficult for my mother as she began to suffer from a painful case of varicose veins. There seemed no other solution but for me to leave school and get a job.

"But what kind of job?" my mother protested when I told her my plan. It was at another family conference with Uncle Rudi, but fortunately without Uncle Otto. It had become more and more apparent to my mother that Otto had mismanaged our family fortune. When a financial transaction went well, it was his money; when it went bad, it was ours.

"There is a man your father once helped," Uncle Rudi said thoughtfully, "a Robert Rosenbaum—a very decent fellow. He was in financial trouble and your father's help saved him. Now he manages a gigantic publishing empire. I'm sure he would give you a job."

Uncle Rudi called Herr Rosenbaum and asked if he could find work for me. "Of course," Herr Rosenbaum said warmly. "However, he must have a little background to do well in the business. Can he go to the Graphic Academy? It will be worth it to him."

I agreed and attended the academy for two years, and then Herr Rosenbaum, the director of Elbemühl Papermakers, Printers, Bookbinders, and Publishers, saw to it that I got the job he had promised me, a fine position that paid enough to make our little family comfortable again. I became Rosenbaum's personal secretary.

"Now," I told my mother proudly, "it's time for you to quit." She resisted at first, but I insisted and finally she gave in, relieved that finally the burden of supporting the family was off her back. As for me, I enjoyed the work. The hours were loose, and Herr Rosenbaum was not only pleased with me, but was an excellent and pleasant man to work for.

Now that I had a career, my mother decided that the time had come for me to find a rich wife and start a family. "After all, I want to live to see my grandchildren," she told me rather pathetically as she suggested the first of a number of arranged dates with the daughters of old school friends—none of which worked out. One of these arranged affairs ended in such embarrassment to my mother that she finally gave up in despair.

I was to take a ship to the south of Yugoslavia to meet the girl and her family at their summer home. It was during vacation, and I thought the cruise down south would be relaxing, and indeed it was. On the boat, I met a dark-haired girl named Lili who had the most incredibly blue eyes and a smile that was at the same time wicked, innocent, and vulnerable. I started a shipboard flirtation that developed into a full-fledged romance. Lili pleaded with me to stay on the cruise ship, which was headed into the warm Mediterranean and eventually Egypt.

I didn't need much urging, and I never got off where I was supposed to, to meet my arranged date. Lili and I went on to Athens, Crete, Rhodes, and then to Alexandria and Cairo, spending much time in our rooms and very little time sightseeing, and I figured that all those magical nights on the Mediterranean would be worth my mother's eventual wrath.

At Alexandria, sitting on a terrace, Lili and I were approached by a seedy Alexandrian who asked if we'd like to see a circus. We agreed and followed him to a small tent nearby.

We sat down and saw behind us an Englishman and his two daughters, fifteen and seventeen years old. The circus consisted of a few clowns, one or two rather sad and typical circus acts, and then a less typical pornographic note was introduced—culminating in a fat woman having intercourse with a goat!

As Lili and I stood up in disgust to leave, we saw the Englishman, stony-faced, still sitting and watching with his two daughters.

In Egypt, we took a lovely room at a small hotel in Luxor, close to Cairo, and had one more glorious night. The next morning I woke up to find Lili gone and with her all my cash, my gold cuff links, cigarette case and lighter. Chastened and disillusioned, I had to wire my mother for money to get home.

"Never again!" my mother swore when I returned to Vienna. "Never will I humiliate myself by arranging dates with beautiful, not to mention wealthy, girls so that you can break their hearts!" I was deeply apologetic, but secretly relieved that she had finally decided to give up her matchmaking.

I might still be involved in publishing if Herr Rosenbaum, at his son's urging, hadn't left the Elbemühl company to start a business of his own. Out of loyalty, I went with him, and he was delighted to have me. We worked well together, but his son didn't share his father's enthusiasm for me. He saw me as a potential rival, not only to his position in the company, but also for his father's affection. In the end I decided that the wisest thing was to strike out on my own. I had a good reputation in the field by now and had no trouble finding another very good job.

I was in my twenties, and though the work was easy and I was good at it, I felt that basically it was dull and unexciting. There was no challenge, and looking around at the older men I worked with, I realized uneasily that they had settled into their jobs and their comfortable middle-class lives even as I was doing.

Remembering Uncle Rudi's suggestion, "You can always study acting at night," I thought, Why not? I still loved the theatre. Shouldn't I give it a try? I could still keep my job but add a little excitement to my life. The only theatrical academy in Vienna that had night classes was the Neue Wiener Konservatorium. I enrolled in it and started classes in drama, comedy, speech, fencing, film technique, singing, makeup, and theatrical law and history.

Acting in Austria in those days was considered as much a profession as medicine or law. You had to attend school and study and eventually take an examination to determine not only whether you could act, but also how much you knew about makeup and the theatre, its lore and its history. You had to know the leading parts in eight plays by heart—four classical and four modern ones. Of the classics, two had to be in prose and two in verse. Of the modern plays, two must be comedies and two dramas.

Normally, the acting academy took three years to complete, but since I had passed my Matura, I was allowed to finish the course in two. At the end of my first year, the graduating class asked me to play the captain in *Esther* by Franz Grillparzer, not so much because of my acting ability, I believe, but because of my height. They needed a tall man and I qualified.

It was a fortunate bit of luck for me. These school plays were attended by the managers of all the Viennese theatres as well as those in the provinces. It was their way of selecting the new crop of actors.

Max Reinhardt, one of the top directors in Austria, a man with an international reputation, was in the audience the night I came on, and after the performance he sent his card back with a message scribbled on it. "I expect you tomorrow at three o'clock in my office."

I stared at it in amazement and delight, and all I could think was, Uncle Rudi is wrong. I won't be the one to say, "Your horse is saddled." No bit parts for me!

The next day I went to the Theatre in the Josefstadt, the

theatre Reinhardt managed, and presented myself at the stage door. After a while a secretary came out and asked, "Whom are you supposed to see?"

"Professor Reinhardt," I said proudly. "I'm Paul von Hernried, and he's expecting me."

Unimpressed, the secretary asked, "May I have your card?" and he held out a silver tray. I put the card on it very gently and waited anxiously while he took it in to Reinhardt. In a few moments I was ushered into Reinhardt's small office.

Reinhardt himself was an ugly man, not very tall, but with a charged kind of energy and a sense of brutality about him. I knew him not only by reputation but I had seen some of his work in Vienna and Berlin. He was a theatrical genius who could make or break an actor's career. He had a reputation for ruthlessness, of complete disregard of anyone else's needs, of doing anything to get what he wanted.

Although I knew all of that, I saw him as my savior, especially when he told me, with what seemed like honest enthusiasm, how much he had liked my performance. "I expect to bring in a lot of new plays, many from America, and I'll need a juvenile lead," he told me bluntly. "Would you like it?"

"My God, yes!" I answered, stunned at the chance.

"Good. I can't give you a big salary since you are only a beginner and unknown, but you'll work with the top actors in the country, and you'll be under my direction. I hope you take the job."

"Of course, Professor," I told him quickly. "I'd love to do it!"

I left the office walking on air, the happiest man in Vienna. I, Paul von Hernried, had entered the best modern theatre in Vienna as a juvenile lead! And I really believed, in my euphoria, that I would be given leading roles.

I signed with Reinhardt and passed the theatrical exam. I was now officially an actor, permitted to appear on any stage in Austria and Germany.

◆

Two

Paris and Cannes

*M*y mother was impressed but apprehensive about my new career as an actor. "It's all well and good to be hired by Professor Reinhardt, but how can we get along on such a salary?"

How indeed? My new job with Reinhardt would pay the equivalent of twenty dollars a month. I had been making sixty dollars at the publishing house. Did I dare to give it up? And yet I knew, with terrible certainty, that the stage was what I wanted, where I belonged.

"Give your job up?" My boss, the director of the publishing house, said indignantly when I told him of my new career. "Nonsense! Of course you'll keep your job with us. Acting isn't that steady a profession, and you must make enough to support your mother and brother."

When I tried to explain how much time acting would take, how little time I'd be able to devote to him, he brushed my objections aside. "Your real value to this business lies in your ideas. That red leather and raw linen binding you came up with for Erich Maria Remarque's *All Quiet on the Western Front,* for example—ideas like that are priceless! Then there are your contacts, those aristocratic friends of yours, the business you've brought in, and, my goodness —the prestige of having an actor on my staff!" He waved his hand at me. "No, I don't really need you to oversee production, but I do need your ideas, so I'm going to make you a consultant. You'll sit in on our conferences, and your hours will be your own. You'll be free to give Professor Reinhardt all the time he needs."

It was a wonderful solution for me. I had found the work of overseeing production boring; the brainstorming sessions about how the finished books should look, on the other hand, had fascinated me. This new arrangement sounded perfect, and indeed, in the years that followed it worked out extremely well for me.

I can't begin to say how decent that publishing firm was. They kept me on at my old salary for years, insisting that the prestige I gained in the theatre and later in films rubbed off on them and was well worth the money. Their decency to me, however, extended beyond my worth to them. During the terrible years of World War II when I could send no money to my mother, they continued to pay her my salary.

Max Reinhardt, when he hired me, had praised my performance in *Esther* and had talked grandly about the American plays for which he needed a juvenile lead, plays like *Men in White* and *The First Legion*. However, the first play I was to appear in was a classic, Goethe's *Faust*. I approached the casting with great anticipation. I was bound, I thought, to be given the part of Valentin, the lover of Margarethe, who loses her to Faust—the juvenile lead. Hadn't Reinhardt hinted as much?

Alas for my anticipations. Valentin's part was never offered to me. I was given the role of the schoolboy. I appeared in the first act with a few speeches, walking about the stage with a friend. I appeared again later on, when I had a discussion with Faust, about ten pages of script. It wasn't a lead, but at least it was a well-known part, and when I looked at my situation rationally I knew I couldn't complain. Acting in Reinhardt's company, in any part, was a wonderful opportunity, and best of all I'd be directed by the Maestro himself, a legendary name in the theatre. Could a beginner ask for more?

Reinhardt, however, did not like to work with completely raw material. He had an assistant director, a Dr. Horn, who prerehearsed until the Maestro arrived. When he did arrive, the Maestro demolished everything Horn had set up. In the first scene, when I walked around the stage with my friend, all went well until the great Reinhardt took over. That was the moment I had waited for! I started my promenade, and his voice slashed at me, angry and impatient.

"You stupid son of a bitch! You, the schoolboy. Why don't you look around when you talk and walk? Idiot!"

I was shocked and terrified. Every actor, at one time or another, was at the end of Reinhardt's lashing tongue. Each of us was humiliated, told he was a fool, all wrong, deliberately fouling up the play.

Reinhardt was a man who was easily angered, who could praise an actor in one breath and destroy him in the next. I had been totally secure when I walked onstage. In moments Reinhardt destroyed my ego, and I built up a sense of terrified apprehension during that rehearsal. But I learned. God, how I learned under that man, and the terror he inspired in me kept me in line, kept me doing exactly what he wanted. That was Reinhardt's style.

The terror remained with me for years. I always feared, in the back of my consciousness, that whatever director I was working with would humiliate me as Reinhardt had done. The strange thing is that instead of hurting my performance, this unconscious fear has led to my exploring every play and every character I've played at a deeper level.

Paradoxically, the fear Reinhardt instilled in his actors led many to more creative performances. Before the opening night of *Faust* I was terrified. The terror increased as I waited for my entrance, but once the lights were on me, once I came onstage, the terror disappeared.

What did not disappear was the adrenaline my body had produced in response to the terror, and this adrenaline sharpened my performance. It was true not only in *Faust*, that first time, but in every play I've been in since.

I must say something of Reinhardt's directorial style, since it had made such a profound impression on the theatre. Before his time, most sets were flimsy painted canvas backdrops. He, along with a few other directors of that period, insisted that his stage sets be sturdy and solid, built of wood.

These solid sets brought a new reality to the actors and the performance. Reinhardt also changed the tempo of stage speech, making it faster, with transition and movement and more energy. This too evolved a heightened sense of reality. His direction also stressed reality, and while that approach seems fairly obvious now, at the time it was a very daring and new concept.

His daring extended to the classics as well as modern plays. In a production of Ibsen's *Ghosts,* a rather shocking play about inherited syphilis, there is a final scene where the grown son becomes completely insane and asks his mother for the sun.

Reinhardt decided that the boy should regress to a child. His set had the sun shining through the leaves of a tree outside the window and making golden spots of light on the floor. He directed the son to climb onto his mother's lap as he says, "Mother, give me the sun," and point to the reflections on the floor. He puts his head on his mother's breast as she remains silent, tears coursing down her cheeks, as, childlike, he repeats, "Give me the sun." Curtain.

Reinhardt's staging of *Ghosts* created a sensation. The realism of the son's regression was almost too much for the audience to bear.

And yet, original and autocratic as Reinhardt was, as arrogant and insistent on his own way of doing things, he was not above taking suggestions from the actors.

A year later I was playing the male lead in the final segment of *Lulu,* a play made up of a number of segments about the love life of Lulu. A different director did each segment, and Reinhardt did the last. In mine, I played a psychotic coachman who could only come to orgasm when he murdered the woman he was making love to. In the play, Lulu falls in love with him, goes to bed with him, and he takes out his knife and kills her.

I suggested to Reinhardt that I take out my knife at the beginning of the scene, open it, feel its edge, then close it and put it back in my pocket. It would establish with the audience the fact that I had the knife and the terror would be that much stronger. Reinhardt was delighted with the idea and incorporated it into the play. That was typical of Reinhardt. He would take and use anything logical and in character if it helped the play.

Over the years I have found that almost all first-rate directors are like that. Those who are blind to actor's suggestions are usually second-rate.

One of Reinhardt's peculiar directorial habits was that he liked to work at night. Unfortunately, the actors had tough schedules. They were putting on one play as they rehearsed the next. In our case, there would be an eleven A.M. rehearsal for *Faust* that would go until one o'clock, when we'd break for lunch until one-thirty. We'd rehearse from one-thirty until five, then hurry off for a quick bite before the seven-o'clock performance of the current play. In Europe curtain-time in most theatres was at seven, based on the theory that it was better to view a play and act in one on an empty stomach. Full stomachs meant drowsy audiences and drowsy actors. We'd have a little snack, perhaps a sandwich, before we went to the theatre. Viennese theatres had enormous lobbies with bars and elaborate buffets, and during intermission you could have another snack as you socialized; then after the theatre there would be a late supper at one of the many elegant restaurants.

Paula Wessely, a talented actress who played Margarethe in Reinhardt's *Faust,* was in another play due to close when *Faust* opened. The hellish schedule, pre-rehearsals with Horn, re-rehearsals with Maestro Reinhardt, then the evening performance, and afterward the Maestro's late rehearsals till two or three in the morning exhausted her. Time and again I found her in tears, but she didn't dare protest.

"Why not?" I asked her. "If you tell him how hard it is for you . . ."

"No, you don't understand. It's hard for all of us. I can't ask for special favors, and I want to please him . . . I so desperately want to please him!"

"But if you're exhausted . . ."

"It doesn't matter," she said fiercely. "This is my one big chance. The Maestro can make me a star if he chooses."

At that time I had no other play to perform in after the daily rehearsal ended at five, but I had my job to attend to, and easy as it had been made for me, it was still tiring, since I had to be back for the Maestro's late rehearsal after the evening performance. But I was young and filled with energy and daring, and doing exactly what I wanted. This had to be the best of all possible worlds. If there was a better one, perhaps it was Paris.

I was not one of those Viennese who are passionately in love with Vienna. My love affair was with Paris, a city I had been introduced to much earlier by the Baroness Clarice Rothschild. I had

met Clarice Rothschild during a ball given by a club of former
members of the Theresianische Akademie. It was an annual affair,
and the first one I attended was quite sumptuous. The school's
graduates, as I said before, were from the wealthy aristocracy, and
I had formed friendships with some of them that lasted for many
years and helped me in very troubled times.

Since I was good-looking and a good dancer, besides being tall,
my friends decided that I should lead the opening waltz, and my
partner was the Baroness Rothschild. Clarice was not a beauty, but
she had rich brunette hair, a voluptuous figure, and wonderfully
expressive eyes. She was a happy girl, full of life and vitality, and
always ready for fun or adventure. She knew the best wines, the best
people, the best whorehouses in any city and the best slums.

To my callow eyes she was a "woman of the world." Clarice was
eight years older than I, but she had at least twenty years more
experience. She had that wonderful quality so hard to define, the one
we've come to call charisma. She could attract and charm anyone,
and inevitably she attracted and charmed me. That first time we met
at the ball she insisted that I come with her to Paris. "To my Paris.
It's really the center of the world. I exist in Vienna, but I really live
in Paris!"

Clarice knew Paris thoroughly. She seemed to know every
street, every good restaurant, where everyone went, and where every
skeleton was buried. She ran with a wealthy set that intrigued me,
but whose style, I knew, was far beyond my limited budget. When
I finally gave in to her coaxing and went to Paris with her, I stayed
as a guest at the Palais Rothschild on the Avenue Foche. It was a
French rococo building with an enormous stone-and-marble entry-
way and with walls covered with paintings of the Rothschild ancestors.

During that visit, what had started as a friendship ripened into
an intimate affair; however, I couldn't bring myself to do more than
give her a chaste kiss in that overwhelming palace.

"I feel that every one of your ancestors is watching me and
disapproving," I finally told her, gesturing at the portraits on the
walls.

"Then, for heaven's sake, take a hotel room and we'll be alone."

"I can't afford it," I protested unhappily.

"That's silly. I'll pay."

I said, "No! I can't allow that."

"Of course you can," she snapped, "unless you're trying to tell me that you don't like me."

I embraced her and kissed her where she liked to be kissed the most.

"Then there's no problem. I have more money than I know what to do with. Let's have no more of this middle-class morality. You're my guest here and I'll pay your way." Her voice softened. "And besides"—she put a finger to my lips to stifle my protests— "be fair to me. I want to be alone with you."

She had made her point and I took the hotel room.

The intriguing thing about my visits to Paris, and I did return again and again, was that I spoke an excellent French with a slight Parisian accent and so was readily accepted in every circle in Paris. I had come by my knowledge of the language and the accent because I had a French governess as a child, who taught me to speak French as fluently as I spoke German.

Paris, however, was not enough for me. I fell in love with all things French, and when a dear friend of my late father, Count Maximilian Corwin, invited me to visit his home in Cannes, I accepted eagerly. Count Corwin had married a very wealthy Chilean widow with three lovely children. One of them, Rita, who was recently divorced from an Italian prince, took a fancy to me, and we started an affair that lasted for two years, though we only saw each other in the spring, my vacation time.

Paris was exciting, but Cannes had a quality all its own, a sense of relaxed wealth. With the count as my sponsor, I mingled with millionaires and royalty, attended the finest sporting clubs as the count's guest and became good friends with the "beautiful people" of that time—while being still young enough to be thrilled by it all.

Cannes was filled with wealthy English ladies having "discreet" affairs—and sometimes indiscreet ones—with professional gigolos. There were women like Mabel Pool, a "poor little rich girl" who went through three American millionaires in quick succession. Each died and left her a fortune. There were the Straus girls from Chicago, cousins of Gertrude Stein, and millionaires too. And amid all these rather voracious ladies there were one or two impoverished but handsome young men like me who moved through the magical crowd with open, adoring eyes.

At one point, Edward, Prince of Wales, and his brother George arrived in Cannes, and two of the wealthier ladies, Mabel Pool and Lady Rothermere, got together to throw a great bash for the princes at the Sporting Club. Maurice Chevalier and Lucian Boyer, two top cabaret stars of the time, were flown in for entertainment. It was a gala affair that lasted until four in the morning, an extraordinary production. One hundred little boats had been posted in a circle around the terrace where we ate and drank and danced, and on a cue from the shore a magnificent display of fireworks arose from every boat. It was unbelievably beautiful.

Finally, and reluctantly, the party broke up. I was staying at the Ritz, the guest of a wealthy young friend, Bobby Lenninger, and Bobby and I started walking on the croisette toward the Carlton, both a little tipsy from all the champagne we had drunk.

On our way we were joined by the two royal brothers, Edward and George, who had managed to sneak away from their official entourage. Edward spoke excellent French, and the two of us hit it off at once, talking eagerly as any two young men will who suddenly, in the midst of a drunken evening, find in one another a sympathetic friend. Bobby and George went on ahead, singing raucously.

At the hotel, Edward and I joined the other two in harmonizing on some soggy German love songs, then a few racy French tunes, and then Edward, who had a fine repertory of off-color French ballads, sang a few solos.

At the height of our drunken merrymaking, a door opened up on the hotel balcony, and a famous perfume manufacturer, Mr. Coty, shouted down at us, "How the hell can anyone sleep with all that racket?"

"Well, close your door and try it anyway," I shouted back with what we all thought was hilarious wit. The man slammed his door disgustedly and we four doubled over with laughter. Everything seemed extraordinarily funny.

It was early dawn when we finally kissed each other good-bye, swearing undying friendship, and while the two young princes staggered off, Bobby and I climbed back to our room, suddenly sobered by the approach of the granddaddy of all hangovers.

It was also at Cannes, on a later visit, that I appeared in my first motion picture. I had met Rex Ingram, the film director from Hollywood, and the fading actress Ellen Terry. At that time she still had the beauty that had made her famous, but her body had spread out in comfortable middle age. Her vitality, however, had not diminished and she was still alive and eager.

"Paul," she told me, "you should be in films. Rex is shooting a movie, *Baroud,* about the French Foreign Legion, and you must be a *spahi.* Mustn't he, Rex? Won't he look magnificent in a uniform?" A *spahi* is an Algerian cavalryman.

"Not bad," Rex agreed and slapped me on the back. "Would you like to be an actor? Come on, I'll make a star of you."

I agreed eagerly, and I was fitted with a dashing costume and plunged into the fascinating and difficult routine of making a movie. It was a small part, but ah, that uniform! I wore it constantly, even when I wasn't in the day's shooting, and it was the uniform, I'm sure, that captured the heart of an adorable little woman in the film. She too had a very small part, and that left us both a great deal of free time for our flirtation. The film was shot in the spring, and I remember vast fields of paper-white narcissus spread all around us, the perfect background for our gentle affair.

Those excursions to Cannes were all made in the spring, before the bulk of tourists arrived and while things were slack in the publishing business, the best time for me to get away. But the trips and all the delightful flirtations and romances in Cannes stopped once I began to work in the theatre. There was no more time to parlay my name and appearance into freeloading visits to the Riviera, nor did I need to. I found enough excitement onstage, and I began the most serious romance of my life, my affair with Lisl Edthofer.

On the night that *Faust* opened, the fourth of September,

1933, an old friend, a lovely woman in her forties, said, "I am going to throw a big party for you, Paul, and I want you here after the show."

"Even if I'm a dud?" I laughed.

"Especially then. We'll cheer you up, but I'm confident you'll be superb."

If not superb, I was at least adequate in my part, and I came to the party in a flush of heady victory. The play itself had been very well received, and I was carried along by its success. Everyone congratulated me, especially a beautiful young American actress, Virginia Field. We danced a bit and flirted a bit, and then I was introduced to Elizabeth Edthofer, whose nickname was Lisl. She was the ex-wife of one of Reinhardt's very successful leading men, Anton Edthofer, but Lisl, I was told by our hostess, was a celebrity in her own right. She had a very successful couturier shop in Vienna and had designed costumes for some of the most popular stage productions. Lisl was a tall brunette with brown eyes, and I think it was her eyes that attracted me most. They were large and surrounded by shadows, making them very sexy and exciting. She had short hair in the very popular *Bubikopf*, or, in English, "child's cut."

No sooner had I been introduced than memory came rushing back. "Why, you're Lisl Glück," I said, "Hofrat Dr. Gustav Glück's daughter."

She smiled, a delightful smile. "And I know you. You're Paul von Hernried. We met at your school."

"Exactly!" We stood there staring at each other, and I remembered our meeting very well. It had been several years ago at one of the school dances. We had had a wonderful time and I had often thought of her since, and now here she was, a grown lady, beautiful and poised and with an indefinable quality that intrigued me.

I spent a good part of the evening either talking to her or staring at her covertly while she talked or danced with other men. But of course there was Virginia Field, and she was quite beautiful too, with the added attraction of that Hollywood glamour, and of course she was studying at the Reinhardt Seminar to become an actress, and I—why, tonight I was a genuine actor myself. It was a dilemma indeed, but such a lovely dilemma! Two beautiful women to flirt with and each available, I thought.

At the end of the evening, we three and another young man were the last to leave. In the darkened street, I said, "I'll get a cab." But Lisl shook her head. "Don't bother. I have my car across the street. I'll drop you all off."

We took off, the four of us in her convertible, and as chance —or was it design?—had it, Lisl dropped Virginia off first at her hotel, then she dropped off the other young man. We were alone.

Our flirtation had grown to the point where we were both obviously interested in each other, so I took my courage in hand and asked, "What shall we do with the rest of the evening?"

Lisl smiled enigmatically, and I tried to be very offhand as I went on. "Since we have your car and it's such a fine night, why don't we drive up to the Kobenzl?"

The Kobenzl is a mountain of the Vienna Woods, and there is a castle on it that had been converted into a hotel, restaurant, and bar. It had a terrace for dancing that overlooked all of Vienna, and this was a beautiful summer night with an almost full moon. We sat on the terrace and drank champagne and talked and danced and talked some more, had coffee and pastry and still talked!

We drove home and kissed each other good-bye, a lingering kiss full of promise, and at six in the morning I left her apartment, excited and exhilarated. I had been a success in my first proper acting part on the stage—and I had fallen in love!

Three

♦

Lisl

*T*here is an old belief in Vienna that if you stay up late and drink too much, a good herring the next morning will keep your stomach in order. The day after I met Lisl I slept late, then bought a lovely herring and took it to her apartment as a gift. She made breakfast for me and served me the herring, but wouldn't touch it herself. Leaning over the table in her dressing gown, her eyes still clouded with sleep, she looked even lovelier than the night before.

"Herring," she said thoughtfully. "Not flowers, not candy, not even perfume—herring. Paul, you're a very interesting man."

"Won't you try the herring?" I asked. "It's delicious."

She made a face. "I hate herring. Tell me about your work, Paul, I mean your publishing work. I think I've had enough theatre talk with my ex-husband to last me a lifetime."

And so we talked again. We spent the whole morning talking, while both of us slowly realized that this was it, for us.

Until then I had been going out with a beautiful young lady named Cissy Rudolf, a blonde with blue eyes and very thick red lips. Cissy had a full, rounded figure, not at all like Lisl's slim build, and although she was usually sweet and pliable, she could also be arrogant and demanding.

In spite of my mother's promise never again to meddle in my love life, she had finally relented and fixed up a date with Cissy, the daughter of an old schoolmate—and fabulously wealthy.

"Not that money is that important," my mother assured me, "but it never hurts. At least go with the girl and see if you like her."

I went, and I liked, and I thought, why not? I'd marry Cissy and live wealthily ever after—but that was before I met Lisl. I did like Cissy, and one of the things I liked about her was a quality of sensuality, but it was a deceptive quality. When we had been going together for a month, I brought up the question of sleeping together, but Cissy was not taken with the idea.

"But I couldn't marry a woman I had never slept with," I told her. "I think I love you and I do want to marry you, but I think we should sleep together first and find out if—well, if we're compatible."

"I couldn't, Paul," she had protested at first, and then, uneasily and reluctantly, she had agreed to go through with it. Her reluctance took some of the edge off my desire. After all, it wasn't something distasteful, like medicine. It should be a warm, wonderful experience for both of us, I told Cissy.

She tightened up at that. "Look, Paul, I agreed to go through with it. Let's not discuss it."

Her agreement was one thing, but where could we go? Her home was out. She was terrified at the thought, and my mother was always home, so my place was out. She shivered delicately at the thought of a hotel room. "It's too demeaning."

I suggested that when I went on vacation, I'd go by train to a small resort town I knew of in Italy. The train would go by her country home at midnight; she would join me and we'd arrive in Portorose in Italy together. It was just the sort of foolish, romantic plan that I knew would appeal to her, and she agreed. But two days before we were to meet she called and said she couldn't go through with it. "Give me another week, Paul."

I was furious and said, "Let's forget it!" and I hung up. The next week I met Lisl, and Cissy, along with all the other girls I knew, left my mind. The vacation I'd planned to take with Cissy would have been a very brief six days because of the play, but before the play moved on to Salzburg and the summer festival, I got a real vacation, and it fortunately matched Lisl's. "Will you let me show you the French Riviera?" I asked her. "I adore it."

Lisl, with no artifice, looked straight at me and said, "Yes. I'd like that. First we'll visit my parents and then drive through Italy to the Riviera."

Lisl's father, a remarkable man, was the curator and director of the famous Vienna Art Museum. He had accumulated the largest

Breughel collection in the world for Vienna and had written many books on art, on old masters, on the understanding of art, and a critical approach to painting. Her mother, too, was a warm, generous, intelligent person, as I later found out, but I was unprepared for their unequivocably modern viewpoint.

Lisl dropped me off at a hotel in the same town where her parents had a summer house and drove off to tell them about us and our plan to drive to the French Riviera. But that same evening they said, "Why doesn't Paul come for dinner and you can both stay here overnight?" They knew we were sleeping together, and they accepted it without the slightest censure. I had a great evening with them, and it started a lifelong friendship and mutual love.

When we left to drive to the Riviera, Lisl's father gave her a sizable roll of bills. Grinning at her, he said, "When you get to Monte Carlo, go to the first table and place all this money on whatever number comes to mind."

"But what if we lose?" Lisl asked, looking at the staggering amount of money.

"That's my headache."

She looked up at him slyly. "And if we win?"

Gustav Glück spread his hands. "It's all yours!"

We had a grand time on that trip, and I showed Lisl what I considered "my Cannes" very proudly and lovingly. We joked about her father's money and kept dreaming up different numbers and spending our imaginary winnings, but when we finally reached Monte Carlo, Lisl said, "I just hate to gamble all that money."

"Don't look at me," I said as she got that coaxing expression on her face. "I'm a born loser. Go ahead and do it. Your father wanted you to."

Lisl took the money and went into the casino, and I waited outside nervously. When she finally came out, she looked stricken, and I put my arms around her gently. "You lost, right?"

"Oh, Paul, I did just what Father said. I went to the first table and played the first number that came into my head—and I won!"

"You won? Fantastic! Now you can buy that fancy Cord convertible you were admiring yesterday. So why the long face?"

I could see tears well up in her eyes. "Because at the last minute I lost my nerve. I only put a third of the money down!"

We drove back to Vienna in Lisl's old car while I tried to joke with her about her sudden lack of faith, but she couldn't see the humor of it. "If I'd only done what Father told me to, I'd be driving that lovely Auburn Cord back home instead of this miserable old junkheap."

"I think this is a pretty fine car, and it's taken us just where we wanted to go. Now cheer up. It was only money."

Back in Vienna I got a frantic phone call from Cissy Rudolf. "I've thought it over, Paul, and I've been an idiot about this whole thing. I want to marry you at once!"

I swallowed. After meeting Lisl I had no desire to see Cissy again, but I couldn't tell her that. Stalling for time to think, I said, "You know what I said before . . ."

"Paul," she interrupted, "I won't sleep with you until we're married. I've decided that. Now listen, Paul, there's someone else who wants to marry me, and if you say no, I'll marry him."

"That's emotional blackmail," I answered firmly, trying to hide my relief. "I'm sorry, Cissy. If you want it that way, it has to be no."

She hung up and within the week she had married the other man. It was a tragic marriage because on their honeymoon in Sicily, Cissy drowned while swimming in the Mediterranean. The doctors diagnosed her death as heart failure, but the gossip in Vienna was that her husband had drowned her to inherit her fortune.

Once Cissy was out of my life, I informed my mother that I was moving in with Lisl, but I would still keep up our apartment. I expected great things of my new career. My mother was less than ecstatic about the news. "Who is this girl, Paul?"

"Mother, you've met her. Her father is Hofrat Dr. Gustav Glück, the former director of the Imperial Gallery. Every important museum and every collector and dealer—even Lord Duveen—everyone who buys an old master tries to get his authentication!"

My mother looked very unimpressed. "Lord knows, you could have married an heiress, Paul. My friends . . ."

"Mother, I'm not talking about marriage. I'm going to live with Lisl, and I want you to learn to love her."

My motherr looked at me and of course had the last word. "A divorced woman!"

I moved into Lisl's apartment and, cramped as it was, it seemed heavenly to both of us. Everything was going right for me. Our company of *Faust* was so successful that we had played at the Salzburg Festival, and there, for the first time, I heard Arturo Toscanini conduct Wagner's *Lohengrin.* He replaced Wilhelm Furtwängler, who had become sick. I listened from the fourth gallery on opening night, and I was lifted out of myself by the brilliance of Toscanini's conducting. He had put enough dramatic power into the music to change its character and quality. It no longer seemed slow and ponderous, but strident and much faster. I loved it, but the Viennese critics were outraged.

"How dare Mr. Toscanini, an Italian, distort Wagner to this degree?" they wrote, yet his interpretation of Wagner changed the concept of modern opera by making it faster and more dynamic.

I returned to Vienna after our stint in Salzburg prepared to go into rehearsal for Reinhardt's next play. Instead I was called into his office. He was not present, but Otto Preminger, an assistant of his, was waiting for me. "I have some bad news, Hernried," he said, avoiding my eyes.

My heart sank. Had my performance displeased the Maestro? "What is it?"

Preminger sighed. "Anton Edthofer has told Reinhardt that you stole his wife Lisl from him."

I was stunned and angry. "But that's a lie! I didn't meet Lisl until a year after they were divorced."

Preminger shook his head. "Perhaps. But Edthofer insists you stole her and he's told Reinhardt that if he has Paul von Hernried in his theatre, he won't have Edthofer. As simple as that."

"My God, I can't believe that!"

"I'm sorry," Preminger said, sounding very sincere. "Of course, Reinhardt says he will honor your contract and pay you, but after *Faust* you won't play anything else in this theatre, so you'd better start looking somewhere else."

"Would it do any good if I talked to Reinhardt or Edthofer?"

Preminger shook his head. "I'm afraid not. Reinhardt won't talk to you. If it's a toss-up between you and Edthofer—well, he's too big a star to lose. I don't think he wants to know your side of the story. That's just the way things are."

I walked out completely shattered at the injustice of the affair, slowly becoming aware that my promising career at Reinhardt's theatre was finished.

♦

Four

UFA Makes
an Offer

*W*hen Lisl heard what had happened to me because of Edthofer, she was shocked and angry. "It's so typical of him," she said furiously. "Why I ever married him—"

"Why did you?" I asked, kissing her. "A nice girl like you?"

"But I was only a child! I was sixteen and what did I know? He was forty-two and so handsome—he still is, the bastard, and charming, and I thought it was all going to be magic. He knew everyone in the theatre, and he introduced me to everyone, showing me off, I realize now. It took years before I understood what a son of a bitch he was—and still I stuck it out for seven years! I really tried to make that marriage work, but, Paul, this is so unfair. We were divorced a year before I met you."

"I think Preminger believed me when I told him that, but Reinhardt wouldn't talk to me. Anton is much more important to him than I am."

"Well, Anton's doing this to you is just like him. So petty! He's a vindictive man, and do you know, Paul, he's really very strange."

"Strange? How do you mean?"

"Well, for one thing, he doesn't believe in banks. He carries all his money around with him, a small fortune in Swiss francs, and he keeps it in his hip pocket and closes it with a safety pin!"

"Well, it's over and that's that," I said. "Let's not worry about it. I'll just start job hunting. At least Reinhardt will keep paying me, and I always have the publishing job to fall back on."

"Well," Lisl said, still angry, "I'm not going to take this lying down. I won't let Edthofer force you off the stage!"

"It's no use," I protested. "Reinhardt is firm about that."

"Reinhardt? Is he the only director in Vienna? What about Dr. Rudolf Beer? He likes me. He always has, and I know he'll give you an interview if I call him."

Lisl did call and Dr. Beer said, "Of course. Send him up to see me."

Dr. Beer, the director of the Volkstheater, was in the process of opening a new and modern theatre, the Scala, with the play *A Woman Who Knew What She Wanted*. When Lisl told Dr. Beer about Edthofer's edict, Dr. Beer laughed. "Well, if Reinhardt liked you well enough to put you in *Faust*, that's good enough for me. I'll give you a part in my new play."

It was a small part, but at least I was on the stage again. Reinhardt had brought *Faust* back from Salzburg and I started rehearsing for the Beer play while I was still appearing in *Faust*. The new play opened in 1933 and it caused no great storm among the critics, but I did my part competently and Beer was pleased, and a few of the theatrical agents who always scouted the Vienna theatres noticed me. One found me a part in a revue opening at the Casino Theatre called *Always Love*. It was a better deal because the revue consisted of a number of short plays and I had the lead in one, and to my delight one of the newspaper critics was impressed enough by my performance to write about me.

"In Paul von Hernried," he wrote, "we have a gifted actor who promises much for the future."

The play as a whole received excellent notices, though I thought it was rather miserable. The notices were seen by Professor Beer, who phoned Lisl and said, "Send your boy over to me quickly. I have another part for him."

It was another small part, but I was the understudy to the lead and, to my delight, after two weeks the lead was too sick to go on, and I played the lead for the rest of the run! It was a long run, too, a very successful play, and automatically I moved up another rung on the theatrical ladder. I entered the category of "Leading Man." "Paul von Hernried," a critic wrote, "is a very talented and sympathetic lover. He makes every one of the scenes his own. He also has a lovely singing voice that could do more difficult songs very well indeed."

I fairly glowed at the notices and Lisl was impressed. "Obviously you're going to be an enormous success and become rich enough to buy me that beautiful new convertible roadster."

"Obviously, but first there are a few little bills that must be taken care of."

The play, *Ball at the Savoy*, opened in January of 1934, a momentous year, politically, for Austria. The play, a musical, was a big hit. Indeed, it was so successful that it moved to another theatre when its run at the Scala ended. Another play had been booked into the Scala, and the theatre had to be prepared for it.

During the run of the play, on February 12, 1934, a stunning incident shocked all of us out of our complacency. The fascists in Austria, a group we had all scorned and shrugged off, joined forces with the government, and seventeen thousand troops of fascist militia and government soldiers turned their artillery on the Austrian Social Democrats in the workers' flats in Vienna.

They slaughtered a thousand men, women, and children, and wounded thousands more. Democratic political freedom in Austria was dissolved and the government was taken over by a clerical-fascist dictatorship under Engelbert Dollfuss, who had become chancellor in 1932. The nation had barely recovered from that when in July 1934 a gang of Nazis dressed in Austrian army uniforms murdered Dollfuss while other Nazis seized a radio station and announced that he had resigned.

It was a premature Nazi putsch and it failed, mostly because they bungled everything. The government forces were led by Dr. Kurt von Schuschnigg, who took over as chancellor. Some of the murderers of Dollfuss were eventually caught and hanged in spite of Germany's protest. The attempted putsch, though unsuccessful, shook us all up. It is astonishing, in retrospect, to realize how little of what was going on around us penetrated to those of us working in the theatre. We were so much in our own world, so involved in perfecting our craft, that the enormous political upheaval that was to culminate in World War II seemed nothing more than a dark shadow on the horizon.

I, as a struggling actor, had thrown myself completely into my work. Lisl had a firmer grip on politics, and I know that her parents —after all, Gustav was half Jewish—were deeply concerned. For me, however, the most important thing was my performance in *Ball at the Savoy.* Eventually it ran for 106 performances, a record for Vienna in those days. Perhaps the deadly political events caused people to search for something light and amusing. At any rate, Professor Beer, delighted at my performance, hired me to play an important role in *Lulu,* by Frank Wedekind.

Lulu was one of three plays that Beer was presenting at the Scala in February of 1934. In an unusual theatrical concept, the three plays—or rather the last act of each play—were presented in one evening. The beginning of each play was told by a narrator, and the entire, slightly experimental, approach was intended as a tribute to Karl Forest, a famous character actor. Each play was directed by a different man, and as luck would have it, *Lulu,* the play I appeared in, was directed by Reinhardt.

I thought it would be an awkward situation, but Professor Reinhardt was most gracious. He made no reference to the problem with Edthofer—indeed, he acted as if it had never happened. I mentioned earlier that I had made a suggestion about that business with a knife in *Lulu,* which he accepted with a great show of delight. We came to know each other a bit during his direction of *Lulu,* and it was then that he invited me to his upcoming party in the summer at Salzburg.

Max Reinhardt was an extraordinary man, and I've always regretted that I didn't get the benefit of his directing because of the Edthofer affair. Reinhardt had been one of the first to stage the work of the German Expressionists after World War I. In 1920 he founded the Salzburg Festival, where his unique staging of *Everyman* became an annual affair. He used the Austrian Alps as a backdrop to the play. Reinhardt was Jewish, his original name was Max Goldman, and in 1933, the same year he hired me to play in *Faust,* he had been forced by the Nazis to flee Germany.

Reinhardt owned an enormous castle, Leopoldskron, near Salzburg, and every year, at the festival, he threw a magnificent party to which he invited not only the leading directors and most famous actors, but also the cream of the European aristocracy.

I was delighted at the invitation. Reinhardt's parties were legendary all through the industry, and invitations were rare and eagerly sought. I'm sure mine was tendered as an apology for the Edthofer affair, but unfortunately we could not attend that year or the next. Each year, however, a new invitation, beautifully engraved, came to us, and finally, in August of 1936, we were able to go.

The party was an extravagant affair and lived up to its reputation. The food was lavish, and the rooms were lit with hundreds of candles. All the guests were beautifully clothed, the women lovely in evening dress, the men handsome in tails, wearing their medals.

Berlin, where Reinhardt had started, was the center of the theatrical world, or had been before Hitler. Producers from every country came to attend Reinhardt's openings, and even after Reinhardt moved to Vienna, they still came, certain that any Reinhardt play was destined to be a hit, and they fought for the international rights. His parties were just as popular, and at the one we attended I met two producers I knew, Gilbert Miller from New York and Henry Shereck from London. Shereck, a round little man, was very charming but unable to resist making practical jokes.

At one point in the evening, he and Lisl and I were talking to Gilbert Miller, who was very impressed with the party. "It's the first time I've been to one of Reinhardt's affairs," he said, "and I must say I'm overwhelmed. It's really an exciting thing for me, an American, to meet all these dukes and counts and barons. Really exciting."

Shereck winked at me and said, "Now come on, Gil. You don't really believe they're royalty?"

"What do you mean?" Miller sputtered. "I was introduced to them by Reinhardt and his wife in the receiving line."

"Gil, Gil—this whole party is just another of Reinhardt's productions," Shereck went on.

"I don't understand," Miller said, turning pale.

"Now you don't really think that's the Prince of Hohenlohe?" Shereck nodded at the prince, "or that that's the Duke of Liechtenstein, or that she, that woman there with the tiara, is the Baroness Salvotti? Why, they're all made up, all his actors and actresses playing a part for Reinhardt."

Miller stared at Shereck, then, muttering an oath, wheeled and stormed out of the room and out of the castle. "These crazy Americans!" Shereck exploded with laughter. "They go to pieces over royalty."

Later, I heard that Shereck sent Miller a letter: "It was all a joke, Gilbert. They really were royalty." But from that day on Miller never again spoke to Shereck.

Lulu was another success, and my next play was at the Komödie Theatre, a play whose German title translated into *Annie Under Pressure.* By now I was an established leading man on the Viennese stage and the offers began to come in, not only for plays, but to do commercial advertisements, to endorse products—a clothes valet for gentlemen, a hat, a tie—anything that could be linked to a suave young lover.

In 1934, the year that started with *Ball at the Savoy,* I did six plays. After *Annie Under Pressure,* I was asked to do *The Master of Millions,* a play in which Albert Basserman, a world-famous character actor, starred. I was the leading man in a role that, for the first time, I was able to create myself. No one else had done it before me.

I had had a number of successes now, and with the advertisements I had achieved a certain notoriety, and to a degree I began to develop an inflated ego. After all, I was on my way to being a star.

My old friend, Professor Beer, was directing *The Master of Millions,* and after I made my entrance during the second reading, script in hand, he stopped us and told me to do it differently. I did, and again Beer was dissatisfied. We began to discuss the interpretation of the role, a discussion that very quickly turned into a furious argument. Finally I lost my temper, threw the script at Beer and stalked off the stage.

I reached home considerably chastened and shocked at what I had done, and I sat down next to the phone waiting for Beer to call me—but no call came. I went to bed that night miserably certain that I had blown my opportunity and lost the part. Behavior like this, I realized, was completely unprofessional, and if Beer were vindictive this could easily spoil my chance to work with Basserman, an actor I admired tremendously. It might also ruin my career.

I had been a fool, I thought, too puffed up with my own importance to understand what I was doing. I hardly slept that night, and the next day I was mooning around the apartment when, at ten-thirty, the phone rang. It was Professor Beer, and when I said, "Hello?" he asked abruptly, "Why aren't you here? We're starting rehearsal."

I said, "Professor, I'll be there immediately!" and I ran all the way to the theatre. There was a five-minute break when I arrived, and Basserman sent his valet to me to ask me to please come to his dressing room. He wished to talk to me. I was both apprehensive and pleased. Basserman was a figure to be treated with awe—and he wanted to talk to me! My only hope was that he wouldn't scold me for my outrageous behavior yesterday.

But that was precisely what he talked about. "I heard you and Dr. Beer arguing yesterday," he began with no preamble. "No, wait." He held up his hand against my explanation. "The fault is both yours and his. He was unable to explain what he wanted, and you failed to understand him." Again I started to defend myself, but he cut me off. "I will explain one basic thing to you because in spite of your youth you show some talent and ability. The important thing about acting . . ." He paused portentously. "The important thing is that you stand on the stage with the weight of your body in your legs, not in your head. Your weight must be toward the center of the earth. As long as you learn this and practice it, you will become an important actor. Remember that."

He paused and frowned. "I believe that is what Dr. Beer was trying to tell you. When you entered yesterday, your head came before your body. Now remember, when you enter, your weight must be in your feet."

At the time I was bewildered. Was this the final word on acting from the great Basserman? I didn't know whether to laugh or get angry. Was it a joke? But there was no humor in his face, and I left his dressing room after mumbling some sort of thanks. But when I had to play the scene at rehearsal, I remembered his advice and did as he had suggested, and to my surprise, Beer was delighted.

"You see, Paul," Basserman said, with a friendly arm around my shoulders. "You took my advice and it's perfect. Very good."

I know now that all the teachers I ever had never gave me as good a piece of advice as Basserman did that day. I have studied many forceful actors—Brando, Tracy, and older character actors; Wegener, Jannings, and Basserman himself—and all of them had the solidity Basserman described to me. They all had the quality of being part of the earth. I'm glad that I was chastened enough that day to take Basserman's advice, and I honestly believe it was the most important advice about acting I ever received.

There was a political and literary nightclub and cabaret in Vienna in the 1930s run by a brilliant satirist, Karl Farkas. In addition to his own witty monologues, he would put on short sketches that he wrote himself. He would hire well-known actors to appear in them, and after seeing me on stage he approached me to join his cabaret act. I accepted eagerly. His reputation was excellent and the exposure could only help my career, and the extra money was more than welcome. The cabaret started at eleven-thirty, and my stage play, whatever it might be, was finished by ten o'clock at the latest. It left me plenty of time to get to the nightclub.

It was about this time that a film producer, Joseph Than, saw me in a play, *The Queen in Love,* and approached me to do a motion picture called *High School.* It had nothing to do with high school as we know it in this country, but was the story of a former calvary officer who trained Lipizzan stallions in the remarkable art of dressage and performed with them in vaudeville theatres around the world. Dressage is a form of riding where the horse responds to almost imperceptible movements of the rider and does unbelievable jumps and other maneuvers.

The breed of beautiful white Lipizzans used is descended from an Andalusian strain. The Roman Legions brought them back to Rome from Spain, and over four hundred years ago the Spanish Riding School was established in Vienna to train them. Dressage is an exquisitely difficult job and usually takes three to six years. There were performances every Sunday at the Spanish Riding School.

In the movie, a superb actor, Rudolph Forster, tours the country with the Lipizzans and falls in love with a young woman. I play her brother, a man who opposes the marriage and is killed in a duel with Forster. My death breaks up the romance.

It was a juicy part, and I enjoyed the experience. This film was far ahead of the early movie I had done in Nice for Rex Ingram. It was not only more professional, but it brought in a lot of money. Still, profitable as it was, it was not as satisfying as my stage work, and I knew that that was where my interest lay.

High School was a great success and I received some fine reviews. Ufa, the large and important state-owned German studio, sent a scout to Vienna, a man named Kurt von Ried, to see me perform on stage. He watched *The Queen in Love* and liked my work. After the show he came backstage and told me that Ufa would like to offer me a star contract.

"It will make you a big film star," he told me. "You have the looks and the ability."

I hesitated, pointing out that my first love was the stage. "Ah yes," he told me. "But the movie industry is where the money is."

We haggled over terms, and I finally agreed provided I did only two films a year so that seven months of my time could be devoted to the stage. There was some question of billing, and once we had settled that, he agreed that I could be paid two thirds of my salary in Austria instead of Germany. In the end it was decided that I would come to Berlin, all expenses paid, to see the Ufa studios and to sign the contract after the play closed.

I have said before that, as an actor, I was not involved with politics. My father, before he died, had told me, "Stay clear of politics, son. The men who are involved in it are power-hungry and unprincipled. It's a dirty game." I had tried to follow his warning. Perhaps, if I had paid closer attention to what was happening in Germany, I would have refused to go to Berlin, but Ufa had a fine reputation as the biggest and most experimental studio in Germany. It had turned out films like *The Cabinet of Dr. Caligari, Scherben (Fragments), Dr. Mabuse, The Gambler,* and The *Mountain Cat.* I was elated at the thought of a studio that had made films like these offering me a contract.

Ufa stood for Universum Film Aktiengesellschaft, and it was a state-owned combine that came into existence after World War I. The Deutsche Bank, Krupp, and I. G. Farben were among the outfits that initially financed it, and gradually it bought out all the other German studios. During the twenties it was the only film organization in the world to offer Hollywood any serious competition.

Ufa attracted some extremely talented directors, men like Ernst Lubitsch, F. W. Murnau, Fritz Lang and G. W. Pabst, and actors such as Emil Jannings, Conradt Veidt, Pola Negri and Henry Porten.

What I didn't realize was that, when Hitler came to power, he found in Ufa a ready-built propaganda machine with a distributing system that encompassed all of Europe. In 1933 Goebbels began the takeover of Ufa, and by the time I was offered a contract, that takeover was complete. However, Goebbels had a great deal of difficulty in forcing his propaganda on the industry, and the movies that were filled with it were box-office flops.

I must also say that although we had our own Nazi party in Austria, we had only an ominous foreboding of the terrible anti-Semitism going on in Germany. Indeed, I had many Jewish friends in Austria who shrugged off the specter of Hitler even as they agreed that there was little doubt that eventually he would take over Austria and come to Vienna.

Later, as things grew worse and the stories of the Nazi concentration camps began to filter in, I asked my friends, "Why not leave now? You have the money to go and you can still get out." But most just shook their heads. "We are Viennese and we love Vienna. We don't want to leave, to uproot our families—and perhaps it won't happen after all."

Many kept up that attitude until their last chance to leave was lost, and eventually they ended up in the Nazi death camps. But at the time of Ufa's offer, all of that was still vague and shadowy. I myself, unlike Lisl, had no great love for Vienna itself, but the stage there was magnet enough to hold me.

Lisl had opened a shop in Berlin called Margarethe. It was in a fashionable part of town, and she was eager to see how it was doing. When the Ufa offer came, we decided that both of us would drive to Berlin and she'd look over her shop while I went to the studio.

"Once the contract is signed," I told her, "and I have to go there to do films, you can come with me and look after your shop. It will be a perfect arrangement."

When I arrived I was given the grand tour of the studios before the signing of the contract, and I was dutifully impressed. It really was a magnificent operation, with fantastic equipment and elaborate stages. Afterward Herr von Ried took me to the commissary for some lunch and we talked a bit about the contract before he left me to see if the studio heads were ready for the signing. "I'll be back in a moment."

Sitting close to us was Paul Wegener, one of Berlin's most distinguished actors. When Ried left, Wegener shouted a welcome to me across the room and introduced himself. I was thrilled to meet him and, shouting back at him, told him my name. Wegener was one of the biggest stars at Ufa, a handsome man with a wide Mongolian look to his face and piercing eyes.

"I couldn't help overhearing you and Ried," he called out without apology. "I take it you're planning to sign up with Ufa?"

He spoke in a loud, carrying voice, the voice he sometimes used on the stage and in films, and I was somewhat embarrassed, especially when I saw other people in the commissary turn to look at us.

I said, "Yes, sir, it's a great opportunity."

"Opportunity for you? Ridiculous. It's just another spoke in their Nazi propaganda wheel. If you sign, you're a fool. Hitler and these Nazis are a curse. Be sensible, boy. Stay in Vienna and don't come here!" He stood up abruptly and left without a good-bye as the entire commissary fell silent.

I was amazed at his frankness and at his courage in shouting this out. He seemed to me a man who didn't give a damn, and I admired that—and it started me thinking.

Herr von Ried returned and suggested we go to his office. The contracts were ready to be signed. I followed him and at his desk checked over the contracts, almost hoping I would find something we hadn't agreed on, but they were in order. They contained all the additions I had asked for.

Disregarding Wegener's warning, I began to sign them. As I

signed the last copy, Herr von Ried indicated another paper tucked under the contracts and, without meeting my eye, said, "Now this one."

Surprised, I looked at it and found a statement, apart from the contracts, saying I was willing to become a member of the National Socialist Actors' Guild of Germany and pay hefty dues into the organization. It also bound me to uphold the Nazi ideology.

I put down my pen calmly, although my heart began to race. "This wasn't in our agreement," I told Ried.

"No," he said uncomfortably. "But you understand that this is normal procedure. You can't be a part of Ufa unless you are also a member of the National Socialist Actors' Guild."

"Nevertheless," I said tightly, "I will not become a Nazi. I have nothing to do with politics. I am an actor, not a propagandist!"

His face paled, and he said, "If you don't sign that agreement, there will be no contract."

I had a brief flash of Wegener's face as he told me I was a fool, and I felt a vast sense of relief as I saw my film stardom fade away. "You could have told me that in Vienna," I said, trying desperately to keep my voice steady. "It would have saved me this trip to Berlin."

"Ah, but Berlin is a lovely city," Ried said as he quickly recovered his temper. "Now don't do anything hasty. I'll keep the contract. You talk it over with your wife and see how she feels."

"She will feel exactly as I do," I assured him as I left his office —and I was right. Lisl agreed completely.

"Of course the money would have been nice, Paul," she said as we drove back to Vienna. "But I'm terribly proud of you."

"I wonder what Paul Wegener will say when he finds out," I mused. "Well, there goes a career and stardom—and I'm glad."

◆

Five

The First
Play in London

*I*n Berlin Ried had called Lisl my wife, and many of our friends considered her that; but we were not married, although we were living together in Lisl's apartment. It was a beautiful little place decorated with Lisl's tasteful and unique style and taste. Actually, it was what we now call a penthouse, an apartment on top of Vienna's first high-rise. It had a roof garden with trees and flowers, and the apartment itself was delightful, but very small. Lisl's old nanny had lived with her as housekeeper, but when I moved in there was no room for her and she had to spend the nights sleeping at Lisl's parents' house, then commute to the apartment each morning.

Our moving in together—in those days it was considered "living in sin"—upset some of our friends and associates. We were both well known, Lisl for her couturier work and I for my acting, and Viennese society professed to be shocked by the openness of what we had done. Many of our friends, especially my old aristocratic ones, stopped seeing us, but the real explosion came from my mother. She was appalled at what I was doing, and she told me so when I moved my clothes out of her apartment.

"It's not that I don't like Lisl," she said in that tone that meant she really didn't, "but how can I respect her if you do this, Paul?"

"Don't respect her, Mother," I said seriously. "Just love her."

"Paul, it's not funny. What will my friends say? How can I hold my head up in polite society?"

I said, "Mother, it's my life, not yours, and I have to live it as I see fit, not as you do. Tell your friends the truth, that you disapprove of what I'm doing and can't forgive me."

"How can I tell them that? Of course I forgive you!"

I kissed her. "There. Then it's all right, isn't it?" But she just threw up her hands in despair.

However, as shocked as my old school friends and my society friends were, our theatrical acquaintances simply shrugged it off. What mattered to them was my public performance, not my private life, and publicly, on stage, my career seemed solid, and in films, even without the help of Ufa, I seemed headed for success. *High School* was a big hit, and the producer Joseph Than, whom I liked a great deal, approached me to do a second film. Than and I are still close friends and, since he now lives in Hollywood, we see each other frequently.

Only a Comedian was a movie about actors, and it also starred Rudolph Forster, the star of *High School,* and was done by the same producer and the same company. In general, actors were looked down on socially and called comedians no matter how successful they were. That explained the title. My part was good, but it was not the lead and not as pivotal a role as the one I'd had in *High School.* In that movie the plot hinged on my death.

"But if it's not a leading role, why take it?" Lisl asked. "Why not wait for a better offer?"

I thought uneasily of my refusal to sign the Ufa contract, and I wondered how much influence the Nazis could have over my future career. I told Lisl, prophetically, as it turned out, "There may not be another offer, and besides, the movies pay for all the extras, like that wonderful car you have your heart set on."

My apprehensions about my film career in Austria were justified when *Only a Comedian* appeared. The reviews were excellent, and I was offered a leading role by Henry Kosterlitz, a leading director who changed his name to Koster when he came to America later. At the time he was doing a film with a famous Hungarian actress, a big star, in the female lead. It would be a tremendous leap ahead in my film career if I was starred with her. But after I agreed, Kosterlitz told me he had to withdraw the offer.

"But why?" I asked, knowing the answer.

"Because the German distributors have turned you down. If I insist on putting you in it, Berlin will refuse to distribute the film, and we'd be dead. I'm heartsick about it, Paul, but that's the way it is. You're blacklisted in Germany. Goebbels has heard about your refusal to sign with Ufa and has declared he won't have you in German films—or in films Germany distributes. I'm sorry."

I was even sorrier. *Only a Comedian* had been filmed before the producer found out about my refusal to join the National Socialist Actors' Guild. Once Goebbels' decision was known, before *Only a Comedian* was given German distribution, my name was taken off the film. I never appeared on the list of credits, but I was there on the screen, acting in the film. The unknown actor. It was too expensive to reshoot the picture or to cut me out, so reality was tampered with and I simply wasn't there!

My career on the stage, however, continued without interference. Austria was still independent, a free country, and I appeared in six plays during 1935: *Something Is Wrong, The Hour, Waltz Paradise, Where Love Blooms, The Unknown Girl,* and *Mizzi. The Unknown Girl* was later made into a film by Hollywood and called *The Bride Wore Red.* It starred Joan Crawford.

I continued to support my mother and brother Robert, who was now able to go on to the university and study industrial chemistry. He was offered a job with a perfume company in Vienna and worked there until Lisl's mother, who liked him very much, asked him to go into business with her. She had some money to invest and wanted to start a small drugstore. Robert agreed, and he ran the shop while she was the chief investor. They got along splendidly.

Lisl's tiny apartment grew more and more difficult for the two of us, especially since our hours were so different. She worked during the day and was usually asleep when I came home from my nightclub stint. I hated to wake her up, but in a place that small I usually had no alternative. "What we need," I decided, "is a larger apartment."

Reluctantly, Lisl agreed. She hated to leave her charming apartment with its roof garden, but we desperately needed more room. After a good deal of searching we found a house for rent with two spacious apartments and a garage. The top apartment was much larger than we needed, but the bottom one was perfect for the two of us. By coincidence, Lisl's parents were looking for a smaller place at the same time, and they fell in love with the top apartment in the house. We decided that we four could live together and we took the house. There was even room for Lutzi, Lisl's housekeeper, and two other servants, and we decided we would try a ménage where we shared the servants.

Those years in the early thirties were lived in the shadow of the Nazi rise to power in nearby Germany, yet somehow the shadow was not as dark as it might have been on the Viennese stage. Men like Reinhardt, who was Jewish, continued to be admired and lionized, and there was little distinction among actors in terms of politics or religion. As for me, I was far too busy to concern myself with politics until they concerned themselves with me.

A typical day for me would start at five or six in the morning when I was doing a film. A car would pick me up and take me to location. There I'd work from seven until it was time for my performance at the theatre. I'd be driven there, perform that evening and, after the evening's performance, hurry to the nightclub, where I'd pick up a bit of extra cash doing sketches and singing songs. I'd come back to the apartment exhausted and fall into bed, to be picked up again the next morning at six.

It was hard and grueling, but I seemed to have boundless energy, and I looked on it all as fun as well as work. I must mention that somehow, in between, I always managed to give a few hours to my infinitely patient publishing firm.

But with films closed to me I began to get apprehensive. How long, I wondered, before the stage, too, fell under Goebbels' dictates? Perhaps I'd better start looking for some alternatives. "What do you think of Paris?" I asked Lisl. "I love it there, and there are all sorts of movie opportunities, and I am positive that Hitler will never influence the Parisians."

"No," Lisl said firmly. "I'll live in Vienna and die here. I love this city, Paul. It's my home."

I didn't press the point, but I was ripe for change of some kind and it came about late in 1935 when I was doing a play called *Mizzi* at the Deutsches Volkstheater in Vienna. The play was a little piece of fluff about the son of a rich family falling in love with the daughter of a middle-class family—a favorite stage them of the thirties.

I was the leading man and Henry Shereck, the English pro-

ducer who ran His Majesty's Theater at the Haymarket in London,
came to see the play and afterward went back to my dressing room.
Shereck spoke French and German fluently.

"I liked your performance," he told me in German. "Do you
sing?"

I said, "Of course. I've done a number of musical plays. I'm no
opera singer, but I have a decent voice."

"That's splendid." He bobbed his head. "I'm going to produce
a play in England called *Café Chantant*, and there's a marvelous part
in it—an impoverished Austrian aristocrat waiting tables at a good
restaurant in Kitzbühel. He falls in love with an American millionaire's daughter. The parents, who don't know he's a count, are dead
set against it. They've brought her to Europe to marry a title, but
finally someone tells them he's a count, and it all ends happily. Do
you like it?"

"It's very original," I said drily and Shereck laughed. "It's pure
corn, what you call schmaltz, but it's bound to be a hit. The Prince
of Wales discovered Kitzbühel in the Tirol last year, and every little
girl in London is wearing a Tyrolean hat. I'll pay you a hundred
pounds a week. What do you say?"

What could I say? A hundred pounds equaled five hundred
dollars then. I signed the contract without telling Lisl. This, I realized, was how I could escape the growing Nazi menace. What
Shereck never asked, however, was, could I speak English? We had
discussed the project in German, and I didn't know a word of
English!

That little problem didn't bother me. I was young and arrogant
and confident in my ability to do anything. I promptly hired an
English coach when the script came, and he taught me the words
in English. That was the extent of my knowledge of the language
except for a few stock phrases. It worked, too, except that at the first
rehearsal in England, I, who had always been proud of my beautiful
speaking voice, gave my lines in a timid little squeak.

The director said, "Mr. von Hernried, speak up, please."

It took me a moment to understand him. Then, concentrating
on the words, I said, "I am speaking up."

"But we can't hear you." He frowned.

"Are you sure you want to?" I muttered in German, then took my courage in hand and put some volume into the lines. Amazingly, it worked, and by the second day I was managing to make myself understood. Today I would be appalled at anyone who tried a trick like that, but when you're young you'll try anything.

I hadn't told Lisl about the English contract until I was ready to leave, then I confessed what I had done and said, "Those English girls are very attractive, I hear. Don't you think we should be married before I go?"

Lisl, who had been badly hurt by her first marriage, was reluctant to enter into another, and although I had suggested marriage a number of times, her answer had always been, "It will spoil everything, Paul. I know."

Now she said, "I don't want to tarnish this beautiful relationship, Paul."

"I promise you marriage won't spoil it," I said. "And remember those English girls."

Finally, reluctantly, she agreed. We were married on Saturday, and on Sunday I took the train to London, nearly missing it because we had been up all night celebrating. The porter threw my suitcase on the moving train and Lisl, teary-eyed, waved farewell from the platform. It was, I couldn't help thinking, a little like a scene from a motion picture.

The musical in London was successful and played for a long run. Lisl came for the first night and then came over frequently to visit, and very slowly she began to know London and admit that, although it could not begin to compare with Vienna, it still had some good things about it. "But whatever you say in its favor," she told me with a shake of her head, "you must admit the food is god-awful!" I had to agree.

In the play, in the part of the count as a waiter, there were two scenes where I would move from table to table, singing. This bit in the play was particularly successful, and the manager of the Ritz Hotel contacted me through Henry Shereck to ask if I would sing nights at the Ritz Cabaret. I called my English agent, whom Shereck had helped me find, and I asked whether I should take it on. "They're offering me a hundred pounds a week, as much as I get in the play."

"Grab the money and run," she advised with a laugh, and my income rose to the astonishing height of a thousand dollars a week, a fantastic amount for the times—and my appearance at the cabaret was a success.

I sang the same songs in the cabaret that I sang in the play, starting onstage and then moving from table to table, and the customers loved it. Lisl, during one of her visits, came to hear me and sat at a front-row table. Afterward I asked, "Did you like it?" and she shrugged. "I was embarrassed."

"Why?" I said, astonished. "The songs were all proper. Maybe a bit suggestive, but nothing that would embarrass you."

"Oh, it wasn't the songs. It was the claque they hired. Was that necessary?"

"Claque?" I was puzzled. "There wasn't any claque."

"Wasn't there? Come on, Paul. I heard them stamping their feet and clapping. No respectable audience in evening clothes who can afford the Ritz does that."

"But this is England." I laughed. "They do it here, honest!"

She wouldn't believe me until she came back herself one night and sat at the rear of the cabaret. Then she actually saw the men and women in evening dress applauding, stamping, and whistling, and she was finally convinced. "Give me Vienna," she said sadly. "They're a proper audience."

One night, shortly after my opening, the cabaret manager came to me and said, "This is a big night, Paul. The rumor is that Edward, the Prince of Wales, is coming, and the place is packed. Do your best. Something like this is fantastic publicity!"

I remembered Edward with a touch of nostalgia from that drunken evening long ago in Cannes, but I thought, he won't recall it, and if he does he won't possibly tell the press about it.

But I was wrong. At the end of my routine, Edward stood up and came to the podium where I was. We shook hands and he said, "Do you recall that wonderful evening in Cannes?"

I grinned and said, "I couldn't forget it, Your Royal Highness."

"Nor could I!" He laughed. "Paul, I enjoyed hearing you sing tonight almost as much. It was so good to see you again."

We talked for a while longer and, of course, all the newspapers picked it up the next day and it was in every gossip column. My reputation was made and the manager was delighted. "This does it, Paul," he told me. "You can sing here at the Ritz for as long as you want. Having the prince recognize you and chat with you like that is a fantastic break for us, fantastic!"

My original engagement at the Ritz Cabaret had been for one season, from September until June, and though I could have stayed longer—especially after the attention shown me by the Prince of Wales—one season in the cabaret suited me, since *Café Chantant*, the musical play that had brought me to London, was scheduled to close at the end of June. Nothing else was offered to me in London, and I knew I'd have to go back to Vienna to get work—provided it was available. London was far enough away from Germany to make Hitler and his crew seem less important. I could almost forget about him unless it was driven home to me, as it eventually was.

The cabaret at the Ritz had a constant parade of distinguished visitors, and one night Baron von Ribbentrop appeared with his wife and entourage. At that time Ribbentrop was ambassador to London for Nazi Germany. He had qualified as ambassador, and later Foreign Minister for the Third Reich, because of his familiarity with foreign customs and languages, a familiarity gained as a traveler for the champagne merchant Henkell. He married into Henkell's family and owed his title to a paid-for adoption by a relative. As Goebbels said of him, "He bought his name, he married his money, and he swindled his way into office."

And now here he was at the Ritz Cabaret. I wasn't aware that he was in the audience until a note was brought to me by one of the waiters asking me to come and dance a waltz with Ribbentrop's wife. "Is there any answer?" the waiter asked as I stood frowning at the note.

I shook my head. "No, I'll answer this myself."

I had thought that for at least this period in London I had left the horrors of Nazi Germany behind. And now here was this dull-witted Ribbentrop strutting through the diplomatic circles of London. More and more of the stories about what was going on in Germany had begun to filter out, along with the truth about what was being done to the Jews. I had so many friends who were Jewish, and because of it I felt not only an intellectual hatred of the Nazis, but an emotional one as well.

I approached Ribbentrop's table and said, "Baron, my name is Paul von Hernried, and I'd like to let you know that I am an actor, an artist, to be exact. I am not a gigolo, and I am not for hire to dance with a guest."

I turned to his wife, a blond, good-looking, somewhat horsey German woman with very large teeth, and I said, "If I were to meet you socially, Frau von Ribbentrop, I might ask you to dance—but then again, I might not because I don't care for Nazis, and I have never cared for the Third Reich, so if you will excuse me . . ." I bowed and turned away.

Ribbentrop never moved a muscle. His face grew white, but he just sat there staring at me with his cold blue eyes. I walked away feeling quite good about it. Even now, I think it was one of the high points of my life. But it was also a reminder that even in London I was not completely free of Germany's reach.

During the run of the play *Café Chantant*, Lisl would come to London and stay with me for a week or two or even longer. We spent our holidays together and even the enforced separations weren't too bad. They made our meetings all the sweeter. I had taken a small apartment at the Mayfair Court, an annex of the Mayfair Hotel, and one of the nice things about it was that it not only had the hotel maid service, but room service as well. In fact, I had my first disastrous experience with English food at the Mayfair Court.

I called room service my first night there and ordered a trout. It came with anchovies on top! To me it was an absolute sacrilege to assault the delicate flavor of trout with the overbearing taste of anchovies. I must say that in later years I came to love England and eventually to forgive the English almost everything, their weather, their language—everything except their cooking.

Lisl, who had always been positive that she could never exist outside of Vienna, began to admit, though grudgingly, that she enjoyed her vacations in London and in the English countryside, especially the weekends we spent in the great luxury of the large mansions and castles that were the country homes of some of my new friends. Lisl was a magnificent horsewoman and loved to ride across the English countryside. I, too, was an excellent horseman. At school I had ridden in the Theresianium riding quadrille every Sunday morning. Later I played polo, using the polo ponies of my friend Count Ulrich Kinsky. In fact, I was a "ten-goal man."

But all good things must end, and eventually *Café Chantant* closed, and that first wonderful season in London came to an end. I would have to return to Vienna, though I decided to put that off as long as possible. I had a good deal of money saved up and one or two ideas about spending it.

Six

◆

The Fall
of Austria

W hen *Café Chantant* closed, I found myself with enough money to buy the car Lisl had always dreamed of, the Renault Viva Grand Sport. I called Lisl and asked her to meet me in Paris at a time convenient for both of us, then made arrangements to pick up the car at Renault in Paris. Both of us flew into the city the same day, met at the airport, had dinner with an old friend at Fouquets, then checked into the sumptuous Hotel Raphael, our favorite. "We are really doing this up properly," I told my beautiful, delighted wife.

"I'm very impressed," Lisl said, looking around our exquisite suite. "But what are you going to do for an encore?"

"My birthday present for you will be an encore tomorrow," I assured her, and the next morning presented her with the Renault Viva Grand Sport. Lisl couldn't get over the car, a four-door convertible with a motor that ran like a dream, as smooth as a whisper. I was a hero in her eyes.

We set out to drive to Cannes, and it was an unforgettable trip, though it started out badly. We drove to Vienne, a city on the Rhône, where we had lunch at La Pyramide, one of the ten best restaurants in France. It was so good that we decided to splurge and stay the night in Vienne's best hotel and have dinner at La Pyramide as well. It was a brave decision, but the problem was that there was no "best" hotel in the entire town. The place we ended up in had bedbugs, as we found out very quickly.

"What are we going to do?" Lisl asked miserably, scratching the red bites on her body.

"I've read of a peasant remedy," I told her. "We'll fill four glasses with water and put a leg of the bed in each glass."

She looked at me as if I were crazy, and I explained. "The

bedbugs will drown when they try to climb up the legs of the bed."

Lisl was doubtful, but I thought the idea brilliant. I got the glasses from the management, and we filled them, slipped them under the legs of the bed, and went back to sleep—or I should say we tried to sleep. We didn't realize that the bedbugs didn't need to climb up the legs of the bed. They were firmly ensconced in the mattress and came out the moment the light went off. We ended up sleeping fitfully, with all the lights on and no covers, to wake up the next morning not only bitten all over, but freezing as well!

We drove on through Provence to Cannes, nursing our rashes of bites but delighted at the smooth performance of the Viva Grand Sport. At Cannes we were able to afford one of the very best hotels, the Miramar. But we didn't have much time to enjoy our stay. No sooner had we settled in when I got a call from Franz Zwonik, a well-known Austrian producer. "We've all read of your success in London. When are you coming back to Vienna? I have a wonderful part for you in a brilliant anti-war play."

I accepted over the phone, all my fears about being forgotten in Vienna disappearing, and we headed home ten days later. The play was called *Der Etappenhas* in German, the story of a private who managed, by all sorts of tricks and devices, to stay away from the front. I played the romantic lead, and the play was as much a success as Zwonik thought it would be. It played at the Raimund Theatre for an entire season, a remarkably long run for Vienna. Lisl was delighted to have me home, and although I missed London, I liked the play and my part, and there was the compensation of seeing all my old friends and family.

The next summer we decided to drive the Viva Grand Sport down to Cannes again, but this time we insisted on Lisl's parents' coming along. There was plenty of room in the car, and they were grand company. Gustav, Lisl's father, had an endless fund of information about every architectural style we passed, about every cathedral and every museum. It was most exciting.

"You mustn't bore the children," Lisl's mother would say anxiously as Gustav launched into some involved historical anecdote about a town or fortress, but he would brush her objections aside. "They should know these things," he insisted, and he was really too nice a person for us to object. And in truth, the facts we learned were fascinating—there were just too many of them! But sometimes, when he wanted to see just one painting for his studies or a new book, he and Lisl's mother would go in alone while we waited in the car or, if possible, had an espresso nearby.

One time when we stopped in Italy, there was no café or bar close to the museum, so we stayed in the car smoking. Suddenly I noticed a half dozen young children clustering around the car, touching it and whispering among themselves. I started to shoo them off, but another group materialized on the other side of the car. Within minutes there were fifty or sixty little Italian urchins swarming over our precious Viva Grand Sport, rubbing their greasy little hands over it in admiration and asking eager questions about it.

I was frantically trying to get rid of them when Lisl took my arm and said, in what was to me a totally unfamiliar voice, "Aren't they darling, Paul?"

I wasn't that happy about children in general, and less so when they were smearing our beautiful car with dirty handprints. "They're fine until they're three years old," I muttered, scowling at the ragged kids. "Then they should be given away and new ones produced!"

"You'll feel differently about children," she said in that same, foolishly maternal voice, "when we have one of our own."

"Children are highly overrated," I said, but I felt a cold chill go down my back. Our own children? We had never talked about children when we discussed marriage, and I dropped the subject at once, hoping Lisl would forget it too. The truth was, I had no interest in having children of my own. I was sure that there was nothing paternal in my makeup. As it was, I spent little enough time with Lisl. I didn't relish sharing that precious time with children.

That trip with Lisl's parents had some important advantages. We ate better and stayed in better hotels because they insisted on it and made up the difference with their own money. They enjoyed treating us, and I must say I enjoyed being treated.

Again in Cannes I received a call from Vienna, this time from Professor Beer. "When are you coming back? I have a great play for you."

"Very soon," I told him. "I'll call you in two days and give you the exact day of our arrival in Vienna."

The play Professor Beer had for me was called *The Mistress of La Paz*. "Take the script, Paul, and read it. You'll love it," Dr. Beer said when I saw him at the Scala.

I did love it. The star was a famous Hungarian character actress, Sari Fedak, a woman of sixty. I also was intrigued that the woman to play opposite me was Hortense Raky, a delectable Austrian actress. Even though I was a happily married man, she managed to excite me. My own part was fat and juicy, and I could see just how I'd play it. But Lisl, who had been asked to do the costumes for the play, had other ideas. She read the script and tossed it aside. "I'll do the costumes. It pays well, but I tell you, Paul, the play is trash. It won't last a night."

"I don't tell you which type of dress will sell, and I don't think you ought to tell me which play will go," I said rather pompously.

Lisl shrugged. "Suit yourself, but you'll see that I'm right."

I wouldn't believe her. She's just jealous of Hortense, I told myself, and went into rehearsal enthusiastically. Then, two weeks before we opened, I received a wire from my agent in London. "I have an offer for you to play Prince Albert in *Victoria Regina*. It will be at the Lyric Theatre, and it's bound to be a success. Pamela Stanley will play Victoria. Wire me your reply."

While Edward was still Prince of Wales, *Victoria Regina* had opened at the Gate Theatre, a club, because there was a rule in Great Britain that royalty couldn't be portrayed on the public stage—at least British royalty. Pamela Stanley had played Victoria, and Vincent Price, Albert. Gilbert Miller also bought the play for New York to star Helen Hayes and Vincent Price. Although it received rave notices at the Gate, it didn't play long because there wasn't a big-enough audience available. There were only so many club members.

Now Edward had come to the throne, and one of his first acts was to rescind this foolish decree. After all, he said, Shakespeare constantly portrayed royalty, and he was always performed.

As a result, *Victoria Regina*, produced by Gilbert Miller, was moved to a legitimate theatre, and I was asked to play the part of Albert, Victoria's husband. It was a fabulous opportunity to my way of thinking. I was one of the most popular leading men on the Viennese stage, but this would make me in London, and pay me much more money.

I went to Professor Beer with the telegram and asked him to release me from my commitment. Frowning angrily, he asked, "When do rehearsals for *Victoria* begin in England?"

I swallowed and said, "Two weeks after we open here with *The Mistress of La Paz*. That's why—"

He cut me off abruptly and furiously. "You dare to do this to me?" he shouted. "I took you in when Reinhardt refused to give you work. I've nursed you along and made you a star, and now you dare to ask me to release you? Do you understand what damage that would do to me? I could never replace you at such short notice!" He threw the telegram back at me. "I'll pretend I never read this. No! You signed a contract and I'm holding you to it."

I was devastated. I went home and told Lisl, "This is terrible. I want that part of Albert so much! Do you know what an opportunity it is? It would really make my name in London."

Lisl studied the crumpled telegram and said, "Now listen to me, Paul. I know the stage, maybe better than you do. I was involved with it when I was married to Edthofer, and I've done costumes for heaven knows how many plays—and I've watched you in every play you've been in."

"So?" I shrugged. "What has all that got to do with this?"

"So this is what you're going to do. Wire Gilbert Miller that you'll be delighted to accept his offer and you'll make arrangements to be free for the rehearsal date."

"But *The Mistress of La Paz* opens in a couple of days and the rehearsal for *Victoria Regina* is only two weeks away. Don't you understand? Beer is holding me to my contract."

"Trust me," Lisl said with supreme confidence. "*The Mistress of La Paz* is a disaster. It won't last two weeks. Never! You'll be free to go to London."

And she was right. The play opened to disastrous notices, and to my delight it folded in just two weeks and I was free. After I wired my acceptance to Miller, I went to the Viennese English tutor who had coached me for the last play I did in London. But after one session with him I grew uneasy. I had spent some time in England and his pronunciation no longer sounded accurate to me. In London I began working with a woman who had taught English at Cambridge.

Glancing through my part, she told me, "Forget the way the words are spelled. English is a barbaric language and doesn't sound anything like it's written. Just imitate me. Sound out the words after me."

She was excellent and I learned my part so well that the director in England was a bit disappointed. "Albert was German," he told me, taking me to one side. "Actually, I had hoped you'd have a thicker accent. Well, no matter. Let's get on with it."

A clever PR man released this story to the press, and in typically exaggerated form it hit all the gossip columns. I became a "master of the English language. No trace of an accent."

Another exaggeration of the press was apparent when the first publicity story about me labeled me a baron, Baron Paul von Hernried. "I am not a baron," I told Gilbert Miller in some annoyance. What on earth would my friends back home think of me if they read this?"

"But that 'von' in your name . . ." Miller started.

"In the first place the 'von' is no longer official in Austria since the World War, since we became a democracy. Sure, it's used, but it doesn't mean much."

"Then what does it mean?"

"It means *from,* or *of.* Look, I can be called *Ritter,* the German for 'knight.' My father was knighted, but you mustn't tell people I'm a baron. It's just not true!"

Miller soothed me down with, "Yes, yes, of course, Paul. You must forgive me . . ." And he went right on with the same story, convinced that I was just modest about being a baron. I heard later that when Gilbert Miller received my telegram saying I'd play the part of Albert, he immediately called Henry Shereck and said, "Do you know who I got to play Prince Albert? The Baron Paul von Hernried. How about that? I've got a baron to play a prince!"

Shereck, a mischievous man, said, "I'll tell you a big secret about Paul, Gil. Paul is really a bit illegitimate. He's a Hapsburg." Miller dropped the phone and shouted across the room to his wife, "Did you hear? Paul is a Hapsburg! Did you know? He's really a Hapsburg!"

There was nothing I could do about it, and all the news stories labeled me a baron. At first I thought my friends would be shocked, but they all thought it was a great joke and teased me about it constantly.

Victoria Regina was directed by Norman Marshall, and though I missed the first two days of rehearsal, I had learned my part well enough to please him. I found Pamela Stanley, the leading lady, a charming woman, and we got along famously. We opened to excellent reviews and settled in for a long, satisfying run.

There was one scene in the play where, at a party, I flirt with a lady-in-waiting. The lady drops a rose and I was supposed to pick it up and hand it to her. But during the second performance, as the rose fell, the theatre cat came streaking towards it, certain it was some kind of food.

I abandoned all of my suave approach and lunged across the stage. I just had to have that rose for my next speech and the following jealous scene with my wife, Victoria. I got one end and the cat the other and there was a brief and hilarious tug-of-war before I straightened up triumphantly with the tattered flower and handed it to the startled actress. The audience was marvelous; hardly anyone giggled!

Aside from that incident, the play went beautifully, and during its long run the Queen Mother decided to come and see us. Before the play started, the curtain went up and we were all assembled onstage to bow to Queen Mary in her box. She, in turn, raised her hand in that languid gesture she has passed down to the present queen, Elizabeth, a half-hearted little wave. The curtain descended and we scurried offstage and the play started.

During the run of the play, Joseph Duveen, the first Baron Duveen of Milbank, one of the world's most-famous art dealers, came to see me onstage and liked the play tremendously. So much so that he asked my father-in-law, Hofrat Gustav Glück, if I would be kind enough to have lunch with him, and would I select the place.

Baron Duveen relied on my father-in-law's advice and know-how in selecting his paintings, and the two were good friends. I was very pleased at the invitation to lunch, and I agreed. I selected the À l'Écu de France in Jermyn Street, and since I brought my car into town each day, I offered to pick him up.

When we reached the restaurant, there was no parking space available, so I suggested he go in and get a table and I would find a place to park. I found a spot nearby, came into the restaurant and joined him. He didn't seem very talkative, so I carried the conversation, telling him how pleased I was that he liked the play and my performance. I chatted about his friendship with my father-in-law, and put myself out to be amusing.

His soup came and I was surprised that he hadn't waited for me to order, then continued talking while he finished his soup. Then, wiping his lips, he looked at me and said, "My dear young man, I haven't the foggiest notion of who you are or what you're talking about. I don't mind your sharing my table, though it is rather odd, since there are so many empty tables.

"Actually, you needn't call me Baron. I'm just a businessman from Liverpool, and I've just come to town this morning—going back tomorrow. Now tell me, just who do you think I am?"

I stared at him. "You're joking, aren't you? You're Baron Duveen, and I just picked you up from your office in Davis street."

He stared at me a moment, then called a waiter over and asked if a Baron Duveen was having lunch in the restaurant.

"Yes, sir, right over there," the waiter said, pointing to a man sitting alone at a table and watching us curiously.

Red in the face, I apologized and hurried over to Duveen's table. Again I launched into an elaborate apology, pretending that the other man was an important producer and old friend and I just had to sit with him for a moment or two.

Duveen was very gracious, and we talked about *Victoria Regina* and my role in it, and all the while I kept looking at him furtively, then at the man I had sat down with. There was absolutely no resemblance! I am either an idiot or losing my mind, I thought. How could I have made such a stupid mistake? But at least both had accepted my explanations, weak as they were. I leaned back and attacked my lunch when it came.

During the run of the play Lisl again shuttled back and forth, from London to Berlin, to check her shop there, then to Vienna and back to London. "It's exhausting," she told me. "We have to settle down somehow, somewhere, Paul."

"In Vienna?" I asked uneasily.

"I'm frightened by what's going on back home," she said slowly. "Our own local Nazis have been carrying on a real campaign of terror. I think, and my father agrees, that it's weakening Chancellor Schuschnigg's hold on the country. You know, back in 1936, Germany promised to respect our independence and not interfere —but I don't think they'll live up to their promise."

Lisl was right. In February of 1938, Chancellor Kurt von Schuschnigg was called to Berchtesgaden for a "personal" talk with Hitler about Austrian independence. There, pressed by Ribbentrop, the newly appointed Foreign Minister, and Franz von Papen, Hitler's special ambassador in Vienna, Schuschnigg signed a document giving Germany unwarranted interference in Austrian affairs. It was, in effect, Austria's death warrant.

Austrian President Wilhelm Miklas tried to resist the agreement Schuschnigg had signed, but he finally gave in. Less than ten days later, Hitler told the Reichstag that from now on he regarded the problems of German citizens in Austria the concern of the Third Reich. At this point Schuschnigg tried to defy Hitler in a speech to the Austrian Bundestag, but while he was talking a mob of twenty thousand Nazis in Graz invaded the town square, tore down the Austrian flag, and replaced it with the swastika. Things grew increasingly worse, and by March 9, Schuschnigg decided to hold a plebiscite and let the people decide if they wanted to be part of Germany.

On hearing of this, Hitler is reported to have flown into a rage and then made the decision to invade Austria. Schuschnigg resigned and Miklas was forced out of office, and Dr. Arthur von Seyss-Inquart, a tool of the Nazis, took over as President. By March 12, German troops were streaming into Austria, and on March 13 a newly formed Austrian government proclaimed, "Austria is a province of the German Reich!" On the fourteenth of March Hitler entered Vienna in triumph after the arrest of thousands of "undesirables." In just a few weeks 79,000 people in Vienna alone were arrested.

We were stunned, and terrified about Lisl's parents. Her brother Gustl had represented the Rockefeller Bank in Berlin, but when Hitler became Chancellor he had asked for a transfer to London and had been there ever since. Now the three of us got together to try to decide what to do.

"Mother and Father must leave Vienna at once," Gustl Glück said. "I just hope it isn't too late."

"I'll go back and bring them out," Lisl decided, and she waved aside my uneasiness at the idea.

"I think it's taking too much of a chance," I told her.

"You can't go, and neither can Gustl. I have my business to wrap up, and I've not been in any trouble with the Nazis."

"I have a good friend in Vienna, a lawyer, a Baron Ettinghausen," Gustl said. "He's high up in the Nazi party, but I know he'll help you if there's any trouble."

"There won't be any trouble," Lisl said firmly, but she took the Baron's name anyway.

"And my mother," I said. "Beg her to come along with you. Robert, too—and for God's sake, bring the car!"

Lisl went back to Vienna and found that her parents had already made plans to leave and were eager to go with her. My brother Robert had received his induction notice to the army, but he had decided he wouldn't serve under Hitler and had managed to join an import firm owned by the father of one of his friends from the Teresianium. He took off for South Africa to buy coffee with a temporary permit to leave Vienna.

My mother, characteristically, refused to leave Vienna. "I

speak no English," she told Lisl. "What would I do, an old foreign woman in a strange country? Here I am among my friends. There's nothing the Nazis can do to me."

As a matter of fact, my mother stayed in Vienna throughout the war. The publishers I had worked for, in unusual generosity, continued to pay her the commissions on the sales to my old customers, and somehow she got along. After the war, General Mark Clark, whom I had met at several parties and who had become a fan and friend of mine after my Hollywood pictures appeared, looked her up and provided food and coal for her in the terrible aftermath of World War II.

Lisl's older brother, Franz, an intellectual who had written a number of books and was director of the Art Museum of the Town of Vienna, also decided to stay on in Vienna. He had a magnificent collection of books, and he couldn't bear to leave them. Franz was in the section of Vienna taken over by the Russians after the war, and for some reason they admired him tremendously. They requisitioned some of his rooms, put their horses in his garden, brought food, gifts, and vodka, and sat with him discussing politics and world affairs. He complained later, however, that their horses ate his rose garden.

In Vienna, Lisl packed her parents and some possessions into the Viva Grand Sport and prepared to leave. A Jewish family, good friends of ours, who were trying to get out, took her aside and asked her if she'd smuggle out some of their jewels and money. "It's obvious," they told her, "that if the Nazis do let us go, they'll take everything and we'll be penniless in a strange land."

Lisl agreed and, with her parents and the faithful Lutzi and the smuggled jewelry and money, got ready to take off. "Go out through Germany, not through Switzerland, where everybody is trying to leave," Baron Ettinghausen advised her. "From Germany go to Switzerland or France, and no one will suspect you are taking anything out."

Lisl followed his advice and she left Vienna headed for the German border. A short way out of the city they passed a convoy of Nazi soldiers and the four of them tensed up. Lisl drove carefully, eyes straight ahead, and drew a sigh of relief when she had left them behind. But her relief was short-lived. She had hardly gone a mile ahead of the convoy when the car's rear tire blew.

In dismay she climbed out and looked at the spare. She had never had to change a tire before, and her father knew even less about a car than she did—and down the road the convoy was approaching her! What if they were searched now? What if the jewelry and money were discovered? Lisl turned back to the spare tire, struggling to get it off the car, trying to ignore the approaching soldiers.

The soldiers, in turn, saw a beautiful young lady in distress, and one of the trucks came to a halt while the men poured out. They joked with her, changed her tire, and beamed pleasantly as she drove off. "In a cold sweat!" as she told me later.

They drove to Germany and out through Switzerland, as the baron had suggested, then to Paris, where they stayed at one of the best hotels, the Raphael, relieved that from then on the trip would be without danger. But Lisl's adventure wasn't quite over. At the hotel she received a call from France's Deuxième Bureau, the intelligence section. They asked if they could come to see her, and she said yes.

A very smooth but distinguished man appeared at the hotel to "pick her up," and he led her downstairs to a large limousine, its windows curtained off. He ushered her in, and once the car took off, he produced a black silk handkerchief.

"Would you permit us to blindfold you, madame?" he asked.

Lisl agreed, thrilled at this real-life spy drama, but a bit uneasy too. How could she be sure he wasn't a Nazi agent?

"It was the strangest trip," she told me later. "It must have taken a half hour, though how could I tell exactly with that silly blindfold? When we finally stopped and they took the blindfold off, we were in front of a beautiful château, but whether it was in the country or a block from the hotel there was no way of knowing. They could have been driving around the block all that time.

"They led me into a roomful of solemn men who explained what they wanted."

"You seem able to come and go in Vienna, Madame Hern-ried," they told her. "We would like you to work for us."

"Work for you how?" she asked.

"Well, we know you have entry into the Viennese aristocracy, and you might overhear some important information. We'd like you to become an agent for our intelligence service. There would be a generous allowance, and we would pay your expenses."

Excited and thrilled, seeing herself as a Mata Hari and mentally designing some sleek and elegant black frocks, Lisl said, "I would be delighted to accept and do my part, but you must let me talk it over with my husband."

They agreed, and she was transported back to the hotel in the same blindfolded fashion. In London, a few days later, she told me about it and I was aghast. "Under no conditions, dearest Lisl, will you do anything that stupid and dangerous," I said. "Absolutely not! You're not trained for this dirty business." And I refused to be coaxed by persuasive arguments, tears, or wild talks about patriotism. In the end, reluctantly, she gave the idea up and wrote to tell them of her refusal.

"I could have been such a glamorous spy," she said sadly as she sent the letter off.

"And I could have been a widower," I reminded her. She stared at me for a long moment, then shook her head. "I never really thought of that. Well, I guess you're right."

Seven

◆

England:
Stage and Film

$\mathcal{I}$n London, Lisl's parents moved into an apartment next to ours in the Mayfair Court, and then Lisl and I went house hunting. In Hampstead, we discovered a large, lovely house with four stories, where all of us could have our privacy and share a large kitchen. It also had a splendid garden and was located in a good neighborhood. We rented it immediately.

In Vienna, Lisl had an excellent partner, a woman whom she trusted to run the business for her now that we were in England. "But I can't continue to manage things from abroad," she told me. "I'm going to let her take over the entire Berlin-Vienna operation, and I'll look for work here."

Reluctantly she had decided that I was right. There was no future for either of us in Austria. The trade papers in the garment industry had heralded Lisl's arrival in England and had interviewed her. She had no trouble finding work, and the job she found paid an excellent salary. She began to design clothes for a large company that made ready-to-wear dresses. She was to design models that could be made simply, and it was something of a challenge for someone who had only designed custom-made clothes. She spent a week in Manchester, where the firm's factory was, and then worked out of Portland Square in London.

Although her salary was excellent, Lisl found the work boring. She was used to couturier work, and mass production never appealed to her. So, although her designs were best-sellers and she received a bonus for each one that sold well, she was far from happy about her job. When a friend from Vienna who had come to England with a sizable amount of money to invest approached Lisl about a partnership, Lisl was ready and eager. They opened a London branch called "Lisl's."

Once we were all settled in London, Lisl decided to go back and see if she could get our furniture and her parents' possessions out of Austria. I said, "That's insane! We're doing well here. Why take a chance?"

Lisl shrugged. "Why not? What kind of a chance is it? They've nothing against me, and they may be Nazis, but they aren't monsters. I have some lovely pieces of furniture there, you know. I'll crate them and send them here. And there's my father's library and furniture and paintings. They can't be replaced. And besides, when we get the furniture here, we can move into the house we rented."

"None of that matters compared to your safety," I told her, "and if you think they aren't monsters, you should hear some of the stories beginning to come out of Germany."

She shrugged. "Stories! Anyway, there are things about my business I must settle. I want to sign the shops over to my partner."

We argued for days, but her mind was made up, and the final argument she used was the dogs. We had three Skye terriers back in Vienna who were being cared for by a neighbor. "Can I just desert them?" she asked.

"What on earth will we do with three dogs here?"

"All right. You win, as usual," she said. "I won't take all three. Just one." Somehow I had lost the argument by winning it.

Lisl got into Austria with no trouble. She made arrangements about the furniture, and then began negotiations with her partner. This woman was a decent sort, but her daughter saw Lisl's return as a threat. Unaware of Lisl's intentions, she was sure she would take the business away from her mother, and in an attempt to stop her, she denounced Lisl to the Gestapo.

"Frau von Hernried has helped Jewish families escape. She's smuggled jewelry out for them and has let them sleep in her shop overnight when their homes were burned," she told them.

Lisl was picked up immediately and taken to the nearest Gestapo headquarters. When she was told of the charges, she tried to laugh them off. "These accusations are nonsense," she blustered.

"Perhaps," the Gestapo agent told her. "But you are on your way to prison and the concentration camps, young lady. It doesn't pay to help the enemies of Germany's Third Reich!"

"Well, if I must go, I will," Lisl said tensely. "But it won't be good publicity in London, where my husband is starring in *Victoria Regina*. He'll tell this idiotic story to every newspaper! Anyway, let me call Baron Ettinghausen. He'll notify my family."

The Gestapo man knew Ettinghausen was high up in the party and, afraid of offending him, allowed Lisl to call. The Baron explained to Lisl, "I can't come over because I'm tied up with government work, but I'll send my deputy, Karl Albrecht Majer."

The baron was a powerful man, and his deputy, Majer, moved swiftly. He got Lisl's partner and her daughter down to Gestapo headquarters and said, "Let's get all this straightened out. There must be a misunderstanding. I cannot conceive of a dedicated citizen like Frau von Hernried conspiring with enemies of the Reich. There must be a reason behind the accusation." Looking directly at the daughter, he asked, "Is it because your mother wanted the shop?"

"That's nonsense," Lisl said. "I came back to Vienna to sign the shop over to her before I joined my husband. You must realize that as an actor he must go where the work is, and as a good wife I must go with him. He's in a play that may run for years in London."

When the daughter heard this, she burst into tears and retracted what she had said. We never found out if she was punished for her lies, but Lisl was freed with gracious apologies, and she left Austria immediately by plane—with all three Skye terriers. She had already made arrangements for shipping the furniture, pictures, and books. Now all she wanted was to get out of the country, but to our amazement all of our furniture and Gustav Glück's valuable library, all packed and crated, arrived a few weeks later, courtesy of Karl Albrecht.

We found out later that, although Ettinghausen had initially expected great things from Hitler and Nazism, he eventually became disillusioned and fell out of favor. He was sent to the Russian front and was killed there—shot in the back.

In June 1938 we went on tour with *Victoria Regina*, and the play was received with excitement wherever it played. There were also some funny moments. In one scene Victoria is told by an old archbishop that she is queen. The archbishop was played by an aging actor who not only had trouble remembering his lines, but was afflicted with a bad case of arthritis. When he knelt before the queen, all of us in the cast held our breath until he had struggled back to his feet. Some nights it seemed as if he'd never make it.

Then, in one performance, he knelt, started his speech—and forgot the end of it! There was a long, dreadful pause while he looked toward the wings where the prompter stood, but this was our three hundred and seventy-sixth performance, and the prompter wasn't even bothering to follow the play. We were all so sure of our parts. He turned the pages of the script desperately, looking for the place, until finally, with all the dignity he could muster, the old man struggled to his feet and marched off into the wings while Pamela Stanley, as Victoria, stood there dumbfounded.

There was a whispered colloquy, and then the old man marched back, knelt again, and delivered the rest of his speech. We had done all we could do to keep from applauding as he struggled to his feet for the second time.

To me, the curious thing about that tour was that Pamela Stanley and I, as Victoria and Albert, were never treated as two actors. We were treated like royalty. It was as if the thin line that separates the actor from his part had disappeared, and we had become the queen and her prince consort in the eyes of the public.

At one point in the tour we were invited to lunch aboard an aircraft carrier of Britain's fleet, and to our amazement we were actually piped aboard, a procedure reserved for royalty or high naval officials.

This confusion of role and actor has always amused me. Some actors and actresses are carried away by it; they come to believe themselves something special because of the adulation they receive. I could never understand that. To my mind, being a star was a big bother, except for three things: you receive an enormous amount of money for your work; you get the best table in every restaurant; and the studio always sends you first-class wherever you go.

When the tour for *Victoria Regina* was over, I started my first English movie, *Goodbye Mr. Chips*, a story about a dedicated Brit-

ish schoolteacher. I played the German master at the school, a man
who becomes Chip's friend and takes him on a walking tour of
Austria. There we meet two English girls, and one, played by Greer
Garson, becomes his wife. Robert Donat played Chips.

It was Greer Garson's first movie role, a leading role in the film,
and she was understandably nervous about it. I had seen her in a play
in London and didn't think much of her performance, though I
must admit that at the time I thought acting on the London stage
was generally poor. The German stage had been the center of the
theatrical world until, under Hitler, the best directors fled to America. For a time New York was the theatrical center, and then it
shifted back to London. But in those days England had few good
stage actors, and Greer was not one of them.

In the *Chips* film, Greer was extremely nervous about her
ability and came to Bob Donat and me in tears at least twice a week.
"I'm just not getting it. What shall I do? Please, Paul, Bob—help
me out." And we did, and Sam Wood, the director, an excellent
director, helped her too. "Be simple," we all advised her. "Just
remember, you can be more effective by throwing away a line than
by emoting over it."

It was a pleasure to work with Bob Donat. Not only was he a
delightful person, but he was also a very talented actor, and he
brought out the best in all of us. Sam Wood, an American, is, to my
way of thinking, one of the five best directors I've ever worked with.
He taught me a great deal about acting for the films and even more
about directing.

But in spite of his talent, he was an impatient man and eager
to get the picture done on schedule. One morning, shooting a scene
that was supposed to take place in Austria at a railroad station but
was actually done on the back lot at Denham, the enormous studio
where this MGM picture was shot, I noticed a glaring anachronism.
Donat and I are saying good-bye to Greer and her friend, and on the
railroad coach in the background the art department had lettered "Ö·
B·B," which stood for Östereichische Bundes Bahnen, the postwar
name for the Austrian Railroad. The trouble was, I realized as I
stared at it, that the picture took place before World War I, when

the cars had all been labeled K·u·K·Ö·B—Kaiserliche und Königliche Östereichische Bahnen. I pointed out the discrepancy to Sam.

"Christ, you're right, Paul," he said with a frown, and called over the art director. "How long will it take to change it?"

"I can have it for you after lunch."

Sam scowled and looked at his watch. "Too much time. To hell with it. Shoot it the way it is. Who'll notice?"

It was shot, and literally hundreds of people did notice and wrote me letters. "How can you, as an Austrian, stand in front of a coach marked like that in such a scene?"

I made copies of all the letters as they came in, and I forwarded them to Sam. Let him feel guilty! I must say, however, that not only was Sam a fine director, but he had a great quality; humility. In my first scene, when I tried to persuade Donat to go on a walking tour, I thought the scene should be played one way and Sam disagreed. He had an entirely different concept. I was bothered by it, but he was the director, and in Austria we were taught that the director's word is law. But when we had finished the scene and Sam said, "Print it!" I couldn't help telling him, "You won't be happy with it."

He said, "We'll look at the rushes together." And we did, and he nodded, "You were right, Paul. We'll reshoot the scene your way." To me, the ability to admit a mistake is the sign of a very good director.

Goodbye Mr. Chips was a great hit, and because of its success Albert de Courville asked me to appear in a movie he was directing, *An Englishman's Home.* I was to play a Nazi, a rich, villainous part. In the script I, as a German spy, came into an English household, made love to a young woman, and gave her young brother a gift of a kit for a homemade radio. I help him put it together, and it turns out to be a beacon to lead the German planes to this house in the center of London for a bombing attack.

Edmund Gwenn was the star of the film, an excellent character actor and a perfect gentleman. He lived at the Carlton Hotel in Haymarket, and we often had him to dinner or dined with him at his hotel, one of the rare places in London where the food was good.

We became close friends during the filming and remained friends for years after, when we met again in Hollywood.

The director, De Courville, had some strange ideas, and at one point I listened to his direction and couldn't believe what he was saying. It was a piece of unimportant business that just didn't make sense. I tried to talk him out of it, and finally I threw up my hands. "I'll do it, but I think you're nuts!"

"I am not!" he cried out, his eyes suddenly gleaming, and he drew himself up to his full height and pulled out a document from his inside pocket. Thrusting the paper at me, he said, "See. If you think I'm nuts, look at that."

I looked, and to my amazement saw that it was a discharge from an insane asylum!

While we were filming *An Englishman's Home*, Alexander Korda, the head of Denham Studios, came to watch our work, and the two of us, both foreigners, found we had a lot in common. We became good friends during that period. Korda, a Hungarian by birth, had done wonders for the British film industry and very well for himself in the process. A film producer in London, Victor Saville, some years later told me an amusing anecdote about Korda that illustrates his keen business sense and his ability to manipulate people.

When the war started, Korda could no longer get American stars, and as a result his business began to slip. He called a meeting of his stockholders, all wealthy British lords who had invested in his films only to improve Britain's reputation as a filmmaker. They knew nothing about the industry.

"I've brought you here," he told them, "because with the war on and the lack of American name actors, I don't think our business will be profitable any longer. I must be honest with you."

They protested at this. "No, no, Alex. We all understand that this whole thing is not to make a profit, but to help the British film industry," their spokesman assured him.

"Nevertheless, I don't want to steal your money," he insisted. "Taking more money from you for films I can't sell would be as bad as stealing. After the war it will be different, but for now I've had a document prepared for your signatures that will disband the company without any further losses. At least then you won't lose any more than you've invested."

They all agreed, impressed with his basic decency and honesty, and while they were signing, he innocently asked, "And the old negatives—what shall I do with them?"

The lords looked at one another in bewilderment. What did one do with old negatives? Finally one of them said, "Well, you made those movies, Alex. They're all your films."

"You mean I can have them," he said, his voice choking up. "How kind of you—yes, they are my life's work."

"Well, you must keep them then," they insisted at once with true British decency. "Of course you must!"

All choked up with emotion at their kindness, he still managed to say, "I'll send a release for you to sign." He did, and Korda ended up owning all the negatives of the films his studio had made. They brought him five million pounds during the first year after the war in re-releases!

After *An Englishman's Home* I was asked to appear again as a Nazi in a film called *Gestapo,* made in London for Twentieth Century Fox. Hitler had made such a fuss about the Aryan race that anyone who was slim and tall and blond, with Germanic features, fit the stereotype of a Nazi. I felt that I owed my appearance, as well as my name Hernried, to Swedish ancestors on my father's side, but I fit the image in the producer's mind, so the suave stage lover became the suave Nazi villain. And I must admit, the villain usually has the best lines.

Gestapo had, as its well-known stars, at least in Britain, Margaret Lockwood and Rex Harrison. I played a Nazi planted in a concentration camp to make love to the imprisoned daughter of a scientist in order to convince her to persuade her father to cooperate with the Germans. All nicely involved.

The film, which was finally released under the title *Night Train to Munich,* and in the United States as *Night Train,* played a decisive role in my life, but more of that later. The director, Carol Reed, was another of the greats in his profession. One of his directorial tricks was to approach an actor in an unguarded moment, usually at lunch, and start a discussion about the next scene to be filmed. With this kind of relaxed, low-key approach, there would be no tension between actor and director, and very little resistance on the part of the actor.

Rex Harrison, who masquerades as a German officer in the film, is a charming man, a light but excellent actor in all the parts he plays. He always had the good sense to pick parts that did not require any great depth of characterization, and they suited the image he was best able to project.

I liked Rex and we became good friends, but never very close friends. Although he had a great sense of humor, there was a quality of aloofness to Rex that seemed to discourage any intimate relationship.

Eight

◆

An Offer
from America

*N*ight Train to Munich was a tremendous success in England; since it was backed by Twentieth Century Fox, it was sent to Hollywood. Darryl F. Zanuck, who headed the studio, saw it at a private screening and, turning to his entourage of yes-men, said, "It's a good picture, but there are no stars in it. Whoever heard of those three leads, this Harrison, von Hernried, and Lockwood? What can we do with it?" If Zanuck didn't know, none of his men were about to make suggestions, so the film was buried in Twentieth Century's vaults.

The Brandt brothers of New York, who owned the Globe Theatre, used to make regular trips to Hollywood to ferret out neglected films they could buy cheaply for their theatre. On one of these trips they came across Night Train to Munich and fell in love with it. They asked for it, and since it was only gathering dust in the vault, they got it for very little. They brought it to the Globe and in 1940 released it as Night Train where it drew sensational reviews and block-long lines. It was an instant success and they showed it day and night. I received the Film Critics Award as Best Actor of the Year in a foreign film, and Lockwood, Hernried, and Harrison, the unknowns, became instant successes in the United States. But all that happened later, when I was on the New York stage.

Back in London, when it was released, Night Train to Munich was voted the best commercial film made in Britain since the war began. I was in danger of becoming typecast as a suave Gestapo agent, and I was relieved when Norman Marshall, who had directed Victoria Regina, approached me with a new play, The Jersey Lily. It was the story of Lily Langtree and her romance with Louis, the Prince of Battenberg, after she had been the mistress of Edward VII, then the Prince of Wales. It was a beautiful play, and I was offered the part of Louis Battenberg. The play takes place around the turn of the century, but later, during World War I, Louis Battenberg changed his name to Mountbatten and renounced his German title. He was created Marquis of Milford Haven and became Lord-Admiral of the Royal Navy.

The problem with the play was that same edict that had prevented the first production of *Victoria Regina* from being shown on the legitimate stage. The Prince of Wales, when he became Edward VIII, lifted the ban, but in 1936, hardly a year after he succeeded to the throne, he abdicated, and now the ban was back in effect. Because of it we were forced to open in a club theatre, the Gate, a small place underneath Charing Cross Station. Every time a train went by, the entire theatre rumbled, and since this was a club theatre, our salary was limited to one pound a week—and a lot of prestige. Apart from that, I took the part because the play was superb, and I had made a good deal of money in films and could afford it. Lisl's dress salon was working out as well.

The play received wonderful reviews and became a tremendous success, limited, however, by the size of the Gate Theatre. The author of the play, Sir Basil Bartlett, had married Lily Langtree's granddaughter, the daughter of an illegitimate child of Lily and Battenberg. Because the play was their family history, they took a great deal of interest in its performance, and Sir Basil and his wife Mary became close friends of ours.

At one of the performances I saw a thin, white-bearded man in the first row who applauded each act, and when the curtain came down on a moving prayer I made at the end, I could hear the old man shouting, "Damned fine, damned fine!" He was George Bernard Shaw, as I found out later, when he came around to my dressing room to congratulate me on my performance. We had a fascinating talk and agreed to meet for lunch.

We had quite a few lunches together, but Shaw was a very busy man and not at all inclined to socialize. At that first lunch I was delighted with his brilliance and wit. He had a vast fund of ideas for plays, and I suspect his main concern with me was to tap my reaction to them as an actor. I, in turn, was fascinated and intrigued by his views of the theatre. He was a Fabian socialist, a group opposed to the revolutionary theory of Marxism. They held that social reforms and socialist permeation of the government would bring about socialism in a natural way.

I was intrigued by his theories, and a bit overcome by his outspoken denunciation of all politics. "Are you political at all?" he finally asked me with some impatience after I had listened to a long lecture without comment.

I shrugged. "I have been forced to be. My father, however, when I was just a child, advised me to stay away from politics. He claimed that politics was the dirtiest business in the world."

Shaw laughed. "He was right, and sometimes I don't know which are worse, politicians or patriots. This terrible war!"

The "terrible war" was gathering steam then, and England was becoming an embattled isle. This was 1940, and London was under attack. Blimps were sent up to form an aerial net against the German planes, and at night the sky was laced with fingers of light probing for enemy aircraft.

I heard of a legion of Austrians being recruited to fight for Great Britain, and after some discussion with Lisl, I decided to join. But the examining doctor discovered an ulcer and informed me that not only was I unfit for service, but I could also expect not too long a life. "I'm surprised that you've made it this far," he told me. "You really shouldn't be alive." Fortunately his prognosis proved wrong, but I was rejected for service.

Lisl and I enlisted as air-raid wardens and walked around Hampstead in our tin hats with gas masks hanging from our shoulders during our tours of duty. However, our patriotic fervor suffered a severe blow. "You are," the government informed us, "German citizens now that Hitler has invaded Austria." Not only were we German citizens, but we were also enemy aliens!

We had to register as enemy aliens, and all of us received classifications, either A, B or C. The C's, considered immediately dangerous, were interned at once, and some were sent to the Isle of Man, others as far away as Canada. The B category was next to go, and the A's were last. Fortunately, we were classified A, and that gave us a respite to think and plan.

It was a terrible time. All the Jews who had fled Germany and taken refuge in England were picked up and put into camps, a black chapter, I feel, in English history, a chapter that has received little publicity. To my mind, one of the most terrible things about the internment of the Jews was that the British came around and picked them up in open trucks, just as the Nazis did in Germany before carting them off to the death camps.

I was apprehensive about my own fate, especially when a local Hampstead policeman, a plainclothesman, took to dropping in to tell me just how my papers were doing. "I'm a great admirer of yours, Mr. von Hernried," he'd tell me, "and I'll make sure your paper is on the bottom of the pile, the last to go—so to speak." And in almost the same breath he'd admire one of our possessions, usually a beautiful record player we had bought and he'd say, "That would be nice to have if you could get away to America, or if, heaven forbid, you go into a camp." It was unnerving to Lisl and me, and there was always an implied threat behind his seemingly subservient words. Unless we managed to get him the record player, we might not stay out of the camp much longer!

Gilbert Miller, the producer, had come to London and he saw *The Jersey Lily*. Coming backstage, he said, "It's a beautiful play, Paul. I want to bring it to New York. Will you come and do it?"

It was just what I had been hoping for, a chance to get out of England and escape internment. I said, "Of course I'll do it, Gil. Just send me a contract."

He had to do more than send me a contract for me to get into the United States. He had to guarantee the government that I would be self-supporting and that, if I wasn't, he'd take care of me. The contract, when it came, delighted me. It paid me $500 a week and guaranteed a run of six weeks, or my salary for that period. He also agreed to pay my fare to New York, and he wrote, "There is only one actress in New York who can play the Jersey Lily, and that's Katharine Cornell—and I have her!"

I didn't know who Katharine Cornell was, but I was delighted at the contract, and Lisl and I prepared to leave. Things had gotten very bad indeed. The local policeman who had come hinting for bribes informed me that I was close to the top of the list of future internees. The government also wanted to intern Lisl's father, Gustav, but Lisl called Lord Duveen, the art dealer, and Duveen had enough pull to have him taken off the list at once. Nevertheless, we made arrangements for Lisl's parents to join their son Gustl, who was in Buenos Aires representing a British private bank.

"From here," Gustl wrote his father, "I can get you into the States without trouble." We felt that there was no alternative. Who could tell? With all the terrible patriotic fervor of the war, even with Lord Duveen's intercession, the government could pick them up and send them off to internment.

Lutzi, Lisl's housekeeper, couldn't get permission to leave either, and so we had her apply for a visa to visit Canada. We thought that from there she would have no trouble slipping into the States and joining us.

Those days of planning and waiting were terrible. We jumped at every ring of the doorbell, and each time a friend or neighbor went off to internment, an apprehensive dread took hold of us. How long before it was our turn? From a friend, or the pretense of friendship, the local policeman became threatening, and we knew it was only a matter of days before our papers reached the top of the pile.

Sir Basil Bartlett had gone to war and now, wounded at Dunkirk and back in England, he and his wife came to dinner at our house. At the end of the meal, rather dramatically, I'm afraid, I said, "I must drink a farewell toast to you and Mary, Basil."

"A farewell toast, Paul? What do you mean?" he asked.

"I'm afraid my internment number is almost up," I explained. "Our local policeman came here today and told me I should be prepared to go any day now."

"But that's nonsense," Sir Basil said angrily. "Look, they've put me into military intelligence since I was shot up, and I know who's safe and who isn't. I know enough about you, Paul, including your stage work here—why, you've done wonders at popularizing our royalty at a time when we sorely need it. You just wait a moment." He picked up the phone and put through a call to intelligence headquarters.

"I want to know the facts on the case of Paul von Hernried," he asked abruptly. "The local police are threatening to pick him up and intern him. Yes, will you see that this nonsense is stopped at once?"

When he hung up, he smiled at me and said, "It's all fine now, Paul. You can stay in England as long as you wish. We'll be proud to have you as a citizen."

I spread my hands. "My dear friend, thank you, but I've already signed a contract to go to America."

He shook his head. "What a pity. Well, at least you'll have no more trouble with the police until you leave." And he was right. From then on the attitude of the Hampstead police changed drastically. For one thing, there was no more wistful talk about our beautiful record player.

When our tickets to America arrived, I took my passport to the American consulate for permission to leave, but the man in charge of immigration shook his head sadly. "I'm very very sorry, but we can't give you a visa."

I felt as if someone had kicked my legs away. Stunned, I asked, "Why not? Everything is in order." When he continued to shake his head, I said, rather desperately, "Here are the papers from Mr. Miller in which he guarantees me employment. I was told there would be no trouble."

"Oh, there's no trouble with Mr. Miller's guarantee," he said, inspecting the paper carelessly. Then he smiled at me, slightly apologetically. "The trouble is with the Austrian quota to the United States."

When I looked blank, he explained. "Every Austrian in England is trying to get over there, and the quota is full—backed up, in fact. It's going to be at least two years before you can leave."

I was so shocked I could hardly speak. We had counted so on this. Sir Basil's reprieve from internment was all well and good, but how long would it last? And I had wanted so to do *The Jersey Lily* in the United States. All my plans were washed up, finished! I turned away in complete frustration.

Then the immigration officer, who had been studying my application, called out, "Wait a minute. Where were you born, Mr. von Hernried? Your passport says Trieste."

"Yes," I said dully. "My parents had a winter villa in Trieste and I was born there."

"But that's now Italy," he said, still frowning down at my papers.

I started to the door, my mind still blurred with what had happened. What would I tell Lisl, and what about her parents?

"Mr. Hernried?"

I looked back at him and shook my head. "No, no—when I was born, Trieste was still Austrian territory."

"Oh well." He laughed. "We don't pay any attention to what countries once were. It's what they are today that counts, and today Trieste is Italian. You're Italian!"

"I am?" I shrugged and turned back to the door. "What difference does it make?"

"Just this: You go on the Italian quota now, and that's wide open."

I walked back to him in disbelief. "What do you mean, wide open?"

"Just what I said. There aren't that many Italians putting in for the United States. You can leave England today. Here, let me stamp your papers."

"And my wife?" I asked bewildered.

"Well, of course she goes with you, no matter what her citizenship is. Congratulations, Mr. von Hernried." And I walked out in a daze, staring down at the visa as realization and excitement grew inside me. I was going to America after all! At home, I embraced Lisl and kissed her again and again until her tears were gone and she could smile back at me.

Nine

♦

New York City

*L*isl and I packed everything we owned, except our furniture and car, and prepared for our trip to America. Immediately we ran into a financial problem. Originally I had kept all my money in dollars in the City Bank of New York. I started this when I was still in Austria because of my memories of the terrible inflation after World War I. The monetary system in the States seemed the most stable in the world.

I continued keeping my money there once I came to Great Britain, but when war started, the government appealed to every citizen to turn in all foreign currency for pounds. I felt it a duty to my new country to do this, and so I converted all my dollars to pounds.

Now, however, I discovered that there was a law forbidding anyone leaving the country from taking more than £25 with him. I realized that we'd need more than that to get settled, even with the salary Gilbert Miller had promised in the contract he sent me, so I decided to smuggle a larger amount out. I had suffered financially from an excess of patriotism and, I thought grimly, I should have taken Shaw's advice about patriots and politics more seriously.

How to smuggle the money out? My toilet case, a leather affair with a built-in mirror, seemed the best bet. I pried up the mirror and pushed £2,000 in large bills behind it, then carefully glued the mirror back along the edges. It was a rather neat job and I was sure it would escape detection. "It will be our nest egg in America," I told Lisl. "Just in case . . ."

"Let's hope there's no 'in case,'" she answered.

Our trip to America on a large passenger ship was an enjoyable one. There was some tension until we passed the Azores. We traveled in a convoy and were followed a number of times by German

U-boats. Fortunately, the captain spared our feelings and reported the U-boats presence only after they had been spotted and chased off with depth charges. The other passengers, mostly English, proved delightful companions. Lisl and I were recognized and treated like celebrities, and I was still naive enough to enjoy the fuss.

We arrived in New York with all our luggage and one of our championship Skye terriers, Maxi. A customs officer approached Lisl as she walked Maxi on the dock, but he wore no uniform, so she thought him a friendly stranger in this new country. "That's a beautiful dog," he said admiringly.

"Isn't he?" Lisl beamed at him. "And he's a champion. He won so many prizes—and his father was a champion, too."

"Oh . . . a valuable dog?"

"Priceless," she told him warmly, and he whipped out his little book and informed her that we would have to pay $25 to bring him into the country.

"But he seemed such a pleasant man," Lisl wailed in the taxi to our hotel. "Not at all like the European customs men."

"Just smarter," I told her glumly.

I had asked my London agent to recommend and reserve an inexpensive and pleasant place to stay, but she wouldn't believe we had no money, and so she booked us into the Gotham, one of New York's more expensive hotels at $8 a day. August 12, 1940, the day we arrived, was an unbelievably hot day, and although a monstrous contraption called an air conditioner made an enormous amount of noise, it did little to cool the room. I called Miller to tell him we were here, and he asked me to come to his office at once. Lisl had undressed and was lying naked on the bed. It had suddenly hit her that she was thousands of miles from her parents and friends. I tried to console her, but nothing I said helped, so I put on my jacket and went off to Rockefeller Plaza, where Gilbert Miller's office was. No one had met our boat, because sea schedules at that time were kept secret due to the war. When I walked into Miller's office, he sat me down and said, "So here you are! It's so good to see you, Paul—but I have some bad news."

With a sinking heart I sat down and said, "What is it, Gilbert?"

"We've decided, Katharine Cornell and I, not to do *The Jersey Lily.*"

I stared at him blankly. "Why not?"

"Well, we just thought it wasn't in good taste to portray an English prince having an affair with an actress at this particular time, with the blitz on in London and all that. We've called it off." He patted my shoulder reassuringly. "But don't worry. Everyone knows you're here. I've spread it around, and you'll have a better play in no time!"

I stood up to go, bewildered and a little frightened. Here we were in American with no source of income, and how long would our smuggled nest egg last? Also there was the guarantee. Did Miller intend to pay me? He'd made no mention of it, and I hesitated to ask. What was the custom in America?

At the door, he slapped me on the back jovially and said, "Now you mustn't worry, Paul. The war can't last long, and as soon as it's over I'm going to revive *Victoria Regina* with you and Helen Hayes. She was always my favorite Victoria, and you're my favorite Albert."

Somehow I got back to the hotel in a terrible state of despair to find Lisl almost overcome with the heat. "Well, when do you start rehearsing?" she asked.

I said, "Everything is fine—as soon as the war is over, Miller is going to revive *Victoria Regina,* and I'll play Albert again."

She looked at me as if I were mad. "What about *The Jersey Lily?*"

"He's not going to do it."

"Oh, Paul!" She sank down on the bed in tears, and I couldn't stop her crying. She hated the heat. She hated the hotel. She hated the customs and New York, and most of all she hated Gilbert Miller!

Although the New York newspapers had ignored my arrival, the trade papers for the garment industry announced LISL ARRIVES IN NEW YORK in great headlines. "I suppose I'd better find work before we starve," Lisl said grimly, and to my surprise in two days she was designing a collection for Bergdorf Goodman. To economize, we moved across the street to the Shoreham Hotel, where we got a dreadful little kitchen apartment looking into a dark and dirty courtyard for $8 a week instead of the $8 a day we paid at the Gotham.

I began to receive plays as Miller had predicted, but none of them were any good. Jacob Shubert sent me a play called *Boyd's Daughter,* a play I thought was horrible, and when I turned it down he asked me to do him the honor of coming to his office at the Shubert Theatre. When I got there he said, "Well, Mr. von Hernried, welcome to America. Now why don't you want to do this beautiful little play?"

"Because this beautiful little play stinks," I told him bluntly.

"Why, you hadn't even met me when you sent it. How did you know I was right for it?"

He laughed softly. "Well, I've met you now and I'm sure you are right. Will you change your mind?"

"No," I told him firmly. "It's a bad play."

The good humor faded away and he stood up angrily. "Young man, you come here from England, a foreigner, and you dare to tell me, an old hand like me, an American theatrical producer, you dare to tell me which plays will be good for the New York stage?"

I said, "Forgive me, Mr. Shubert. All I can say is that this is a bad play. In England or Austria it would still be a bad play. I'm very sorry and I hope we can be friends and that you'll call me when something better comes up."

He wouldn't be placated. "You'll regret this," he warned me as I left, but I never did. The play closed out of town, and I felt justified. After that my London agent found a New York agent for me, Jane Broder, and she began to sift through scripts. But still nothing decent turned up.

Somewhat desperate now, I wrote to all my friends in Hollywood to ask if any film work was available. Greer Garson, who had come to Hollywood to do *Mrs. Miniver,* wrote back saying, "I wouldn't know what you could do out here. We have all the leading men we need, excellent English, French, and American actors. I don't see any chance for you." It was a cruel blow.

Sam Wood, however, wrote a more encouraging letter saying he'd try everything possible to get me a job. I wrote back and said, "I'll take anything, even a bit part." I had discovered that Actor's

Equity had a law that a foreigner could do only one play a year. If I chose the wrong one and it flopped, I'd be out of work for a year. Anything I could get in Hollywood would at least keep me going financially.

However, it shortly became apparent that I wouldn't have to worry about finances or even broaching our nest egg. Lisl managed to support us in style. After her work at Bergdorf's, she got a job with Charles James, the number-one designer in New York.

James was a strange man. His clients included some of the country's wealthiest women and the top movie and stage stars: Mrs. William Paley, Jennifer Jones, Gypsy Rose Lee, and many others. But he always operated on the edge of bankruptcy. When Lisl came to work she found only a vast, empty room. There was a beautiful carpet on the floor, and a magnificent rocking horse in one corner. His clothes were expensive—$500 for a small scarf, an incredible price at that time.

Very gay, very affected, James carried a little lap dog inside his vest, and there were always those beady little dog eyes peering out at you when you talked to him. When she first came into the empty salon, Lisl asked, "Where are the chairs? Is the furniture on order?"

"There is no furniture," he snapped. "I want nothing to spoil the empty ambience of the room."

"Where will the customers sit?"

"They don't have to sit," he minced. "If they must, they can sit on the floor."

If there was no furniture in the room, Lisl thought, he must be either broke or about to go broke, so she insisted that her salary, $60 a week, be paid in advance.

He paid her grudgingly and then said, "Oh yes. I'm giving a show tomorrow. I've invited everyone who's of any importance. Here's the order book. Your job will be to take the orders at the show."

"But what will the models wear?" Lisl asked as James took her back to an empty workroom.

"Oh, for heaven's sake! Don't worry. I have the dresses at home, and I'll bring them. I had twenty girls working for me." This surprised Lisl because she could see only one girl working in the back room and no fabric, no clothing at all.

James lived at the Chelsea Hotel, and the next morning he arrived with curtains, draperies, and blankets from the hotel. Picking them up and examining them, Lisl was flabbergasted. She said, "Curtains? Where are the dresses?"

"Isn't their texture incredible?" James asked, depositing his load of material in the workroom. Avoiding Lisl's questions, he turned to the models who had just arrived. "No, no, no! Off with the bras. I want you wearing only underpants."

Then he went to work, furiously draping the models with the material he had brought from the hotel, pinning everything together. Watching him openmouthed, Lisl realized that the man, for all his affectations, was an absolute genius. Within a few hours, using the curtains and draperies pinned about the models, he put on a stunning fashion show for an excited audience of wealthy older women.

The orders came in like crazy, but there was no way, Lisl realized, that she could cut dresses from these crazy pinnings, and she took James aside to tell him that. "Now just write the orders, dear," James paused in his fluttering to reassure her. "Every dress is twenty-five hundred dollars, and don't worry about how soon they want it or the color. They'll take *what* I give them *when* I give it to them."

And he was right. Women would come for their fittings, and he'd tell them what color he wanted them to have and when they'd get the dress, and they submitted meekly. As for the cutting, he told Lisl to forget the dresses he had draped and cut regular dresses. Then, at the fittings, he'd slit a dress here, drape it there, with a truly remarkable result.

Once Lisl got the hang of it, she breathed easier and finally decided she could take enough time off to go apartment hunting. "I've finally got things under control," she told me. "But it's controlled madness! What a man."

She finally found a lovely apartment on Beekman Place with a wonderful view of the East River. It was just luck, neither of us realizing that this was one of the most elegant areas in Manhattan.

In the meanwhile the good plays continued to elude me, and then one day I received a call from Helen Hayes. "I just tracked you down," she told me. "Gilbert Miller told me you are the best Albert he ever saw, and I'm starting my own radio theatre. I'm putting on *Victoria Regina*, and you must play opposite me. No one else will do!"

Pleased, but bewildered, I said, "Miss Hayes, you haven't even met me!" Was everyone in America like this, I wondered, accepting you before they had met you?

"We'll correct that," she said brightly. "What about next weekend? I'll send my chauffeur to pick you up with your wife, and you'll come to visit me here at Nyack."

Her husband, Charles MacArthur, would be there, she told me, and so would Ben Hecht. He had written the hit play *The Front Page*. "Charles wants to meet you, and my son is here. We'll have a wonderful time."

And we did. Helen was a gracious and warm hostess, and we all got along splendidly. In fact, we've remained friends ever since. I did the radio show with her and received $150 for the performance, not bad pay in those days. I also received some very good reviews, and the producer of a daytime soap opera called *Joyce Jordon, Girl Intern* asked me to come on for a guest appearance, a character who would be on the show for two months. It paid $60 a week, and I took it. It occupied only a brief hour each day.

In spite of all the publicity about my appearance on the Helen Hayes Radio Theatre, there still were no decent plays offered. Finally, rather desperate, I went to Jane Broder, and asked, "What's the trouble? Why can't you find anything decent for me?"

"It's very difficult, Paul," she told me. "There's just nothing worth doing. I have received one terrific script, but there's no part in it for you." She hesitated. "It's by a very fine playwright, Elmer Rice. Why don't you read it anyway? You'll be interested in the subject. It deals with Jewish immigration and the Nazis."

I read it through in her office. It was called *Flight to the West*, and there was a Nazi diplomat in it. "He's thinking of Otto Preminger for the Nazi," she said. "He played that terrible villain in *Margin for Error.*"

I shook my head. "He's all wrong, you know—Elmer Rice, I mean. He depicts the Nazi diplomat as an uncouth, miserable character. They aren't like that."

Jane said, "What do you mean?"

I shrugged. "The Nazis were too smart to send people like that abroad. They sent out their suavest, most polished men." And I recalled Ribbentrop in the Ritz Café, a typical example, exquisitely tailored and coldly elegant, no matter how shallow he was inside. "That's why they were always accepted by British society. But the rest of the play," I told her, "is a fine job."

Thoughtfully, Jane said, "Do you mind if I tell Mr. Rice what you said about the Nazi diplomat?"

"Not at all," I assured her, and she called Elmer Rice and after a moment's talk put her hand over the phone.

"He's very interested in what you said and wonders if you could have lunch with him today?"

I agreed, and we met at the Algonquin, a horribly crowded place with dreadful food, but for some bewildering reason the literary meeting place of New York. I found Rice a witty, pleasant man, a wise old owl, as I privately dubbed him, and over that miserable lunch I explained what I thought about the character of the Nazi diplomat.

"If we go back to my office now, and I give you a script," he asked, "would you read it for me the way you see the character?"

I sighed. I had never read for a part in my life, and I told Rice that. "But I'll make an exception now because I want you to see the changes I have in mind, but I won't do it cold. The play deserves better than that. Let me take it home and study it very carefully and make some notes. I'll read for you tomorrow if you're available, or the next day." I laughed ruefully. "I have no job right now, so I do have a lot of time."

He hesitated. "That's all fine with me, but there is one problem. If we change the character and you play him, I don't think I can meet your salary requirements. Jane tells me it was five hundred dollars in London, but this is the Playwrights' Guild. We have our own theatre—not such a good one—but we do have a tight budget. Betty Fields, the star, gets a substantial salary, but the rest get only two hundred and fifty dollars, and I've budgeted that for the Nazi-diplomat part."

I said, "I'm glad you're frank, and I'll be frank, too. I won't pretend I'm overwhelmed with work. I haven't found another play I like, and I do like yours. Equity allows me only one play a year, and I have to choose one that will last. I believe yours will. So let's talk salary after I've read the part to you."

I took the script home and I read it out loud to Lisl, my faithful critic, and she agreed that the play was exciting, but the part of the Nazi was unreal. "Do you think you can change it?" she asked.

I said, "Yes, I'm sure I can," and I sat down and worked over the script, then read it to her again. "I see him wearing a gray pinstriped suit, white shirt, black tie, gray sideburns, a small mustache—very conservative."

Elmer Rice, when he heard me read the part as I had changed it, said, "Yes! That's it. That's exactly how it should be. I'll rewrite it using your words. Can you start rehearsals in two weeks?"

"I can—and have you thought about the salary?"

"I did," Rice said, "and I've decided to put another hundred in out of my own pocket. It will come to three hundred and fifty a week. Is it a deal?"

We shook hands on it, and in two weeks we started rehearsals. It was a wonderful feeling to be back on the stage, and I found the New York stage superb. I saw a few other plays, and in general I found it more alive and superior to the English stage. As for the American playwrights, they simply overwhelmed me—Sherwood Anderson, Elmer Rice, S. N. Behrman, George Kaufman. And the actors, I felt, were smoother and closer in style to what I had been used to in Vienna.

The bad side of it all was the construction of the buildings. Every theatre seemed an auditorium with a tiny stage tacked on. The stage gave the director no chance to do anything, and though there were excellent scenic designers, they were hampered by the lack of adequate room.

The night *Flight to the West* opened, I was keyed up, not only about the performance, but the reviews, too. They could be terribly important. This was my first attempt on the American stage. How would they receive me?

After the show, Hugh Marlowe, the male lead, and his girl-friend and Lisl and I had supper at Sardi's and at eleven forty-five we took a cab over to Times Square and had the cab wait while we sat there biting our nails in glum silence waiting for the early edition of *The New York Times* to come off the press. It was a miserable, rainy night, which made us even more anxious and uneasy.

Finally we saw the papers being delivered and Hugh Marlowe dashed across the street through the rain and grabbed a paper. He opened it there by the paper kiosk, the rain pouring down on him, and turned to the reviews. Then he waved the sodden paper at us and, as he paid the newsseller, he yelled across Times Square, "It's a smash! And you're a top smash, Paul! We've made it."

It was true. Every newspaper praised us, they all loved the play, and each reviewer—Watts, Brooks Atkinson—singled out my performance. It should have had a long and fantastic run, but none of us had realized that the premise of the play was too intellectual. The afternoon papers didn't like it very much, and they carried a lot of weight. It made a thoughtful statement about the condition of Germany, the Jews, and the world, and most New Yorkers were indifferent to that, or they didn't want to be upset by being forced to think about it.

The intellectual audience came in droves, but eventually we exhausted them. The play moved from the creaky Playwrights' Theatre to the Royal, where the prices were lower and there were no reserved seats. Again we packed in an audience, mostly students attracted by the reasonable admission, but then attendance dropped off once more. We all took a salary reduction in an attempt to keep it alive, but the play, in spite of its critical acclaim, was dying.

Luckily for me, just after the play opened and the great reviews began pouring in, *Night Train* opened at the Globe, and the New York film critics stood up and cheered. I became the actor of the day.

Suddenly Hollywood awakened to my existence and offers

started pouring in, and so did newly interested Hollywood agents. One of them, Lew Wasserman, who was with MCA, even then a very large and important agency, impressed me very much. When he approached me, I said, "If you can get me the kind of Hollywood contract I want, I'll sign up with you."

"You tell me what you want, and I'll get it," he said confidently.

"First of all, I want a check from your agency for two thousand dollars. I'll give you two weeks to get the contract. If you do, I return the two thousand from my first Hollywood check. If not, I keep it. Okay?"

"What else?" he asked, without blinking a lash.

"I am, as you Americans say, hot now, so this is the best time to go after it. In this business I could be forgotten in another two weeks."

"Fair enough. And the contract?"

"I want the male leading role in any film I do, the actor who gets the girl. I want to do one film a year at any major studio, and it must be shot between May thirteenth and September first."

He raised his eyebrows and I explained. "Because I must be available for the Broadway stage. That's one film a year for the next seven years."

"And salary?" he asked blandly.

"I'll leave that to you. Anything from twenty-five thousand a picture is okay."

"I'll get it for you," Wasserman promised, and the next day he brought me the check for two thousand dollars and we shook hands. I thought he was crazy and I was sure no studio would accept such terms. I was prepared to dicker if they made a lesser offer, or take it. But two days later Wasserman called.

"You're going to star opposite Ginger Rogers in a picture for RKO. I bettered your price. You'll get thirty-two thousand, and you're expected out on the coast by May fifteenth."

Ten

◆

Hollywood

$\mathcal{M}$ y contract with RKO was to start on May 15, and that was perfect for me. My play, *Flight to the West,* was scheduled to close on May 5. The fact that I was to play opposite Ginger Rogers was another tremendous break. Rogers had just won an Oscar for her portrayal of Kitty Foyle, and that was an assurance that the studio would put everything they could behind the making and promotion of the film.

As for the two thousand dollars I had received from Lew Wasserman, that would buy me a new Cadillac convertible. We had left our beloved Viva Grand Sport behind in Europe, and we decided to drive out to California and see this intriguing new country firsthand. Lisl's parents, who were on their way to the States after having first gone to Argentina, wrote that they might arrive in New York in time to drive west with us. The Cadillac would hold us all comfortably.

A canny car dealer, however, talked me out of the Cadillac and sold me the new Chrysler convertible with fluid drive. It was larger and cost almost six hundred dollars less. Not only that, but it was a beautiful car, and we couldn't resist it.

Unfortunately, Lisl's parents didn't arrive in time, and we had to leave without them. We made plans for them to take a train to the coast to join us, and we set out on our journey. In a way we hated to leave New York, but we reassured each other that we'd return. "There will be at least one play a year. My film contract has assured me of that."

"If you can find a play."

"Oh, there'll be no trouble with that after the success of *Flight to the West.*" And I was sure I was right. There would be plenty of offers. Lillian Hellman, when she was getting her play *Watch on the Rhine* ready, had approached me to play the part Paul Lukas eventually took. I was unable to do it because of my commitment to Elmer Rice. She offered to buy out my contract, but I didn't think that was proper, nor was Rice willing.

With that much interest, I thought, the good scripts are bound to come in, and we'd both return. New York City, or at least Manhattan, was one of the most beautiful cities we had ever seen. It was impressive and colorful, and the people were alive and fascinating, the restaurants excellent. It was such a continental city; all we had to do was stroll down Fifth Avenue and we'd meet any number of friends from London, Paris, Vienna, or Berlin.

But beautiful and exciting as New York was, the rest of America was even more so. Driving across it was the most memorable experience of our lives. The scenery, particularly in the West, was breathtaking. There was a quality of grandeur that equalled the Alps, though in a different way. The people were generous and friendly, and since we were crossing in the early spring, the weather was rare and fresh and the air fragrant.

The only fly in our ointment was the food. It was uniformly horrible. The only gastronomic pleasure between the two coasts was the baked potato, something new to both of us. Done properly, and it was the one food that was always done properly, it was delectable, and we lived for it during the entire trip.

When we finally reached Los Angeles, we stayed at the Beverly Hills Hotel, and I got in touch with my agent to learn the sad news that Ginger Rogers had said no to the script we were to do together. At the time, I was puzzled and a little amused by her refusal. In Europe films were considered a number of degrees below the stage. I would never consider appearing in a play if I didn't like the script, but a picture, I thought, was a different story. In a way, I suppose, we considered it slumming. It was a means of making money, the extra car, the new house, but the stage had a certain purity. That was where you displayed your craft and received your inner satisfaction.

I must say that after a few films in Hollywood I changed my mind. Perhaps I saw filmmaking in a new light, or it may be, if I am completely honest with myself, that I sold out. Whatever the reason, I became as concerned with scripts as anyone else.

"Don't worry about Ginger's refusal," David Hampstead, the producer, assured me. He explained that RKO had a substitute picture for me, a movie called *Joan of Paris*. I was to star with Michelle Morgan, the sultry French sexpot. Robert Stevenson had agreed to direct, and would I come and meet Michelle? She had just arrived from Paris.

When I left for the studio, I said to Lisl, "This may be the end of our marriage."

Unimpressed, Lisl asked, "How come?"

"I've been madly in love with Michelle Morgan on the screen ever since I saw her in that film with Jean Gabin. If she's anything like her film image, I may never come home."

"Good luck," Lisl said drily, and I went off to the studio. I entered Hampstead's office, and he asked his secretary to show Miss Morgan in. I stood up as a very young, lovely girl, more like an American bobby-soxer than a French sexpot, came in. In fact, she actually blushed when we were introduced. This couldn't, I told myself, bemused, be the same woman I'd seen on the screen. I had underestimated the illusion-making magic of the movie camera, and I had underestimated Michelle's acting ability.

Michelle turned out to be a splendid actress, and the rest of the cast—Thomas Mitchell, May Robeson—all the rest, or almost all the rest, were fine, competent performers.

Before we started work on the picture, the production head of RKO called me into his office. "We have a little problem with your name," he told me.

I was puzzled at that. "You mean Paul?"

"No, no," he said quickly. "Paul is fine. It's the von Hernried that's difficult."

"Difficult in what way?" I asked, still puzzled.

"Well . . . for one thing, it's rather long for a theater marquee. We like short names. And also, it sounds very . . . well, German."

I smiled at that. "Actually, it's Austrian."

"Austrian, German—it's the same language, isn't it?"

"Yes," I said slowly, "though my ancestors were Swedish. Hernried is a Swedish name."

"Well, perhaps, but we think you should drop the 'von.'"

In Austria, I explained, when the country became democratic after World War I, the use of "von" was eliminated from all official documents. I had democratic leanings myself, and I was indifferent about keeping or losing it. But Hernried was another matter.

"It's hard for Americans to pronounce," the production head assured me. "That funny *r* in there. Would you consider Hammond?"

"I wouldn't consider it for a moment."

"Hmm." He fiddled with a pen and pencil. "Henry?"

I shook my head.

"Well, what if we dropped the *r* and made it Henried?"

I didn't want to be stubborn, and perhaps he was right and Hernried was hard for Americans to pronounce. I said, "All right," and he beamed.

"And we'll change the *ie* to *ei.*"

"But why? Why a silly change like that?"

"Pronunciation," he said. "Henried would be pronounced Hen-ride. Henreid comes across as Hen-reed. Do you see?"

I didn't see at all, but I decided there was no point in any further argument. He knew the language better than I did, so I became Paul Henreid. I have regretted it ever since. I liked my original name much better. Shortly after that I was asked to take Lisl to dinner at Romanoff's restaurant to meet with the publicity department of RKO. "Perhaps they want me to change my name, too," Lisl said with a touch of sarcasm. "It may be too German, or not glamorous enough for Hollywood."

But their request, which did concern Lisl, was much stranger and more outrageous than a mere change of name. Lou Wasserman was there with a few other studio people. It was rather elegant for a business dinner, which was what they assured me it would be. After the meal, as we sat over brandy and cigarettes, the publicity people began to talk about how they'd build me up, what sort of image they would create. "The suave ladies' man." They assured me that they knew what was important for the job and what wasn't.

After a lot of talk filled with hints and suggestions too subtle for me to understand completely, I realized that though I might be in the dark, Lisl knew what was going on and was stiffening up a bit.

"Just what are you suggesting?" Lisl asked finally. "Perhaps my English isn't good enough. Can you talk plainly?"

"Well, we'd like to have your husband not married," the head publicity man said to Lisl with what he thought was a charming smile.

"I don't understand how you're going to do that," I said in bewilderment.

"Yes," Lisl put in, "I don't think you know what you're talking about. Am I to go back to Europe? When do I meet Paul, or do I meet him at all?"

When no one answered, she continued, "Do I meet him at all —and will we be married again?" In spite of her suppressed anger, she kept her voice calm. "I think your suggestions are ridiculous!"

"And so do I," I added.

"We thought," the publicity man said, not seeing any of our annoyance, but taking her questions at face value, "we'd have Paul go out with Hollywood's leading glamour girls, the stars, you know. You see, we're grooming him to be a big star himself."

I looked at Lew Wasserman, but he avoided my eyes. Lisl said, "I understand completely, and of course I'm all for Paul becoming a star, but since I'll be living without Paul, I'll need some money myself. After all"—she shrugged—"without Paul I'll have to pay different gentlemen to take me out, and I'll need a decent salary for that."

I leaned back, holding my laughter in, and I listened. I didn't have to say anything. Lisl was handling the situation beautifully. Still not realizing what she was doing, the publicity man nodded seriously. "Of course. How much would you need?"

Lisl considered a moment, then very brightly said, "Why, to be fair, I should have exactly what Paul is getting." At their dumbfounded look, she explained, "You see, I spend more than he does. He's rather tight, not at all a big spender."

No one answered that, and the next day the Los Angeles newspapers announced MR. AND MRS. PAUL HENREID ARRIVE.

I started work in *Joan of Paris* soon after that. It was the first "A" picture for a new young actor, Alan Ladd. He played a member of a squad of Free French fliers shot down near Paris. I was the captain, and we try to hide out from the Nazis in the city. Michelle and Thomas Mitchell, who played a priest, are in the underground and help us escape. Ladd is shot, and he has a death scene in the sewers of Paris.

It was an unfortunate scene. Ladd simply couldn't die properly, and Stevenson shot and reshot the episode. Ladd's eyes showed no expression. They were like glass balls, no matter how much Stevenson worked on him. Later, watching another scene being shot, Stevenson asked me, "Those three young actors who play the airmen —which of them, if any, do you think will make it?"

I shrugged. "Certainly not Ladd. Maybe Dick Frazier."

"Yes," Stevenson agreed. "I think Dick has the right stuff!"

How wrong we both were! Frazier never got a break, but in his next picture, *This Gun for Hire,* Ladd was cast as a glassy-eyed gangster who showed no emotion. He was an instant success, but so much of success in Hollywood is based on just that one lucky break.

Joan of Paris introduced me to one of the roughest methods of shooting motion pictures. Alexander Granach, who played the Gestapo agent who finds me, had an exciting chase scene with me through the streets of Paris at night. The scene was shot at the RKO ranch, where they had built the streets of Paris for the chase and rigged the whole set for rain. Since the chase took place at night, the filming was done at night. I didn't realize that though the days were warm out in the valley where the ranch was, at four in the morning an ice-cold wind comes in—and four A.M. was when we shot!

Since we had to shoot most scenes again and again, we were dressed first in woolen underclothing, then a rubber suit, and over that our costumes. Hampstead, the producer, brought a bottle of brandy into my tentlike dressing room, and between takes he poured it into me. I've a good head for liquor, and the hard work, the stunts I did myself, as well as the activity of the chase, burned the alcohol up.

Making the film, on the whole, however, was a pleasure, and it was done with great care. Afterward we went on a tour to publicize it, a new and strange custom of this very strange land I was in. I took the first part of the tour alone by luxury train to Chicago. Once in the city I was booked into the Ambassador East Hotel, and the RKO publicity man and my travel companion, Terry Turner, who was to supervise my appearances and act as a general nursemaid, took out a small black book and tossed it to me.

"Now take your choice, Mr. Henreid. Brunette, redhead, or blonde?"

Puzzled, I thumbed through the book. "What do you mean?" It seemed an address book with curious notations after each name, and all the names were female.

"Well—don't you want a woman after that long train ride?" he asked me in surprise.

I could hardly believe him. "You mean a whore?"

"No, no, no!" he protested. "These aren't whores. They're all beautiful girls, talented, educated—very elegant girls—and clean, of course. Here we call them Call Girls, and they're perfectly safe, no possible blackmail, if that's what's worrying you. They're checked over regularly, and there's no disease."

"How can you guarantee that?" I asked drily. "Or do you also examine every man they sleep with?" I waved his protests aside and said, "Anyway, I've found it better to sleep with society ladies. They're just as pleasant and much safer, and instead of paying them, they give you presents."

Taking me seriously, he said, "Oh no, you won't have to pay. RKO will pay for them."

I thanked him and somehow managed to get rid of him. Later that evening I went down to the Pump Room, the dining room, alone. But I had hardly settled into my seat when a pleasant young man came up and introduced himself. "You're Paul Henreid, the actor. I'm Ernie Biefield, the owner of the hotel. May I join you?"

"I said, "Of course," glad of any company who seemed intelligent and cultured, especially after the RKO publicity man.

"Now what's your favorite wine?" he asked.

Smiling, I said, "I don't know that until I order. If it's white, I prefer a Montrachet—if red, a Rothschild Lafitte."

He said, "Let's have both, and let me be your host."

We had dinner together and hit it off beautifully as friends. It's that way with some people. From almost the moment you meet, you know you'll get on well together. Ernie Biefield's friendship was one of the pleasantest I've ever had. Among other things, he was the importer for Beluga Caviar, and for years afterward, at any occasion, he would send me a ten-pound gift package of caviar.

What became evident to me very quickly on that tour was the unique quality of the American movie fan. In Europe, the theatrical fans were discreet and diffident. If they ventured backstage after a performance, they would be announced by the callboy, and I'd receive them in my dressing room, where they would tell me how much they enjoyed the performance—or, sometimes, just what they felt was wrong with it.

In America the fans would approach you anywhere—on the street, in restaurants, in the lobby of your hotel. They would approach you blatantly and with frightening enthusiasm. They wanted to touch you, to get your autograph, or even to tear off part of your clothes as a souvenir. It was more a kind of hysterical sensationalism than true appreciation—and I suppose there was more fun to being a fan in America. I have even seen young people photograph the stills put up in theatre lobbies and bring the photographs to me to autograph.

In New York City, Michelle and Lisl joined the tour. We did a number of radio shows, and RKO arranged some personal appearances with our film, *Joan of Paris.* In the city we were approached by a representative of the Treasury Department, who asked us to combine the rest of the tour with a bond-selling campaign. We agreed, and it was one of the first of the Hollywood War Bond tours.

Michelle and Lisl became good friends on the tour, and to all three of us the trip became a revealing exposition of America, all new and exciting and stimulating. It disclosed some unusual streaks of generosity in people. There was Biefield's graciousness at his Ambassador Hotel in Chicago. In New York, the owner of the Stork Club, Sherman Billingsley, not only refused to let me pay my bills, but he also always had a little present for Lisl. The president of RKO insisted that I buy Lisl an extravagant present and charge it to the company. I chose a beautiful silver cigarette case and lighter from Dunhill with Lisl's initials worked in gold on both—though I must add that it was the only time any studio I worked for gave me such an outstanding present.

From New York the tour went to Miami, and there I was faced with another, uglier aspect of America, a sign in front of a palatial hotel on a street that reminded me of Cannes, a street of palm trees facing the ocean. The sign, carefully lettered, said, JEWS AND DOGS NOT PERMITTED. I stood there staring at it, and I thought, My God, could what happened in Germany happen here? I had never realized there was so much vicious anti-Semitism under the cover of warmth and pleasant smiles.

From Miami, the tour went to Atlanta, New Orleans, Houston, and Dallas. In every town RKO arranged a tremendous cocktail party for us to meet the press. The one in Dallas started at three P.M. and at three-thirty half of the press corps and most of the guests were blind drunk.

Lisl, Michelle, and I realized very quickly that these people would have just as good a time without us, so we returned to our rooms to rest. When we came back, two hours later, nobody had missed us. The free drinks provided by RKO were evidently more important than our presence.

Suddenly one of the women began to pull me toward the ladies' room. "Please, you've got to see. This is too funny," she giggled as she pulled me into the room.

The door was open and several men and women, drinks in hand, were staring and laughing. I had been dragged in to see a completely naked lady sitting on the toilet. She was in a very gay mood, laughing and holding out a highball glass, which one of the men was filling up.

She was rather plump and seemed to be having a great time. Grinning, she waved me to her. "Come in, Paul! Come in and be my guest. How about a roll in the hay? You're supposed to be good at that."

The people standing around got into the act and called out, "Go on, give her a good time, Paul. Be a sport!"

I turned away and suggested that some of the women might help her dress and get home. Then Michelle, Lisl, and I left to attend a press conference in one of the best restaurants in town. The food was just edible, but I discovered a superior Montrachet Batard that washed everything down, but didn't quite take away the taste of the party.

Some of the reporters had sobered up and a fairly intelligent conversation became possible, except for one Texan who kept telling me, "Paul, Texas is the last frontier in the world. It's the only place where a cowboy on horseback still thinks he can defeat a tank!" He repeated this profound statement several times during the evening, interrupting my conversations with other members of our party. When we were leaving our private dining room, we had to walk a few steps down to the entrance to the restaurant. One of the ladies lost her balance and tumbled down the stairs, showing us all of her quite lovely thighs. As I tried to help her up, my objectionable Texan pulled me up to tell me once more about Texas being the last frontier, about the tank-fighting cowboys and all the other rubbish.

Later, I remembered how beautiful the country had been when Lisl and I traveled through it by car. I remembered the cactus in bloom in the desert in May, the red sand in Colorado and the pale-blue water flowing over it, the almost mystical beauty of Bryce Canyon and the splendor of the Grand Canyon—and I thought how sad that the behavior of this group of people, these aggressive Texans, should spoil what I felt for America—and then I made a firm resolve that it wouldn't.

Eleven

Settling In

*W*hen the publicity tour for *Joan of Paris* ended, we returned to Hollywood, and I began the long wait for a decent play so I could come back to Broadway, but none came. In the meanwhile we left the Beverly Hills Hotel and rented a house in Westwood. Erich Maria Remarque, the novelist, had been a good friend of mine over the years. Our friendship dated back to my publishing days, when I had designed an edition of *All Quiet on the Western Front,* his remarkable anti-war book.

When Erich found out that I was going to Hollywood, he advised me, "The fools all live in Beverly Hills, a congested place I detest. Do you know, Paul, it's a crime to walk in the streets there! Honestly, the police will stop you—and anyway, there's a snobbishness about the place you won't like. You look for a home in Bel Air, Brentwood, or Westwood. There are larger lots there and you won't hear your neighbors."

So that was where we looked. We fell in love with Brentwood, but there were no houses available, so we settled for a rental in Westwood and thought we would be quite happy there.

At about that time, while I was reading one bad play after another, Lillian Hellman and her producer, Kermit Blumgarden, arrived in Hollywood and wanted to talk to me about playing the lead in *Montserrat,* a new play Hellman had written. They stayed at the Beverly Wilshire, and they asked me to join them for lunch after I had read a copy of the play.

At lunch, Blumgarden was very quiet and let Hellman do all the talking. Afterward, she asked us up to her suite for a drink, and once we had settled down, she said, "What I really want is to have you read for us, Paul."

There was a long, uncomfortable pause, and finally I put down my drink and said, "My dear Miss Hellman. Forgive me, but I consider that an impudence, asking me to read. I think I must refuse to do your play."

"But why?" Blumgarden asked, genuinely surprised. Hellman said nothing, just sat there glaring at me.

What I told them then was very deliberate, even though I realized it would cost me an opportunity to return to the stage. I had very strong feelings against reading for a play. In my experience, the only actors who were asked to read were those who were just getting started, who were still unknown.

"I have never read for anyone except Elmer Rice," I said carefully, choosing my words, "and I only did that to show him some character changes I had made in his script. In Vienna I was hired by Max Reinhardt without reading, and I won't read for either of you any more than I would ask Miss Hellman to write a scene for me in order to test her ability to write, or ask Mr. Blumgarden to stand on his head to see if he can produce! You saw me in *Flight to the West* and thought enough of my acting to try to buy my contract so I could appear in your play *Watch on the Rhine.* I am not an unknown quantity!"

I waited to see what they would say, but neither answered me. When the silence became too long for my taste, I stood up, bowed and left—and still they said nothing.

"It was a very noble speech," Lisl said when I told her what had happened, "but it was the only play that showed any promise, Paul. Now what do we do?"

"We look for another place to live," I told her. "Our sublet here is up—and I look for another film to do."

We moved from the rented house to a rented apartment, and Lisl started house hunting. She had made no effort to involve herself in couturier work in Los Angeles and so had plenty of time to search. We didn't feel pressured, and in fact we rather enjoyed the strange, open quality of the city. Los Angeles, in the forties, was a city of broad boulevards and empty lots and very few traffic lights. It was no effort to get into our car with our friends and drive out to the beach for a day in the sun. If we preferred intellectual stimulation, we had that at hand, too.

It seemed to us that Hollywood, in those days, was a gathering place for some of Europe's most intriguing people. Charles Laughton, whom we had met in London, was there with his wife, Elsa Lanchester. They were both bright, excellent conversationalists, and both had a great sense of humor. There were the novelists Lion Feuchtwanger, Thomas Mann, and Vicki Baum. There was Bruno Walter, who had conducted and directed the Vienna Opera, and Arturo Toscanini, and Gregor Piatigorsky, the cellist—the list seemed endless, and they were all old friends or friends of old friends. Some did well in Hollywood while others faded out of sight, but they were all splendid and entertaining company.

Another good friend, Francis Lederer, the actor who had such a remarkable success with *Autumn Crocus* in New York, came and did one flop after another until his career petered out. But Lederer was a born peasant who had a great love for the land. He bought four hundred isolated acres out in the valley for $7,500, and settled down to grow alfalfa. He married and lived very happily in a caretaker's house on the property.

Los Angeles, however, grew outward, and in a short time his four hundred acres were worth $4 million. He refused to sell for a long time, and the longer he held out, the higher the value of his land rose. Eventually he was able to sell a quarter of his acreage for $4 million!

Bertolt Brecht was in Hollywood, too. Lisl had known him in Berlin, when she was married to Edthofer, and they were very fond of each other. When I met him, I liked him, too. He was a brilliant man, but he had some peculiar habits. He smoked the most horrible cigars and chewed off the ends so that a froth of brown saliva always surrounded his mouth.

In his house, there was a long, narrow room with a high desk at one end. He wrote there, standing up, and pacing back and forth as he composed. The room was filled with ashtrays and spittoons that were never cleaned. The smell was overwhelming, but when we protested, he'd simply smile and say, "I like it. It reminds me of those Berlin coffeehouses where the conversation was always so stimulating!"

Brecht's wife's maiden name was Weigel, and none of us ever knew her first name. We all called her Weigel. She had been a minor character actress before she married Brecht, but she was a first-rate baker, and there was always a rich-smelling kugelhupf ready with coffee when we came to visit. His house was very much like a café. People would drop in and out to sit and talk and eat Weigel's Gugelhupf, and Brecht, in turn, seemed to welcome any excuse to stop working.

The conversation at Brecht's was provoking and witty, filled with inspiring ideas and sometimes outrageous views. Brecht was very much a man of the world, and we all knew that he had a number of girl friends on the side. Weigel knew it too, but never seemed to mind.

In his work, Brecht was searching for some original way of expressing the intonation that should be used for a playwright's words. There were many nights when he talked to Laughton and me about finding the right way. In *The Threepenny Opera*, he felt that his words should not be sung the way they were. "They've made my work into an operetta," he complained. "The words should be spoken over the music, sharp and dangerous, especially 'Mack the Knife.' "

Recently I saw a production of Brecht's *Mahogany*, and as I watched it I remembered his explanation of how his material should be handled, and I thought how wrong it sounds on stage now and how powerful it was when we read it with him, trying to find a way of notating his own ideas of intonation.

Hanns Eisler, the German composer who fled to the United States in 1933 to escape Hitler, was a great friend of Brecht, and we met him and came to know him at Brecht's café-house. Eisler, an immensely talented man, was the musical assistant to Charlie Chaplin, and later, tragically, was forced to leave the United States during the days of the McCarthy witch-hunt. At my request he wrote a splendid score for my film *The Spanish Main*.

Once settled in Los Angeles, we were invited to the home of Jules Stein, the head of MCA, the agency that handled me through Lew Wasserman. MCA stood for Music Corporation of America, and Jules, its head, had started, oddly enough, by studying opthalmology in Vienna.

To make some extra money while he attended school, he played the violin in an orchestra. He got the idea of putting bands together to play at nightclubs and parties, and he took care of the bookings. He soon found that he was making more money representing musicians than playing with them. When he came to America he started MCA, originally to handle big bands. He became quite wealthy and owned a beautiful house in Beverly Hills. I was the third actor the company represented when it started to branch out and cover more than music. Betty Grable was a client, and so was Eddie Bracken. MCA was small then, but later it became the biggest agency in Hollywood.

At Stein's house we met many of the Hollywood "celebrities," among them Miriam Hopkins, Bob Hope, Jack Benny, and Claudette Colbert. We were new in town and something of an oddity in a place where people were quickly jaded, so we were handed around from hostess to hostess in those early days, and although we came to dislike a few of the more pretentious of the Hollywood set, we also made dozens of good and fascinating friends.

One of our best friends was Miriam Hopkins, who gave weekly luncheon parties that were always delightful. We'd all arrive about one o'clock to swim, play tennis, talk, and sometimes stay on until late at night. It was an international crowd, and invariably one of the guests would cook some dinner. I tasted some very unusual dishes there, but one of the best was a fabulous chicken in white wine prepared by Jean Negulesco, the director.

At one of Miriam's parties, on a particularly hot day, we were all in the pool. Fritz Lang, the Viennese film director who had made the fabulous *Metropolis* and *M* and had also become a refugee from the Nazis, had brought a beautiful young woman with him, Virginia Gilmore. She had changed into a bathing suit, but sat at the water's edge without venturing into the pool. She looked so hot and uncomfortable that I sat down next to her and offered her a cool drink, which she took gratefully.

"Now what's a beauty like you doing outside the pool?" I asked. "Come on in for a swim."

She shook her head in alarm. "Oh no, I couldn't."

"Do you swim?" Lisl asked.

"Of course, but I spent yesterday at Elizabeth Arden's," she said with a grin, "and if I got wet, all my beauty would wash away!"

Miriam had an enterprising young son who made his own spending money during those parties. A long drive led up to her house, and it ended in a wide parking space. He would set up a stand with bottled soft drinks where the cars were parked, and he'd sell Coca-Cola to the arriving guests for ten cents. All of us felt compelled to buy a bottle—after all, he was such a cute little boy, but we never drank it. We'd hand the unopened bottle to the butler when we went into the house, and the butler would put the bottle in the refrigerator. After a while, when his supply was low, Miriam's son would empty the refrigerator to restock his stand. It was a continuous circle that Miriam was well aware of but thought quite amusing. I've often wondered what became of her son. He must have had a fabulous career in the business world.

Once we had settled in in Hollywood, Lisl was approached by a woman who wanted to go into business with her and set up a dress salon. "The potential is fantastic," Lisl told me, "but I have made so many changes. First it was Vienna and Berlin, then London, and then New York, first with James and then that fur shop." In New York she had finally left Charles James to set up a fur shop with a partner. It was doing very well when we had to leave for the coast. "I just can't stand the idea of starting another business and nursing it along until it becomes a success and then having to leave it."

"Why should you?" I asked. "I'm making enough money for us to live comfortably now. Why don't you just stop? You've worked ever since you left your first husband. It's high time you had a rest. Look, get to know California and enjoy yourself."

She agreed, and I doubt if she's ever regretted her choice. In the meanwhile I still waited impatiently for scripts of plays. I was unhappy at the idea of my stage experience slipping away, and I didn't want to be "just" a film actor. Jane Broder, my agent in New York, wrote after I had been particularly demanding about her finding a good play:

> Paul, you're living under the illusion that we have a living theatre in America. What we have here is a real estate business. The theatres are valuable pieces of property that are bringing in income. They lose money when they stand idle, so the owners look for a play and an audience to make the theatre pay. Good plays, as you think of them, are just not the rule. What they want are popular plays.

In a way I agreed with her, but I felt that there was a paradox involved because there were so many playwrights in America. By contrast, the European theatre was an ensemble theatre. You were hired for the season and you appeared in whatever play they put on, usually at the same theatre. In Vienna I had done most of my plays at the Scala. From time to time the Scala would hire a big name star to play the lead, but the supporting cast remained the same, the ensemble players. In the end I gave up any real hope of finding satisfactory work on the stage and turned all my energy to films.

"Now that we are settled in an apartment," Lisl said one day, "I think it's time we reciprocated and paid back some of the people who have been inviting us to parties. Let's have a party of our own."

I thought that was a great idea, and we made our plans, checked the guest list carefully, and decided on a dinner party. It was late October, and we thought a month would give us ample time to get it all together. "And time enough so that the guests won't have any previous appointments," Lisl said.

We settled on a Thursday late in November. At first we thought of Friday night, the end of the week, when everybody is relaxed, but, as Lisl pointed out, "Everyone runs off for the weekend and they like to get an early start on Friday after work. I really want this to be a success, Paul, so let's make it Thursday. That way no one will have planned something else."

We invited twenty-four friends, and they all accepted. We

rented tables and chairs and reserved a caterer, and Lisl gave instructions to the cook and our maid, who would wait tables, while I stocked up on some excellent wines.

Then, to our dismay, a few days before the party regrets began to pour in. One by one the guests fell away, and on the night of the party we were left with only one arrival, Leonard Spiegelgass, the writer.

"Is something wrong with us?" I asked him. "Have we committed some faux pas—insulted everyone in some way? The invitations were correct, I know that, but for everyone to cancel out like this . . ."

"It would never happen in Vienna!" Lisl said angrily.

"Well," Leonard said as he circled the table, looking at the place cards, "this isn't Vienna, and here the last Thursday in November is Thanksgiving. I guess none of your guests realized that when they accepted. As for me, I am all alone and I was delighted to come."

"Thanksgiving?" Lisl said blankly. "What's that?"

"Our great family holiday, when we celebrate the first harvest of the Pilgrims in America. It's sacred to the family, and everyone wants to spend it at home with their family and friends."

Before we could recover from the shock, Leonard started an ingenious imaginary dialogue with each of our absent guests, an amusing, witty dialogue that left both Lisl and me, in spite of our devastating disappointment, weak with laughter. It was exactly what we needed to cheer us up.

However, before we sat down to dinner with our lone guest, our maid came in to inform us that she was giving notice. She couldn't stay on with a family that has twenty-three cancellations for a dinner party. Something must be wrong with us.

That started us off on new gales of laughter, and as the door closed behind her indignant back, Lisl said, "Don't worry. She was a terrible maid anyway—a perfect snob!"

Twelve

◆

Two Cigarettes
and One Match

*S*hortly after our disastrous party, Lew Wasserman called and told me he had a script for me from Warner Brothers. "It's a small part," he said, "and I think you should turn it down, but do give them the courtesy of reading it first and talking to them. They really want you to do a movie for them, and if this doesn't work out—as I know it won't—they'll offer you something better."

I read the script and found that although it was indeed a short part, still, like many short parts, it could steal the movie if properly played. Small as it was, it was a fantastic role, I realized, and best of all, Bette Davis was to play opposite me. Davis was one of the top Hollywood stars, on a level with Garbo and Colbert.

I told Wasserman I'd take it, and he was completely surprised. "Really?" he said doubtfully. "I know they're prepared to pay a lot, seventy five thousand, but is it right for you, Paul?"

"Let me judge that," I assured him. "It's going to be perfect."

Jack Warner was delighted. He had seen me in *Joan of Paris*, but he had his own idea of how I should look in this new film called *Now Voyager*. "We'd like Paul to be a cross between Leslie Howard and George Brent," he told Wasserman, and the director of the film, Irving Rapper, asked me where I had my clothes made.

"At Anderson and Sheppard, 30 Savile Row. They have all my measurements," I told him.

Rapper shook his head. "Savile Row? Where is that? Downtown?"

"In London," I said.

"Oh, that's too complicated. We'll do it in our own tailor shop in the studio."

I was doubtful, but Jack Warner assured me it would be just fine. "He does all my clothes, Paul. The man is a genius."

I looked at Warner's suit dubiously, but all I said was, "If you insist."

When the tailor had finished them, all my suits looked like those George Brent wore, broad built-out shoulders and narrow waists—not at all my style. I decided I simply looked ridiculous in them.

"Before you go for the makeup test," Rapper said to me, "I'd like you to have your hair cut. It's much too full."

Again I realized that the "Brent" image was in their minds. He wore his hair slicked down, and while it may have suited him I knew it would look ridiculous on me. For one thing, my ears are too large.

I told Lisl the problem, and she took me to her hairdresser, a young Frenchman named Marcel. He listened to my problem sympathetically, and then gave me a pomade he had developed. "It won't harm your hair," he told me. "Nor will it make it brittle. Just put it on and wear a net over it to bed at night. In the morning it will be so tight against your head it will look as if it had been cut."

"But will it come out?" I asked.

He grinned. "With soap and water—presto!—your hair is full again."

The next morning, when I reported to the makeup room, my hair was as slicked down as if it had been cut. Perce Westmore, who was in charge, told me he had received a note from Hal Wallis, the producer: "Make Henreid look like Brent and Howard."

Following orders, Westmore made me up with lipstick and red cheeks and accented my eyes with mascara. Filmed in black and white, the contrast would be startling. Staring at myself in the mirror, I thought, My God, I look like a gigolo! I can't go through with this, it's too embarrassing. Warner must be out of his mind. What am I going to do?

The best thing to do, I realized as I stared at my reflection, was to shut up and let them turn me into a complete department-store dummy. I was bound to look hideous in the test and one of them would come to his senses—if not Warner, then Wallis, who was no fool; and if that didn't work, then I'd fight it out.

At that point I hadn't yet met Bette Davis. She had a house

in Laguna, was married to Arthur Farnsworth, and was off on vacation. She had seen me in *Joan of Paris*, where I wore my usual makeup—a little base, no lipstick or mascara, and only some darkening on my blond eyebrows. Usually, I was in and out of makeup in ten minutes. Westmore labored over my face for three quarters of an hour. Then I appeared in front of the camera wearing the suit that had been made for me by Warner's tailor.

I was invited to see the results of the makeup tests. "Bette will be in to look at them," Rapper told me. "It's a good chance for the two of you to get acquainted."

I came up with some excuse to get out of it. For one thing, I was too embarrassed, and I asked them to run it for me a day later.

I told my wardrobe man to be there at the showing of the test and to call me afterward. As he reported, Bette saw the test and hit the ceiling. She turned to Rapper and Hal Wallis and shouted, "What did you do to that man? How can I act with him? He looks ghastly, like some floorwalker in a department store. You are two of the most miserable bastards!"

"Now calm down, Bette . . ." Hal Wallis started, but she turned on him furiously.

"I saw him in *Joan of Paris* and I wanted to play opposite him, but you've turned him into a monster. I'm just not available for this kind of crap!"

"Bette, please . . . " Wallis tried to soothe her. "We'll fix him up."

"How? With that short hair . . ."

"We'll get hairpieces for his sideburns and make him look the way he did in *Joan of Paris;* we'll eliminate all that makeup and ask him if he'll be kind enough to use his own wardrobe. . . ."

But Bette stormed out without waiting for him to finish. Later, Irving Rapper called me and said, "Paul, we just saw the tests and they look very nice, but we thought we'd like to go with your style of dressing. The suits we made here aren't doing you justice. Could you use your own clothes?"

I said, "I'd be happy to, Irving, but they're cut differently from

American suits. You know, I have an excellent tailor in town, Eddie Schmidt in Beverly Hills. He's made suits for me, and he's very good. I'll use the clothes he's made, and you can replace the ones I wear in the film."

"That's an excellent idea," Rapper agreed. "Oh yes, another thing—we thought your makeup was a bit on the heavy side."

"I know," I agreed. "I never wear makeup like that."

"Yes," he went on, "and there's one other little problem, but I think we can solve that."

"What is it?"

"Your hair . . . " Rapper said diffidently.

"What about it?"

"It's too—short."

"Now look," I said, "you told me to cut it."

"I know," he agreed miserably, "but it isn't right. Now don't you worry about it," he added hastily. "We'll get an excellent side-piece to make it look fuller."

"Now here's where we disagree," I said firmly. "I simply won't do a film with a hairpiece. If this is a problem, we can wait until my hair grows back—and of course you'll pay me for the time, but Mr. Wasserman can discuss all that."

"But we're ready to shoot!"

"I'm sorry. Remember, it was your idea to cut my hair. I just won't wear a hairpiece."

Strangely enough, nothing happened, and there was no need to call Lou Wasserman. I came to the first day's shooting and walked in with my hair plastered down with the goo Lisl's hairdresser had given me. I rehearsed the first scene alone. In it, I'm supposed to be on a ship looking down at the passengers embarking. They usually shot a picture in sequence in those days, a much more logical way of doing it and particularly good for the actors. It allows you to build up your part instead of racing back and forth through time in the story.

I rehearsed the scene with my hair plastered down, then, before the shooting, I went into my dressing room and combed the dried goo out of my hair. It flaked away easily, and my head looked normal again. When I walked into the scene, Irving was bewildered. "What did you do?"

"I combed my hair out."

"You can't make it full by combing," he protested.

"The truth is, I never cut it," I admitted. "I simply plastered it down. Shall we get on with the scene?"

"Thank God," he breathed. "Is Bette going to be happy!"

"What about Paul?" I said sourly. "Don't you think he's happy too? I still don't understand why anyone would bring in an actor because he looks one way, and then try to make him look like somebody else." But Rapper was too pleased with the results of my haircombing to hear me.

When Bette saw me for the first time, she came up to me and kissed me on both cheeks and said, "I just know I'm working with a good actor! You were right not to come to the screening of the makeup test." She drew back and looked at me wickedly. "You're a pretty smart cookie, Paul!"

There was something about her manner, flirtatious and friendly, flattering and yet honest, that made you think of her as an immediate friend, and a solid master of her craft. I found her a delight to work with, and we got along famously. In fact, a very close friendship started between us, and she has remained a dear, close friend—and always a very decent human being.

Bette met and liked Lisl and the four of us, Bette and Arthur Farnsworth, her husband, and Lisl and I spent many evenings together. Farnsworth, who came from an old New England family, was a perfect husband for Bette. He didn't interfere with her professional life but let her do as she pleased, and we could sense the warmth and love between them.

Tragically, shortly after we finished filming *Now Voyager*, Farnsworth died of a massive heart attack while walking on Hollywood Boulevard. Bette took his death very hard, and I like to think we were of some help to her in that difficult time.

After Farnsworth died, she married William Grant Sherry, a painter. He wasn't very successful at his art, but he was a very good-looking, virile man—today, the word would be macho. I think, after Farnsworth's gentle permissiveness, she was attracted to Sherry's masculinity, but Bette was too strong and intelligent a woman herself to be happy in that sort of relationship, and eventually the marriage became a series of stormy encounters.

There was a scene in the script of *Now Voyager* where the author, Casey Robinson, had invented a bit of business to show the growing intimacy between Bette and me. I was to offer Bette a cigarette, take one myself, light mine, then take her cigarette out of her mouth, give her mine and put hers between my lips.

The idea of a shared cigarette was right, but the procedure was too long, too clumsy. I rehearsed it at home with Lisl and the awkwardness of it made us both laugh, but the correct way to do it occurred to both of us at once. When we used to be out in the Viva Grand Sport, a car without a lighter, and the driver wanted a cigarette, the other would usually feel like smoking, too, and would light two and put one into the driver's mouth. It was an intimate and sensual gesture, or it could be played that way.

On the set the next day, I said to Bette, "Have you thought about that cigarette business?"

"Yes," she nodded. "The sharing is rather nice."

"Only it's awkward. The intimacy Casey wanted to show is good, but when we do it, there's a lot of hands and cigarettes, and I know it's going to end up on the cutting-room floor."

"Well, what do you suggest, Paul?"

"I have an idea," I told her. "First, let's try it the way the script says." We did, and then I said, "Now let me show you a better way." I took out a pack of cigarettes, took two from the pack, put them between my lips and lit them, then took one and put it in her mouth. She immediately recognized the significance and allowed her hand to touch mine. It was just right.

"Sensational!" she shouted and hugged me, then rushed up to Irving Rapper. "Irving, Paul solved it!"

"Oh? Have you?" he asked doubtfully. "What?"

"Yes. Paul, let's show him." And we did the scene for Rapper. Shaking his head, Rapper said, "I don't like it."

"You're crazy," Bette told him flatly. "This is a hundred times better than the other. Can't you see it?"

When he continued to resist the idea, insisting we should play it just as the script had it, Bette phoned Hal Wallis, the producer, and asked him to come to the set. We did both versions for him, and he said, "There's no comparison, of course."

Rapper began to smile, thinking he had won the discussion, but Wallis went on, "Paul's idea is so good that I'll talk to Casey and have him put the same business in three or four more spots. It's something that's going to make an impression with the audience."

Wallis was the only one who understood what would happen. Bette and I simply thought of it as a less clumsy bit of business, but he was right. It became not only a symbol for *Now Voyager*, to be picked up by every film critic and the public, but I myself became identified with the two-cigarette maneuver, and all over the country young lovers began to copy the gesture to show a touch of sensual intimacy. This, I believe, together with the meaty part I had and Bette Davis' intelligent acting, made a star out of me.

The two-cigarette bit, however, began to get out of hand when *Now Voyager* played nationally. One evening in New York, Lisl and I were having dinner at Voisin, then my favorite restaurant, when a woman at a nearby table stood up and hurried over to us. "I know you," she said in a loud, challenging voice. "You're Paul Henreid!"

Before I could answer, she plumped herself down on my lap and shoved two cigarettes at me. "Light them! Oh God, light them!"

I was stunned, and I didn't know what to do or how to act. I realized she was drunk, or at least I thought she was, and I was terribly embarrassed. "Light them," she begged.

I took out my lighter, lit them, and gave her one, then pleaded, "Now go back to your table, please! This is awful."

Bette Davis, when I told her about it later, said, "You were completely wrong to do it, Paul. I tell people like that, 'Leave me alone. I don't know you, and you don't know me. I'm here with friends, and I don't want to talk to you!' "

"But that's so rude . . ."

"Oh, believe me, rudeness is the only thing that works in a situation like that."

I couldn't do that, but the next time it happened at another restaurant with another "fan," I was prepared. I stood up and let the woman slide to the floor. "I'm not a cigarette lighter," I told her with all the dignity I could muster. "I did it in a film, but this isn't a film. Please leave us alone!"

I felt very much in command of the situation—but of course it didn't work. The woman was just as insistent, and it happened again and again, and no amount of pleading for privacy did any good. There was something magical about that two-cigarette scene that seemed to turn intelligent women into complete idiots.

When *Now Voyager* was released, the film magazines and newspapers saw a new lover on the Hollywood horizon. Partly it was because of the picture's success, but also much of it was due to an all-out publicity campaign by Warner Brothers. *Now Voyager* was recognized by the studio to be a hit, and a fantastic amount of publicity was launched. There were tours with the stars, radio shows, autograph parties, talks to ladies' clubs, and a veritable deluge of stories about our private lives, our broken hearts, and unhappy or happy marriages—all manufactured in Warner's publicity department.

I was pleased, but a bit bewildered by some of the rave reviews I got for the picture. It was, after all, a sentimental love story, a plot I would have laughed at in a stage play. But the New York *Herald-Tribune* said, very seriously, "Paul Henreid achieves his full stature as a romantic star. . . . " *Time* magazine called me Hollywood's "likeliest leading man," and went on to describe my formula as "in a tough emotional spot, he acts like a kind and morally responsible human being."

Even before the reviews came out, during the shooting of *Now Voyager,* Warner Brothers approached me to sign a term contract that would last seven years. They would use me in the time left free by the RKO contract, but I hesitated. I felt that if I were to go along with it, I'd be signing my life away. I knew that once I signed a contract like that, I would have to do whatever picture the studio assigned to me. I would have no say in the choice of pictures. If a script was so bad that I absolutely refused to do it, they could put me on suspension. That meant that they could stop my pay for the time the picture was being shot, or for a stated number of weeks if they couldn't shoot the picture without me—or didn't want to.

The last touch was the worst. I was only put on suspension once, and that was when they gave me a terrible script, *The Beast with Five Fingers*. I found out later that this particular script was used on many stars when the studio had nothing for them. It was so bad that almost everyone chose to go on suspension rather than be in it. The studio knew this, but eventually Vincent Price stood up to them, accepted the script and did it. Surprisingly, it turned into something of a hit in the horror genre. Robert Alda and Peter Lorre also starred.

I wanted to turn the seven-year contract down, but Lew Wasserman told me to reconsider it. They were interning Japanese then, even American-born Japanese, and Lew said, "Let's face it, Paul. You've told me how you dreaded internment in England. Well, it's possible that America may eventually intern German aliens, and Austria is a part of Germany now. You have a picture a year with RKO, but they're a company that's not in very good shape. If the question of internment came up, I doubt that they could protect you as well as Warner Brothers could. Along with MGM, Warners is the biggest out here. If I were you, I'd think it over carefully."

When I still hesitated, he shrugged. "Look, it may not be a tasty dish, but there's a little whipped cream on it. They're offering you an absolutely unbelievable deal in terms of money. I strongly advise you to take it."

I sighed. "I suppose I should, and I will, but it's against everything I believe in, and I'm sure I'll suffer for it!" So I signed up for a lot of money and was expected to make two pictures a year—three, counting the RKO deal. The two studios agreed to apportion my time between them.

What I didn't understand because I didn't bother to read the small print was that contracts could be bought and sold. Warners,

Left: Here I am as a baby with my mother, Maria Louise von Hernried (Edle von Wasel-Waldingau). Below left: I am about three-and-a-half years old in this picture. My brother Robert (right) is about a year-and-a-half. Below right: My father, Carl Alphons Hernried, (Ritter von Wasel-Waldingau).

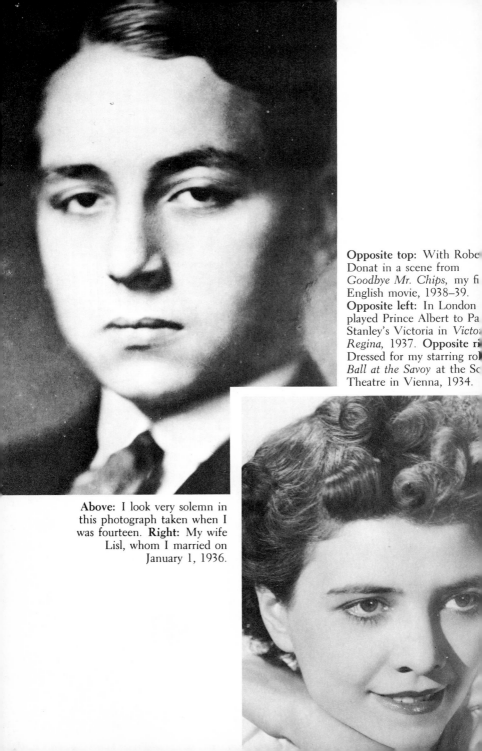

Opposite top: With Robe[rt]
Donat in a scene from
Goodbye Mr. Chips, my fi[rst]
English movie, 1938–39.
Opposite left: In London [I]
played Prince Albert to Pa[mela]
Stanley's Victoria in *Victo[ria]
Regina,* 1937. **Opposite ri[ght:]**
Dressed for my starring ro[le in]
Ball at the Savoy at the S[tadt]
Theatre in Vienna, 1934.

Above: I look very solemn in
this photograph taken when I
was fourteen. **Right:** My wife
Lisl, whom I married on
January 1, 1936.

Above: My first picture for RKO cast me opposite the sultry French actress Michelle Morgan, 1941. **Opposite top:** With Margaret Lockwood in *Night Train*, the film that netted me an award for Best Actor in a Foreign Film. **Opposite left:** With Bette Davis in *Now Voyager*, the movie in which I became famous for lighting two cigarettes at once. **Opposite right:** I played a Nazi in *Night Train*. The other male lead belonged to a little-known actor named Rex Harrison.

Top left: Pictures of my leading ladies (and other friends) adorned a wall of the library of our home. **Top center:** Probably the most famous of all my movies: *Casablanca.* As French Resistance leader Victor Lazlo I ordered the band to play "La Marseillaise" while the Germans sang "Watch on the Rhine." **Top right:** Our two daughters, Mimi Maria and Monica Elizabeth, with Lisl and me in the garden of our home in Brentwood Park. **Opposite left:** The sweet and gentle Ingrid Bergman, who played my wife in *Casablanca.* **Above:** *The Spanish Main,* 1944, with Maureen O'Hara was the first of my many pirate movies.

Top left: *Conspirators,* shot in 1944, was my first picture with Hedy Lamarr, a woman with a rather peculiar outlook on life. **Top right:** Olivia de Havilland played Charlotte Brontë and Ida Lupino played Emily Brontë while I played the curate in *Devotion,* a movie very loosely based on the life of the Brontë family. **Center:** Alexis Smith and I in a scene from *Of Human Bondage.* **Bottom left:** John Garfield, Eleanor Parker, and I in a scene from *Between Two Worlds.* **Bottom center:** Lisl and I with my mother, Marie Louise von Hernried, just after she arrived in Hollywood from Vienna, where she had spent the war years. **Bottom right:** *Between Two Worlds* was a rewrite of *Outward Bound,* which had been done in 1930. Here I'm shown with Eleanor Parker.

Top left: In *Hollow Triumph* I had a different kind of role—I played a gangster. My leading lady was Joan Bennett. Top right: Ever since *Now Voyager*, Bette Davis and I had wanted to work together again. Finally we got the chance in *Deception*. Center left: Ida Lupino and I were together again in *In Our Time*. I played a Polish count; she played an English girl. Center right: I played Robert Schumann in MGM's *Song of Love*. Katharine Hepburn played my wife, Clara, while Robert Wagner played Johannes Brahms. Bottom left: Rita Moreno and I in *So Young So Bad*. Bottom right: As producer for *So Young So Bad*, I gave three talented young actresses roles. They were Anne Jackson, Rita Moreno, and Anne Francis. In this scene Anne Jackson and I appeared with Enid Pulver.

Top left: My third discovery, Anne Francis, in *So Young So Bad.* **Top center:** One movie I did appear in during the blacklist years was *Rope of Sand* with Burt Lancaster and Corinne Calvet. **Top right:** I discovered another actress while working on *Pardon My French*—Marina Vlady, who went on to become a French star. **Center:** *For Men Only* was a film I did with two independent producers. I'm shown here with Kathleen Hughes and Vera Miles. **Bottom left:** In *Stolen Face* I played a plastic surgeon while Lizabeth Scott played a prostitute. **Bottom right:** Merle Oberon and I starred in *Pardon My French.*

Left: My younger daughter Mimi, the tennis champ, pos[es] here with me and Lisl's toy poodle, Schatzi. **Bottom left:** [I] had an opportunity to return [to] the stage with a six-month to[ur] of George Bernard Shaw's *D[on] Juan in Hell* with Agnes Moorehead. **Bottom right:** I[n] *Operation Crossbow* I again played a Nazi—a general thi[s] time. The director insisted th[at] the Germans in the picture speak in German and subtitle[s] would be used. Most of my scenes wound up on the cutt[ing] room floor.

Top right: I directed Ray Charles in *Blues for Lovers* for Twentieth Century Fox. **Center:** The blacklist, which nearly destroyed my acting career, did have one good effect— I found a new career as a director. Here I'm directing a scene from *Take Five from Five* for Universal Pictures. **Bottom left:** Ingrid Thulin played my wife in the 1960 movie *The Four Horsemen of the Apocalypse*. **Bottom right:** *Man in Hiding* was a grade-B movie, but during the blacklist years I didn't have much choice. I'm shown here with Kay Kendall.

Above: Relaxing after a game of tennis. **Below:** My grandson Mario was an astute listener as I practiced for an M.C. performance at Lisl's Trophy Ball at the Beverly Wilshire Hotel.

Mario at age sixteen.

for instance, once I became a big box-office draw, was able to sell me to another studio for one picture and get $125,000. In turn, by my contract, they had to pay me only $75,000. This was not only done with actors and actresses, but also with writers, scenic designers, cameramen, and anyone else under contract.

Shortly after I finished *Now Voyager* and it began to attract such favorable reviews, I was invited to come to the White House with four other stars. I had met Eleanor Roosevelt before at meetings on racial equality and some March of Dimes affairs, but this was an invitation to lunch, and we were also to meet the President, the legendary Franklin D. Roosevelt.

I took the City of Los Angeles luxury train to Chicago, stayed overnight there at the Ambassador East and saw my friend Ernie Biefield again, and then, with the other actors, took a train to Washington. At the station we were met by an impressive escort and driven to the White House.

Lunch, once we got over our feeling of awe, was a warm, generous affair, though, when I called Lisl that night to describe it all, I couldn't, for the life of me, remember what I had eaten or said. But I did remember everything about the President. He was very human and approachable, very concerned about our comfort and completely attentive to us.

I think he must have been well-briefed because he quoted lines to me from *Joan of Paris* and *Now Voyager* and to the other actors from their most recent pictures. Eleanor was gracious and sweet to us, and I was particularly struck by the fact that the President seemed in no pain, though I had heard so many stories about his crippling polio. He was in a wheelchair, of course, but he moved it around easily and gracefully.

When we left, he shook my hand and said, to all of us, "I can't tell you how grateful I am that you took the time to come here and give us a chance to know you." As if, indeed, we were the ones doing him the honor! It made me feel very happy and grateful as we left.

Thirteen

◆

Casablanca

*A*fter I signed the seven-year contract with Warners, I was handed the script for *Casablanca,* and I said to Lou, "Let's forget it. I'll start my contract by going on suspension!"

"Why?" he asked. "What's wrong?"

"What's wrong? Not only is it a terrible script, really rotten, but I don't want to be the second lover in a film, second to Humphrey Bogart!"

I heard later that originally *Casablanca* had been intended as a "B" picture to star Ann Sheridan and Ronald Reagan, but after Bogart had such a tremendous hit with *High Sierra,* the studio decided to use *Casablanca* as his next starring vehicle. Bogart refused at first. The script was bad and they wanted Ann Sheridan to star with him, But Selznick was trying to get rid of a commitment with Ingrid Bergman, who had just finished *Intermezzo,* a delightful movie that made no money. Selznick wanted Ingrid in a major film with box-office stars, and *Casablanca* with Bogart and me seemed just that.

While I was carrying on about the lousy script, Hal Wallis asked me to come to his office. I walked in and was introduced to Howard Koch and Albert Maltz, two very talented Hollywood screenwriters.

"Al, Howie, explain to Paul what you're going to do with the *Casablanca* script," Wallis told them. Koch and Maltz began to talk, Maltz pacing around the room, active and lively, Koch sitting quietly, following him with his eyes and nodding every now and then as Maltz described one of the scenes he wanted to put in. Listening to them, I began to see the film as a very exciting melodrama, and although my part was not the real love in Bergman's life, and not even that good a part, it also wasn't that bad—at least not as Maltz told it. I finally agreed to do it, but asked Wasserman to make sure my contract would stipulate that the ending wasn't changed, at least that part of it where I went off with Ingrid.

I thought Maltz and Koch were a well-matched team, and if anyone could, they would spice up the original Epstein brothers' dreadful script. Maltz had flair; his writing was bold and strong. Koch was more pedantic in his work. He lacked Maltz' élan, but made up for it with his precision. However, Maltz never got a credit on the final screenplay probably because Koch spent more time on the rewrite. Credit depends on a Writers' Guild formula involving how many pages you write.

Shooting started before there was a finished screenplay, in fact, before there was more than the opening scenes. Since we were shooting in chronological order, we were able to do it. The pages usually came out of the writers' typewriters the day before they were to be shot. As a result, there were often different versions of scenes. Nobody knew what would come next, including Mike Curtiz, the director, who did a beautiful job, especially under the wild circumstances. Mike would apologize to us, saying, "Excuse me, I don't know any more than you do about what follows or goes ahead. I'm directing each scene as best I know how!"

We all understood that the picture was being shot against time because Bogart was signed up for a role in *Sahara*, which had precedence, and *Casablanca* had to be finished first or they'd lose him.

"We know the problem," each of us told Curtiz, and we assured him that he was doing a superb job, but still there were confusing moments. I played the part of Victor Lazlo, Ingrid Bergman's husband, a leader of the Resistance who is trying to leave Casablanca. Ingrid, my wife, had fallen in love with Bogart when she thought I was dead, and now she falls for him again. In the end she gives him up to leave with me while Bogart goes off with Claude Rains to join the Free French army. It was all overblown melodrama and romance, but somehow it worked, even though I, as a fugitive leader of the Resistance, had to wear an immaculately clean white suit through most of the picture.

I am described by the Germans as a great leader of the masses, a man who can command obedience. That's the reason the Germans don't want me to leave Casablanca, and it's also the plot hinge. There is a scene in Rick's Café, one of the high points, when I order the band to play *"La Marseillaise"* to counter the Germans' singing *"Die Wacht am Rhein,"* a very patriotic military song. The musicians look away, then back to me before they start playing, and I conduct them, singing myself.

After the rehearsal, I asked Curtiz, "What the hell is going on? Why do they look away and then back at me?"

"Oh yes," Curtiz said. "That—I told them to look at Bogie. I'll have a cut of Bogie nodding, giving them the order to play."

"But why?" I asked, confused.

"Because in the picture Bogie pays their salary, and they don't want to do anything that would get them fired."

"But for heaven's sake," I protested. "I'm supposed to be a leader of the masses, and here I have a stinking little band, and I can't get them to do what I want!"

Curtiz laughed. "Oh, it'll be all right. It will establish that Bogie is on your side."

Curtiz produced a classic with *Casablanca,* but against all odds —one of those odds being he himself. Mike was Hungarian and his command of English was excellent, but his pronunciation left something to be desired. At one point we were supposed to be shooting in a Moroccan street filled with vendors, a cart, a donkey, and a crowd of people. Curtiz reviewed the set before we started and said, "It's very nice, but I want a poodle."

The prop man was upset. "Mike, you never told me that. We don't have one."

"Well, get one," Curtiz snapped.

"All right." Nervous now, the prop man said, "What size?"

"What size? A big one, a big one!" Curtiz turned away in annoyance.

"What color?" the prop man persisted.

Curtiz threw his hands up. "Dark, you idiot! We're photographing in black and white."

"It's going to take about half an hour."

Curtiz rolled his eyes. "You think time is nothing? All right, all right!"

We went back to our dressing rooms, and Mike and I started a game of chess while Bogie kibitzed. In half an hour the prop man poked his head in happily. "I have it now, Mr. Curtiz. Will you come and look?"

"Pauli, don't touch the pieces. I think I have you mate in three moves." And Mike went out. We went with him so he wouldn't accuse us of cheating, and there on the set was a beautiful black standard poodle. Mike looked bewildered. "What do I want with a dog?"

"You said you wanted a poodle."

"I wanted a poodle in the street," Curtiz shouted. "A poodle, a poodle of water!"

"Oh my God, you mean a puddle!"

"Right. A poodle, a puddle—that's what I want, not a goddamn dog!"

All in all I found Mike Curtiz a charming man, balding, in his late fifties, slim with trim features and a tight skin. He was a superb director with an amazing command of lighting, mood, and action. He seemed able to handle any kind of picture—comedy, love story, Western, or giant historical epic.

There was a story that one of the Warner brothers discovered Mike Curtiz after the success of his European film *Moon of Israel*. He signed him up in Germany and brought him back to New York by boat. When the boat docked, Mike looked down at the pier and saw a huge crowd with flags and a band. Touched, he turned to Warner and said, "All this for me, for Mike Curtiz?"

Warner shrugged. "Well—it *is* the Fourth of July."

When I was first introduced to Mike, he said, with all his Hungarian charm, "Please, may I call you Pauli?" and we got along famously. But as charming as he was to his major stars, he was just as rude to the bit players. He treated them abominably, as if he had to let all his meanness out on them so he could be extra sweet to the actors who, in his view, mattered.

There was a bit player, a refugee German aristocrat, a very bad actor, who quickly annoyed Mike. Bogie and I were playing chess one day when there was a knock on the dressing-room door, and Claude Rains walked in.

"Do you hear that?" Claude asked tightly, nodding toward the open door.

We could both hear Curtiz screaming at the German actor. "You stupid son of a bitch! Can't you understand English? Can't you do what I tell you? Don't try to think, you idiot—just listen to me, and don't be such an asshole!"

"Yes," I agreed, moving a pawn. "It's rather awful. I think Mike should learn to control himself."

Very briskly, Claude, who was always a perfect gentleman, said, "We just won't have that kind of behavior, will we?"

Uneasily, Bogie said, "Well . . . no, no, we shouldn't."

"If Mike is going to act like that," Claude went on, "I don't want to have anything to do with the film. What about you two? Bogie? Paul?"

Frowning, but impressed by Claude's moral tone, Bogie agreed, "Absolutely."

"I think," Claude said, "we should tell Michael right now that if he raises his voice like that once more and uses that disgusting language, we'll walk off the set. Are you with me?"

Bogie stood up. "You bet. Come on, Paul, let's do it."

I agreed, and as the three of us walked across the set, I asked, "Does Curtiz do this all the time, talk like that?"

"He can be a real son of a bitch to the bit players," Bogie said, "but watch the way he treats us."

He was right. When Curtiz saw us, his face and manner changed and he smiled. "Gentlemen! What can I do for you?"

We had decided that, since Claude was the oldest, and it was his idea, he would be our spokesman. "Mike," he said, "Paul and Bogie and I all feel we should have a happy set from the first to the last day. We don't want to hear an ugly word from you to anyone on this stage." His voice hardened as he spoke. "Not to a grip, a cameraman, or even, God help us, to a bit player!" He nodded toward the crushed German actor.

Curtiz' eyes widened and his jaw dropped, but Claude went on relentlessly. "What we just heard you say to that man was shameful, and we're telling you right now, do it again and we three walk off the set!"

"Oh no! No . . . I . . . please," Curtiz stammered. Then he collected himself. "Please, I promise you. It won't happen, believe me!"

And for the rest of the shooting he was as good as his word— until the last day. We had to shoot the entire picture indoors, and we used the biggest stage at Warners for the airport scene at the end. To give an illusion of the perspective of distance, small models of planes were used in the background and midgets were hired to look like men far off. Fog machines gave the final touch, softening everything and making the stage walls and ceiling invisible.

The last scene at the airport was a tricky shot. A car with Bogie, Ingrid, and me, driven by Claude, had to arrive, make a turn, and then stop at a certain spot, so that when we all climbed out we'd be at marked places where we all could be seen clearly and the camera wouldn't overshoot the available stage.

It was an extremely complicated shot because of the camera angles. We had been shooting since early morning, and each time Claude would either miss the marks by a foot, or the windshield wiper would be in the wrong place at the wrong time, or the fog would be too thick, or we'd get out at the wrong mark—a series of small disasters at every take! Each time the fog had to be blown out and new fog put in, and this took at least half an hour.

Finally Claude drove in, hit the marks perfectly, we all got in the right place, and a bit player came up, clicked his heels and was supposed to say, "At your service, *mon capitaine*. The plane leaves for Lisbon . . ." A very short line. He had said it perfectly all day, and now he began the line and froze. The thing every actor dreads happened. He simply forgot what he had to say.

Curtiz had a pencil in his hand. He snapped it in two and screamed, "Cut! Cut!" then slammed down the pieces and let loose. "You goddamn stupid fuckin' asshole . . ."

Claude looked at me. I looked at Bogie. Then we three turned and walked off while Curtiz, in horror, shouted, "No! No, please!"

Very calmly, Claude called back, "We'll see you in a couple of days, Mike." And we passed him, then ducked into one of the dressing rooms. Curtiz was frantic. He called the front gate and tried to close down the lot while he had people searching all over for us.

We managed to hide out for two hours, then, at five-thirty, we came back to a chastened, mild director. We reshot the scene, and, miracle of miracles—it worked on the first take!

Mike Curtiz, befitting the reputation of most Hungarians, was a practiced womanizer and was known to hire pretty young extras to whom he promised all sorts of things, including stardom, just to have them around and make passes at them at any odd hours when there was a break in the shooting. He would choose any private place on the set, usually behind some flat in a secluded area. He'd have the grips move a piece of furniture there, a couch, or even a mattress —almost anything to soften his lovemaking.

He thought none of us knew about these little affairs, but Peter Lorre, an inveterate practical joker, found out and went to the sound department, where he coaxed them into wiring up a hidden microphone and loudspeaker at Mike's favorite love rendezvous. We were all resting between takes one afternoon when suddenly, over the loudspeaker, we heard Mike moaning, "Oh God! Oh no, no, no . . ."

We were stunned. For a second we thought he was in pain, and we jumped up, but Peter Lorre, grinning like a madman, waved us back, and we realized what was going on. Mike's moaning became increasingly ecstatic: "Oh yes, yes—oh God, yes." And then: "Take it all, take it all—my balls too!"

The entire cast collapsed in helpless laughter. Fortunately for Curtiz and his status on the set, he never found out about Lorre's trick.

Lorre had a small part in the film, and there were long periods when he had nothing to do, and I think the boredom of waiting around contributed to the intensity of his tricks. We had a cameraman, Arthur Edeson, a very gifted man, the only cameraman I ever ran into who marked the actors' places in a scene with chalk himself.

He would use our stand-ins and fuss over the lighting until he had it perfect, then he'd make the chalk marks even stronger so that the actors, when they did the scene, would know exactly where to stand.

Lorre would wait until the stand-ins had left, then he'd sneak onto the set while the actors were being called, erase the original chalk marks, and put in new ones a short distance away. Unsuspecting, we actors would step up to the new marks and Edeson would look into his camera, then shake his head angrily. "That's all wrong! Are you on the marks?"

He'd rush to examine the marks, hurry back to the camera, sweating and cursing, upset and excited. There'd be shadows on my face while Ingrid would have no light at all. Edeson, furious, but not suspecting anything, would have to correct all his lighting and reposition his camera.

Lorre did this again and again at intervals during the shooting, and eventually all of us, except Edeson, knew what was going on. He never understood why his lighting worked sometimes and at other times simply fell apart!

Lorre, a short man with a round face and bulging eyes, was always typecast as the whining psychotic, the ultimate, slimy, slinking villain; yet in real life he was a cultured, attractive man—particularly attractive to women. When I met him, he had two beautiful ex-wives and had started on a third marriage. In spite of his penchant for sophomoric practical jokes, he was a warm and decent man, yet in the grasp of one of his crazy ideas he could do almost inhuman things.

There is a wild story about Lorre and John Barrymore that I was party to. I first met Barrymore at RKO, when I was shooting *Joan of Paris*. He would come into my dressing room with a bottle of whiskey and two glasses, and we'd each have a drink. Then, while I was shooting my scene, Barrymore would finish the rest of the bottle. My dresser tossed my used laundry into a corner and Barrymore, when he was thoroughly drunk, would stagger over and urinate on the pile of laundry.

It infuriated my dresser, but I shrugged it off. I felt that he was a tragic figure. He had so much to offer, and this curse of alcoholism

made it all impossible. Barrymore, if you forgave him his failings—
and it was easy to do so—was a wonderful man, charming, exciting,
and immensely talented. He would invite Lisl and me to the Shakespeare Society Dinners at the Beverly Hills Hotel, and he would
always have a protégé along, a man or a woman, whom he was doing
his best to help. Victor Borge was one of Barrymore's successful
protégés.

This is all to explain Barrymore's generosity. He spent his
money carelessly on his friends, on women, and on drink, and as he
grew old and the parts became fewer and farther between, he grew
more difficult and irascible. Finally, completely broke and homeless,
he was taken in by Errol Flynn, and lived out the rest of his brief
life dependent on Flynn's generosity. Errol Flynn, in spite of the bad
press he has recently received, was a warm and generous man who
never let Barrymore know what a dreadful burden he was. But he
must have felt a sense of relief when Barrymore died.

I was making *Casablenca* with Peter Lorre the day of Barrymore's death, and he took Humphrey Bogart, me, and two other
friends aside. "I have a fantastic idea," Lorre said, his bulging eyes
glistening. "For very little, maybe two or three hundred dollars, I can
get Barrymore's body away from the mortuary."

"What the hell for?" I asked.

"Yeah," Bogart seconded. "Why would you want his body?"

"Now get this. We take the body into Flynn's house—I know
he's shooting and gets home late, and we arrange it in that chair in
the living room he always used to sit in, then we hide and watch
Flynn's face. Is that or isn't it fantastic?"

We looked at each other and then at Lorre, and our immediate
shock gave way to uncontrollable laughter. We all chipped in, and
Lorre set out to dicker with the mortuary. Later, thinking it over,
I found that I just couldn't go through with it. "I'm sorry," I told
Bogie and the others. "I'll contribute the money, but I can't go
along. It goes against my grain."

The others accepted my excuses, but they went through with
the stunt. They smuggled Barrymore's body out of the mortuary and

into Flynn's house. "We had a hell of a job getting him to look natural in that chair." Lorre giggled when he told me about it later. "He was so stiff!"

They hid behind the doors and waited. Finally they heard Errol's car pull into the driveway, then his key in the lock. He opened the door and flicked on the lights and came in, threw his hat and coat on a chair and walked across the room, past Barrymore's chair to the bar. He nodded at Barrymore and took about three steps, then froze. That moment was fantastic! There was a terrible silence, then he said, "Oh my God!" and he hurried back and touched Barrymore, then jumped. Barrymore was ice cold.

"I think in that second, he realized what was happening," Lorre said, "and he shouted, 'All right, you bastards, come on out!' "

"Was he mad?" I asked.

Lorre shook his head. "Partly mad, but at the same time realizing how funny it was and trying not to laugh. I think, like you, he felt the whole thing was in bad taste. Anyway, he offered us a drink, but wouldn't help us take the body back!"

Peter and I were good friends, but as so often happens in Hollywood, we drifted apart. I found it difficult to keep up many of the very warm and often sincere friendships I made. For a while Peter and I would see a lot of each other, but then commitments would take us to other places, different cities, and our schedules wouldn't coincide. When we were in Hollywood at the same time, it was often for a short period and we would each be concerned with our own family.

I last saw Peter Lorre at the Algonquin Hotel in New York in 1952. He was on his way to Germany, and I was off somewhere else. We had drinks at the bar and said a last good-bye. The next I heard of him was his death.

Ingrid Bergman, who played my wife in *Casablanca*, puzzled me during the filming of the picture. She was sweet and gentle in all her relationships with the other actors, seemingly a retiring, patient woman, wonderful to work with and an excellent actress, but to all of us she seemed terribly vulnerable. We wanted to take care of her, to protect her. She was so amenable to direction, never fussy over lines, never a primadonna—how had she gotten as far as she had? I wondered.

Every actress I knew who had made it had a driving vitality to her personality. If she wasn't ruthless, she was at least stubborn and aggressive. There was no other way a woman could get ahead in such a competitive field. There are too many times an actress must fight for something she wants in a script, or she must have the strength to disagree with a director or producer. Bette Davis had that strength to an inordinate degree. Ingrid Bergman showed no sign of anything like it.

I finally decided she had to have someone behind her, a pushing mother, a good friend or an aggressive agent, perhaps a husband who desperately wanted her to make it. I was convinced it had to be something like that.

After we finished filming *Casablanca* we were called for "still" sittings. One day it would be Bogart, Rains, and me, another day Ingrid and Bogie, and finally Ingrid and me. While we were posing together, I noticed a certain tightness about her, and I asked, "Are you all right?"

"All right?" She bit her lips and I could see tears well up. "Paul, I'm heartbroken!"

Suspecting a shattering love affair, I muttered something sympathetic about men, and she looked at me as if I were crazy. "No, no! I'm talking about *For Whom the Bell Tolls*, the movie they're making from Hemingway's novel. It's going to be a blockbuster of a movie, and I tested for it. It's a fantastic part."

"Well, maybe you'll get it," I reassured her.

"Oh Paul, I've lost it. They gave it to Vera Zorina! I wanted that part so badly, you've no idea." There was a sudden depth of feeling to her voice, an intensity I hadn't heard before off camera. Her voice hardened. "Those idiots! What the hell do they know? Picking Vera Zorina of all people. She can't act, Paul. She just can't, and I'm good. I'm really good!" Her voice rang with conviction. "I just hope they find out how bad she is."

The phone rang then and it was for Ingrid. She went to it and said, "Yes, yes . . . ," then let out a yell I can only compare to that of a tigress who has made a kill, a yell of such joy and triumph that I was stunned. Was this submissive Ingrid? She put down the phone and yelled, "I got it, Paul! I got it! I got it!"

It was an entirely different side of her. I saw her suddenly filled with a triumphant vitality and strength, and in that moment I understood how she had managed to get ahead in Sweden and in the Hollywood jungle.

"What happened?" I asked.

"I got the part of Maria in *For Whom the Bell Tolls!* I just knew that if I fought hard enough they'd come to their senses and see that Zorina was wrong and couldn't act. Paul, we've got to celebrate!"

◆

Fourteen

Our Children

*L*isl had found a small, but charming house in Santa Monica, and we bought it for her parents. We fixed it up with all of their furniture, which had finally arrived by boat from England and by train from the East Coast. When her parents reached Los Angeles after a long trip from Argentina, and we took them to their new house, Lisl's mother burst into tears. "It was as if I had come home at last!" she told us later.

Our own furniture had left Liverpool on an earlier boat that was torpedoed by a German sub and had to limp back to port. Half of our possessions were lost; the rest eventually arrived in California.

Lutzi, Lisl's old family retainer and housekeeper, joined us. She had taken a Greek freighter across the Atlantic. "The filthiest ship I ever saw," she informed us. "Before we landed, I made the captain give me all the officers' uniforms and underwear and shirts, and I washed and ironed them so they'd look neat and fresh when we docked."

"Why did you bother to do that?" I asked her.

"Do you think I wanted to be ashamed of them?"

That was typical of Lutzi. In London, when the bombs fell and we all took off for the shelters, Lutzi refused to leave the kitchen. Why? She had a chicken in the oven and would not go until it was done. "Why should I ruin a good chicken for the Nazis?"

In Canada, Lutzi, a Catholic, was received by a Roman Catholic group in the large refugee camp where new arrivals were processed. "That Catholic section was terribly dull," Lutzi told us. "All such long faces . . . you would think they were the only ones who had ever had a bit of trouble. And the food they served! It was miserable, but I got out of it."

"What did you do?" Lisl asked her.

"I saw another group nearby, the Jewish refugees. They were

full of life, and the smell of the food they were cooking was fantastic.
I went to the head of the camp and said, 'There's been a mistake.
I'm really Jewish.' And before you knew what was happening, I was
moved over to the Jewish section. Such a relief!"

I had hired a New York lawyer to get Lutzi into the States from
Canada, and when she finally reached New York she only had his
office address. Since it was wartime and there was no way of knowing
when her boat would arrive, he told her, when she called him from
Montreal, to take a cab and go straight to his office. She did just that,
but it was Sunday and of course the office was closed.

As luck would have it, her cabby was German, from Yorkville,
and during the ride they had a long, comfortable chat, during which
Lutzi told him her life story and all about her mistress' husband who
worked in Hollywood. When they found the office closed, Lutzi
asked him to take her to a hotel, but he wouldn't hear of it. He took
her home to a good German-American household, where they
stuffed her with sauerbraten and strudel. He refused to charge her
cab fare, and the next day he delivered her to the lawyer.

Lisl and I met her train when it arrived in California, and Lutzi
had fifty dollars left from the money I had sent her. Fifty dollars then
could have bought a good secondhand car, but as Lutzi stepped off
the train, helped by a stout, good-natured black porter, she turned,
gave him a tremendous hug and kiss—and the fifty dollars!

I said, "My God, Lutzi, why such a fantastic tip?"

"Fantastic?" She shrugged. "It's just what I had left of that silly
paper money. Now that I'm here with you, I won't need it any-
more." And she kissed her beloved Lisl again and again.

While I was making *Now Voyager* and *Casablanca*, Lisl had
been searching for a permanent house, and finally she found one in
a section between Palisades and Brentwood, a lovely house in an
orange grove, a place with a great deal of charm. At Lou Wasserman's advice, I offered the owner three thousand dollars less than
he was asking. "Always offer a bit less and then you have room for
bargaining," Lou told me, but instead of bargaining, the owner
simply turned us down. I was ready to raise my offer, when Frances,
Henry Fonda's wife, called.

"I just heard that you're looking for a house. Now you and Lisl

must come and look at ours. We're building another up on Tiger
Tail, and this is up for sale. It's going to be perfect for you."

"I don't know—it's a bit large for just the two of us . . ." Lisl
began, but Frances cut her off.

"We'll give you a very good deal. Come and look at the house.
You won't have to pay any cash down, and I'll give you a mortgage
on the place at very easy terms."

We knew the downstairs of the Fonda house from our visits
there, and it had seemed a very luxurious place, but when Frances
showed us around, we discovered that it was 65,000 square feet, with
a master suite downstairs, five bedrooms upstairs, a living room, a
dining room, a library—it was simply an incredible house. It had
been built, Frances told us, by Paul Williams, a favorite of hers, a
gifted black architect. There were many unusual touches: exquisite
French doors in the living room opening onto a magnificent terrace,
a pool and a pool house, a three-car garage with an apartment and
private gardens with a goldfish pond behind it, and even a tennis
court.

Lisl said, "We're only two people, Frances. It's just too big!"

"But this place is a steal." She laughed, and she named a price
seven thousand dollars above what we had set as our limit. Still, as
Lou Wasserman pointed out when we took him to look at it, "It's
worth at least fifty thousand more than Frances is asking. Buy it. It's
a fabulous bargain."

Frances said, "Just close off the upstairs and live downstairs.
You can give the apartment over the garage to the servants."

During the negotiations, Frances asked us to buy some of the
furnishings, exquisite French colonial period pieces. Her new home
would be early American colonial, and she wanted to redecorate
completely. The furniture would have been another good buy, but
we were at our limit and took only the bedroom set.

Then, almost too casually, Frances said, "And of course the
tennis court is extra."

"Frances," I told her, "you've lost a sale."

"What do you mean?"

"I mean we can't go any higher. We just can't afford it."

"Ridiculous." She frowned. "Paul, you're at the beginning of a great career. You certainly can afford it. Anyway, don't make a definite decision yet. Think it over."

The next day, when I called to tell her we had decided against it, I discovered that she was in the hospital with a broken toe. I went to visit her with two dozen red roses, and she was overcome. "Roses! I can't remember when anyone brought me roses. Paul, you're a darling. Oh, what the hell. I'll throw in the tennis court for the price of the house. You deserve it for being so sweet."

We ended up paying $42,000 for the mansion, a home that today would sell for several million!

My mother, during the war years, stayed in Vienna, sharing her apartment with two maiden sisters, the Baronesses Schenk, who had been her classmates at Sacre Coeur School. The three old ladies were company for one another, and since the war had taken all servants for defense work, they were able to share the housework among themselves.

I wrote to her during the war, and a few of my letters managed to get through, thanks to the Red Cross. At that time I, with most other Hollywood stars, worked in the Hollywood Canteen, a café-type of club set up for the entertainment of the servicemen. Admission was free, and all work was voluntary. Like most movie actors, I was a busboy. Musicians played in the band, and the actresses served as hostesses to dance with the servicemen and talk to them.

I made friends with several of the men, and one of them was General Mark Clark. He had enjoyed my pictures and was something of a fan of mine, and we often had interesting talks. I was as flattered to meet a famous general as he was to meet a famous movie star. During one of our talks he asked me if I had any relatives in Vienna.

"My mother," I told him. "She refuses to leave her home."

"Well, if I get there—or if anyone I know gets there, I'll see to it that she's taken care of," he promised me, and he was as good as his word. He took her address, and later, when the Americans moved into Russian-held Vienna, by agreement, he sent a lieutenant ahead to my mother's address. The lieutenant introduced himself, told my mother he was there by order of General Mark Clark, a representative of Paul Henreid, and did she need anything at all?

She was overwhelmed and thought it was very sweet of the general. She received food and coal, and the three old ladies lived as well as the American army. Clark sent her all the goodies he could spare—wine, meat, chocolate—although he never got to meet her. Eventually, he arranged to have her flown out of Vienna to Paris by the U.S. Air Force.

I had another friend, Leland Heyward, then vice-president of TWA. He got my mother a flight from Paris to Los Angeles by way of Shannon and Iceland. I had to pay her fare, of course, but just getting her on a flight then was a remarkable favor.

When she arrived in Hollywood, we were living in the "Fonda" house (which I understand is now called the Henreid house), but the lavish layout of this Hollywood mansion meant little to my mother. She had been convinced that I would be living in the way she and my father had lived before the First World War, in a castle with our own forests, greenhouses, stables, a mile-long driveway lined with trees, and a small army of servants—a typical Austrian aristocrat's estate. When she saw the Fonda house she shrugged and said, "I suppose you have to live in a suburban place."

"Suburban, Mama?"

"Well, it *is* in the suburbs, and you only have one acre, and there are neighbors all around you—Paul, I noticed you drove here from the airport yourself. Don't you even have a chauffeur?"

"Mama, I like to drive. You know, we have three cars," I said defensively.

She sighed. "And I thought you were a movie star."

Knowing she would want to live by herself, Lisl and I had looked around before she arrived, and we found a charming little house like the one we had bought for Lisl's parents. It had some land and a small garden, and we were sure she'd be delighted with it. A few days after her arrival, I said, "Mama. We have a wonderful surprise for you. When you're tired of visiting us, you have a home of your own."

"A home? But Pauli, I don't want a house with all the work that goes with it. I'm an old woman, don't you understand?"

"Mama, come look at it first," I coaxed. "I'm sure you'll love it." She finally came with us, saw the house and burst into tears. "You do like it, don't you, Mama?" I asked anxiously.

She embraced us both, Lisl and me. "Yes, I like it, and it was sweet and wonderful of you to do this, Paul, but is it possible to undo it now? It's all too much for me. An apartment is all I want!"

We talked to the owners, and they were very kind. They took it back and put it on the market again, and Lisl found an apartment for my mother, a place with two bedrooms and a balcony. Just right, she told us, but she stayed there for less than a year. My brother, Robert, came to visit and stayed with us. He had done very well at first in South Africa, but now he was making a modest living as the director of Hartley and Company, a plant that manufactured auto parts. He had a wife and two children back in Johannesburg.

One day my mother took me aside and said, "I have something to say, Pauli, and you mustn't be offended by it."

"What is it?" I asked.

"I must be honest. I don't like it here. I don't speak English, and I have no one to talk to. It's all too hard for me. When I was at your home I never realized the problems I'd have living by myself —would you mind if I went back to South Africa with Bobby?"

I said, "Of course, Mama. I understand. You must do what you think best. We'd love you to stay, but . . ." I knew that Bobby was still her baby, and she desperately wanted to be with him.

I told Bobby of Mother's decision, and he was delighted to take her back. "But the problem is, Paul, I don't have enough money to buy her a ticket—to tell you the truth, I don't have a return ticket for myself."

"You bought a one-way ticket?" I was shocked. "How did you expect to get back?"

He shrugged. "My brother the movie star might help me?"

There was no question of my helping out, but I would rather have been asked at the very beginning. At any rate, I bought them a first-class cabin on a fine passenger ship from New Orleans to Capetown, and then they went by train to Johannesburg. I intended to go there to visit them, but one thing or another always interfered. However, my mother wrote that she was delighted with my brother's home. There was ample help in South Africa, and Bobby could afford an enormous amount of servants. Mother lived in much the same comfort she had known in old Vienna.

A short time after we bought the Fonda house, in 1943, Lisl said, "Paul, I'm not working, and we seem to have finally settled down here in California. You're doing so well that I want to adopt a baby." We had tried to have children, but although both of us were checked out by a physician as normal, and although we had tried often enough, we had had no luck.

I said, "Lisl, darling, isn't our marriage happy?"

"Very happy, and that's just why I want to share that happiness with a baby."

"Our not having children," I told her seriously, "is not a hardship, and you shouldn't consider it one. Perhaps, Lisl," I continued, trying to comfort her, "it's a blessing from God. It may be that he loves us and is guarding us against the foolishness of having children."

She said, "Paul, be serious! This isn't a matter for joking. I really and truly want a child. There are so many children up for adoption, I'm sure I can find one that will look like us."

"I believe heredity is stronger than environment," I told her unhappily. "I don't think an adopted child will be our own no matter how much it looks like us."

We argued back and forth for days until finally, seeing how much it meant to her, I gave in. I had never wanted children. Perhaps a paternal feeling was absent in me, or it may have had something to do with my own childhood, and yet I remember my childhood with a great deal of joy. It seems to me it was such a happy time.

We went to an adoption agency, and a very remarkable woman there found the perfect baby for us, the most beautiful little girl I had ever seen. In spite of all my protests and doubts, I fell in love with her at first sight. We named her Monika Elizabeth, the Elizabeth for Lisl. She had blue eyes and creamy skin and wispy blond hair, so light it was almost white.

Lisl was ecstatic, and two years later, in 1945, we adopted

another little girl. This time my protests were perfunctory. Monika gave us so much joy and made Lisl so happy that I knew it was the right thing to do. Maurice Chevalier was a close friend of ours, and his favorite song at that time was "Mimi, you darling little Mimi . . ." We loved the song and named the new baby Mimi Maria, the Maria for my mother.

Mimi was born with black hair that fell out soon after, and her new hair grew in blond. She and Monika could easily have been mistaken for sisters, and most people who didn't know about the adoption saw resemblances in the children to me and Lisl.

My work kept me away from home so often in the early years of the children's lives that their care and raising fell entirely on Lisl. I would play with them on Sunday, my one free day, but I was either traveling, on location, or shooting every other day of the week. Lisl didn't mind, for she's a born nurturer, and the children occupied her entire life, so much so that I began to feel pangs of jealousy. I was no longer the center of her world, something I had unconsciously feared from the very beginning.

In the meantime my film career was growing stronger, even as my stage career disappeared. I've often been asked if there is any great difference between acting for films and acting on the stage, and before I became involved with films I looked on stage acting as a purer form of the art.

I thought there was more continuity in a stage performance, and it could therefore be more consistent. But over the years I've come to realize that a film performance can be just as consistent. In very few plays is any character, even the lead, on stage for the whole performance, and even in those few performances there are intermissions to get you off the stage and out of the context of the play. For the average actor, stage acting is constantly interrupted with changes of scenes, changes of costume, and moments offstage and behind the scenes.

I began to realize that there was very little difference in terms of continuity of performance between the stage and film. On film, you play the moment as you think it should be played. There is also the great advantage of retakes. If you or the director are dissatisfied with a scene, it can be done over and over until it's right. Very few, if any, directors will stop an actor from reshooting a scene if he thinks he can do it better. There is also an objective quality to filming. A director can look at a number of takes and decide which is the best, something an actor may not realize or judge correctly.

But on the stage or in film, in my opinion, the most important element is the play or screenplay. The second most important element is the actor. Of much less importance than either of these is the director. A bad actor in a leading role will give a bad performance, and no director, no matter how talented, will get a good performance out of him. But given a bad director, a good actor can often rise above him and turn in a good performance. However, both are helpless unless there is a good script behind them. The best actor or director cannot make a good script out of a bad one, though it has been tried again and again, and I'm sure it will continue to be tried.

When an actor works with a poor director—and he'll usually know it after a day or two of shooting—he'll fall back on the sure things he knows. He won't experiment or try anything new. With a good director, the actor feels encouraged to experiment, knowing that the director will weed out any bad ideas.

I've been frequently asked if there are any special techniques for the stage that don't apply to films, and the most obvious one is voice projection. On stage you must learn to project to the entire theatre; in film there are excellent sound systems to pick up your voice, and the lessened volume required from the actor allows him greater flexibility. The electronic pick-up that is sometimes used on stage is almost always badly controlled.

Gestures on film must always be more controlled than gestures on stage. Time after time we see a splendid stage actor being hired for film, only to produce a miserable performance. In film the camera comes close enough to look into your eyes, and a tremendous amount of emotion can be projected with the eyes alone. On stage you must rely on body language to get the same emotion across.

I have been told by many actors that they rely on method acting to project what they feel on film, and I can agree if it's the

Stanislavski method, as some of my teachers in Vienna taught it, or the method as Kazan and Stella Adler taught it. Both were fine actors, and it takes a fine actor to teach acting. The Strasberg school leaves me cold. I never felt Lee Strasberg could act, and I fail to see how someone who can't act can teach acting. You can be a bad actor and direct well if you have the imagination to see how it should be done, but I can't understand how you can teach an actor to project an emotion when you can't do it yourself.

Another curious aspect of acting in American films was the fan clubs. They wielded a lot of power because they were a built-in audience for any actor and had a direct effect on his box-office draw, and the studios were well aware of this.

My first fan club was started after *Night Train* appeared. As with other fan clubs of male actors, mine was started by a group of young girls who decided I was their actor idol. They put out a small newspaper about me, a collage of things they had culled from film magazines (usually composed out of whole cloth by some imaginative writer), and gradually they interested more and more girls in the club. It spread across the United States, and with the appearance of *Now Voyager*, it literally exploded to include thousands.

Although, like mine, most fan clubs were started by young women and dominated by them, a few were started by men. A group of young men founded the Tortuga Fan Club after I appeared as a pirate in *The Spanish Main*.

From time to time I would have to write a letter of appreciation to the club, telling them I was happy they liked my work and how much I appreciated their loyalty. They'd write requests for pictures with my autograph, and they'd deluge me with hundreds of letters. Warner Brothers kept a special department to take care of answering them, but I felt they were sloppy about it, so I hired my own secretary to handle the mail.

I did indeed feel an obligation to these young people for this rather strange form of hero worship, though I failed to understand it. It was another example of confusing the actor with the role he plays. In time these fan clubs became a very strong pressure group, and there were certain things I could not do in films, certain parts

I could not accept for fear of offending them and losing their support. Years later, when I played a villain in a gangster film, *The Scar*, a meaty part I loved, my fan club reacted strongly, even though I was the "star" and got the girl. The membership dropped at once.

Lisl's mother was intrigued by this whole phenomenon and offered to take over the sending of photos, the answering of letters, and the sorting out of my fan mail. She was a great help. I was bewildered by it then, and I still am, for to this day I continue to receive fan mail, a great deal of it from abroad, from Germany, Austria, Holland, France, and England, and a lot of it comes from well-educated people, as I can tell from the letters.

Some of the early fan clubs were made up of older women, and one such group arranged a coffee klatch and invited me to talk to them. I had some available time, and since it was nearby, I went. I was rather pleasantly surprised. They asked me intelligent questions about acting, about the history of the theatre and the methods of movie production. It was an illuminating experience for me. We film actors tend to denigrate our audience, to think of them all as rather naive. I found out that they could be bright and clever—and still be overwhelmed by the glamour of Hollywood.

◆

Fifteen

The Bond Tour

*O*nce I became a Warner Brothers star, I got along very well with Jack Warner, although I heard many of his contract actors say harsh things about him. As a general rule he treated me with respect; one exception to that rule was his sending me the script for *The Beast with Five Fingers*. Of course he was less than generous in lending out his actors to other studios, even though it would help their careers. As an example, *Gaslight* was sent to me from MGM. I loved the script and wanted to do it. I particularly wanted to play opposite Ingrid Bergman again.

But Jack Warner said, "No, I won't let you make a film for MGM. We'll find something better for you here."

Arch of Triumph, Erich Maria Remarque's novel, was also sent to me, and I wanted to do that, but again Jack said no. I could understand his attitude, but I didn't like it, and I was particularly heartbroken when he refused to lend me to Twentieth Century Fox for *Anna and the King of Siam.* I desperately wanted to do it, but his attitude was, "Why should I help the competition?"

I can't help but feel that those refusals of his set my career back tremendously because most of the parts Warner did choose for me were not as successful.

Another stumbling block in my career was the fact that I wasn't born in America. In Hollywood, the American actors did, on film, what the American literature produced. These parts, though I longed for them, were never offered to me. I think my accent had something to do with it, yet in *Now Voyager* I was believable as a native American. Nobody seemed to notice my accent. I've played Frenchmen, Germans, Italians—but the exciting, top films eluded me. What Warners mainly offered me were concocted pieces written for the screen. Jack Warner had his own ideas about what was good for me, and I was bound by my contract. When that was up, I decided very quickly I would become independent. Never again would I be bound to one or two studios exclusively.

At one Hollywood party I sat next to John Wayne, who had just finished his first big hit, *Stagecoach,* the first picture John Ford made for Republic. Before *Stagecoach,* Wayne had been a secondary actor, but this shot him up to stardom. The talk, as it always does with actors, turned to "How many films have you made this year?" I told Wayne, "Three, and I hope I don't have to make more than one more." As we talked I realized that I had just turned down an RKO script that Wayne had accepted. It would be his sixth picture, and he told me that he had signed up for three more!

Later, talking to Lisl, I said, "The man is foolish. He does everything he's offered, good or bad." But actually, Wayne was right. You can never tell which film will click. William Powell once told me, "Get one hit every five years and you'll be a top star for the rest of your life—but you have to do enough films to guarantee that one hit!"

But I found out that it wasn't that easy to do a "great many films." You had to be offered the scripts. I remember talking to Gary Cooper about just that one evening. It was a time when both Coop and I were, as they say in the industry, "very hot." We were very desirable actors. I complained that the material I got was inferior, and he sympathized with me. "I know just what you mean," he said, shaking his head. "I was offered fourteen scripts recently, and out of all of them only four were any good."

I couldn't say anything. I had been offered four scripts to his fourteen, and not one of the four was worthwhile!

When I was signed up for my first Warner Brothers picture, I was also invited, with Lisl, to my first Warners' party. Jack and Ann Warner lived in a magnificent house in Beverly Hills, a mansion with two swimming pools, one with saltwater and one with fresh, two tennis courts, and immense grounds. Ann was a gracious, knowledgeable hostess, and Jack tried, often successfully, to be a winning host.

There were two tables set up, and since we were the guests of honor, I sat at one and Lisl at the other at Jack Warner's side. I sat next to Ann, and while there were a lot of people we didn't know, there were many faces and names that were familiar enough. Marlene Dietrich was at my table, along with Miriam Hopkins, Charles Chaplin, Gary Cooper, Darryl Zanuck in army uniform, Claudette Colbert, and Irene Dunne. It was a wonderful group, and I was delighted to get to know these stars. The men were handsome in their dinner clothes, the women beautiful in evening dress and magnificent jewelry, and I, still a newcomer to all this, found it hard not to stare.

At one point someone proposed a toast to "Joe Schenk. Farewell, Joe—have a wonderful time!"

I didn't know who Joe Schenk was, but I joined the toast, then turned to Ann Warner and whispered, "Forgive me, but where is this Joe Schenk going that we toast him?"

Ann laughed. "To jail, of course."

"To jail? And we all toast him? I can't believe it. Why is he going? What did he do?"

Ann waved her hand in airy dismissal, as if it were the most natural thing in the world. "He fiddled around with his income tax and made the mistake of getting caught. They'll send him up for a year, but he'll be out in a few months, and it's a farm type of jail. It'll be good for him. He was executive production head of Twentieth Century Fox."

I was speechless. To take something like this so casually! Or was it just another aspect of America?

During that dinner I came to know Charles Chaplin and Gary Cooper, both bright, articulate and intelligent men, and I found a friend in each, friendships that lasted for years. Chaplin disliked Zanuck, who was vice-president in charge of production at Twentieth Century Fox, and he ridiculed and mocked him through the entire meal. Zanuck didn't answer or even protest, and after hearing the company toast a man on his way to jail, then listening to Chaplin mock Zanuck, I began to wonder just what constituted humor in this strange land.

At any rate, Chaplin's ridicule was so witty and brilliant that I couldn't control my laughter. I am sure that my appreciation of

Chaplin's mockery of Zanuck was the reason Zanuck didn't offer me a part for years. He relented with *Anna and the King of Siam*, which Jack Warner didn't allow me to accept.

That evening was memorable. Everything went smoothly. The people were friendly, the talk fascinating, the food exquisite. At Lisl's table someone mentioned a recently released film that everyone began to praise. Lisl was silent until Jack Warner turned to her and asked, "Why so quiet, Mrs. Henreid? Have you seen the picture?"

"Oh yes," Lisl answered.

"And did you like it?"

"Not a bit," Lisl said frankly.

The table fell silent, and Warner leaned toward her with a smile. "But why not?"

"Well . . ." Lisl shrugged. "It was a bad script, bad acting, and very bad directing." She looked around the table. "I'm just amazed that all of you liked it so much.

Jack laughed, delighted. "I'm so glad you didn't like it." He turned to the man on Lisl's other side. "This is the producer." He gestured at another man across the table. "And that's the director. I want you both to meet Lisl Henreid, Paul's wife. The only honest woman at the table!"

Driving home from the party that night, Lisl was very quiet. "Is anything wrong?" I asked her.

"Oh no. I did enjoy myself, Paul. It's just . . ."

"Just what?"

"Well, they're very strange people, the Warners. I mean they're very nice, or at least she is, but that house! Do you know, Paul, I went to the guest bathroom and I was just speechless. I've never seen anything like it."

I glanced at her. "How do you mean?"

"Well, it's an enormous room and it's decorated like a tart's boudoir, and there are five toilets—five! All out in the open, and the women sit on them and talk to each other. It's actually a gossip center, Paul."

"It must have been delightful."

"Oh, it was. At first I was too embarrassed to use one of those open toilets, but nature was too strong. I gave in, and you know, after a while I sort of liked it."

"You did?" Now I was a bit shocked.

"Well, it's not designed so much to pee together as it is to gossip, and I got all the dirt about everyone out here—who's sleeping with whom, and who's a success and who's a failure, and who had a face lift and who needs one—it's really rather intriguing!"

"I guess so. It's very strange but lots of fun. You must admit that. I wish I could have joined you there."

There was another, later party we went to at the Warners' that stands out in my memory. It was given by Ann to unveil a portrait of her done by Salvador Dali. The Warner house had an enormous terrace wrapped around the back of it, and many of the rooms opened onto the terrace. Tables were placed out there with colorful umbrellas. It was a warm June night, and the guests, three hundred of them, seemed to include every star in Hollywood, a fantastic gathering. There were two bands, one for dance music, and the other playing Hungarian gypsy music.

When most of the guests had arrived, Jack stood up and made a little speech about Salvador Dali, "the great surrealist painter . . . who has graciously consented to paint my beautiful wife." He said nothing of what the picture cost, which was unusual for Jack Warner. "To tell the truth," he concluded, as the easel with the veiled painting was brought out on the terrace, "I haven't even seen the picture myself. But"—he pointed to the extravagantly mustached painter—"I have extraordinary faith in the talent of this man, and you all know how good I am at picking talent!"

There was a gentle laugh, and then Jack pulled the string to unveil the portrait. It was an incredible likeness of Ann done in Dali's inimitable style. The background was a desert, and in the distance, but very clear, there was an oasis with palm trees. There was a cage in the oasis with a monkey in it, still very distinct, certainly distinct enough for us all to see that the monkey had Jack Warner's face!

Smiling, he turned to look at the picture, then did a double take. There was a moment's silence, then he swallowed and laughed with false cheerfulness. "I'm so glad I was included." Everybody applauded.

I must add that I never saw the painting hung while Jack was alive.

Later that evening, we were sitting at a table in the library with Errol Flynn when Tallulah Bankhead made one of her grand entrances. She "Dahlinged!" a few people in her husky, whiskey baritone, then spotted Flynn and came storming over to him. "Errol Dahling!" She dropped to her knees in front of all of us and buried her face in Flynn's crotch, then said, "We're going to have a great time together. I can feel it in my bones! Can you feel it?"

Flynn, laughing, took it all with a grain of salt. He certainly wasn't embarrassed, nor were the rest of us. This was a typical Tallulah entrance. She made almost as good an exit. The party had tapered off, most of the guests were drifting home, and Lisl and I were having a late-night brandy in the library with Cary Grant and his wife, Barbara Hutton. It was very quiet, and the four of us were hardly aware of Tallulah necking on a sofa with a young male star until Lillian Gish fluttered into the room looking for the bathroom.

She was dressed in a pale-blue evening gown with pearls around her neck, little tight curls hanging down on either side of her face, and open, white gloves on her hands—a dizzying picture of innocence.

Tallulah sat up in her friend's lap and shouted, "Lillian Dahling! How wonderful to see you. I missed you in the crowd."

"Tallulah!" Lillian paused, put her head to one side and smiled sweetly. "It's wonderful to see you too, and you look so good . . ."

Tallulah smiled with saccharine sweetness. "Dear Lillian, and here we are, surviving after all these years, you with your face lifted and your vagina dropped, and me with my vagina lifted and my face dropped!"

Lillian began giggling and swept out, waving one of her little white-gloved hands. Tallulah stretched and, smiling at us all, grabbed her wrap and stalked out with her escort following. A great exit, we all decided.

They said, of Jack Warner's parties, that anyone invited had to make at least $3000 a week unless it was a young starlet or upcoming male actor, pretty or handsome enough to fill out the room. Certainly an inordinate amount of money was spent on those affairs, and invitations were highly prized.

In September of 1943 I was asked to join a War Bond Tour called The Hollywood Cavalcade, along with Fred Astaire, Lucille Ball, James Cagney, Judy Garland, Betty Hutton, Mickey Rooney, Harpo Marx, Kay Kaiser and his band, and many others. In those days millionaires owned their own railroad coaches, and when they wanted to travel, they had them hitched up to regular trains. A group of them lent their private coaches to the bond tour. I had Rockefeller's, a beautiful car, all polished inlaid wood with elaborate decorations. Lovely to look at, but old. It creaked like mad and almost drove me crazy.

Judy Garland had a steel coach, provided by United States Steel, and it was the most modern one—and the quietest. It just glided along like oil on water. As a result, I cultivated Judy and spent most of my time in her wonderful silent car. But then, so did Jim Cagney and Mickey Rooney and Betty Hutton. It wasn't hard to cultivate Judy. She was delightfully fresh and adorable, but under her pertness there was a quality of sadness.

We had many long talks, and during them we came to know each other and relax in each other's company. She began to let her guard down, and she talked to me about her childhood. "We'd travel at night—my parents, my sister, and I," she told me once, "and it was a hell of a life, Paul. You can say what you want about stage people, all that crap about a heart of gold and a rough outside, but I was just a kid, one of the Gumm sisters, and I saw all that backstage screwing around that went on—even my own parents." She sighed. "It had a terrible effect on me, Paul, and I don't think I'll ever shake it!"

Then, a few minutes later, Mickey Rooney would come in, the

perennial all-American boy, and Judy's black mood would drop away, and she'd become the girl next door, teasing and clowning around.

I enjoyed Rooney, too. He had a brisk, sparkling quality that always made you smile. He was amazingly like the parts he played; you had trouble separating him from Judge Hardy's son.

Our procession of twelve star coaches, plus the coaches for the crew, hairdressers and wardrobe people, would travel at night and arrive in the railroad yards of a city at dawn. We'd continue sleeping until eight-thirty, then we'd either have breakfast sent to our coaches or go to the dining car, a lavish, exquisitely old-fashioned diner. Afterward we'd dress and about eleven o'clock the train would pull into the station.

There would be press interviews at the station, with picture-taking sessions, and then we'd go outside, where a lineup of army jeeps with drivers and attendants, army personnel, waited. Each jeep had a big flag with a star's name on it, and we'd form a procession that would drive into the main square of the city. Our positions were rotated. Sometimes I'd be in the first jeep, sometimes the last. Usually there was a platform erected and we'd all be led onto it to be seated. Sometimes there would be an auction of an American flag autographed by all of us. Big business bidded for the flags—U.S. Steel, Dupont, Ford, General Motors, Alcoa—bids that went up into the millions. The streets we drove through were lined with cheering people, some quite hysterical.

Afterward there would be time off for lunch, and we'd be taken to the best hotel in town, where we each had a room to relax and dress in. MPs would guard the floor our rooms were on, but often they were no match for enterprising fans. I remember one city where I entered my room after saying hello to the MP at the door and started to change.

I had my shirt off and was starting to unlace my shoes when I heard some strange, muffled noises. I checked the bathroom, behind the draperies, and even under the bed—and there they were —two young girls, wide-eyed, frightened and yet thrilled at what they had done.

I scolded them, gave them each a signed photo, then called the MPs and said, "Would you show these young ladies to the elevator?"

In the afternoons during the tour we were asked to make War Bond speeches at different industrial plants, plants like Ford or General Electric, speeches about the war and how much our boys at the front needed the support of the people back home. We were given a general outline of what to say, and we'd present it in our own words.

After the speeches we'd return to our hotel and change for the evening performance, usually outdoors. In Chicago it was held at Soldiers' Field, which seats 125,000 people. The acoustics were dreadful, with echoes coming back from the speakers at every word, but nobody seemed to care. Each of us did a little turn, depending on what we did best. Judy and Mickey sang, Astaire and Cagney danced. For my contribution, I read a letter supposedly written to me by a Free French soldier. It described the horrors of war and told of the gratitude of the Free French for all the help the American people were giving them. During my reading the orchestra played "La Marseillaise."

I don't know who really wrote the letter, but I suspect that Howard Koch did. It smacked of his style, and it always brought a tremendous ovation and left most eyes damp.

Afterward, our procession of jeeps would drive us back to the station, we'd get into our coaches to unwind, and then usually meet in the diner for a late-night snack, a few drinks, and then to bed thoroughly exhausted. The routine was the same in city after city, and the only variation occurred in Pittsburgh. Some incident, we never found out what, took place in a tremendous crowd listening to us, and the crowd began to panic and surged toward the stand where we were doing our turns. The stand started to collapse and we managed to get off just in time to avoid a terrible accident. But many people were pushed forward and badly hurt by the broken glass and the police horses racing through the crowd to break it up.

In New Orleans I was riding in the last jeep, and security had grown lax as we neared our hotel. Then, suddenly, a hysterical woman carrying a baby recognized me and started to cheer. Then, abruptly, she threw her baby at me, shouting, "Touch it! Touch it! It'll bring him luck!"

Fortunately, I managed to catch the child and one of the security men returned it to the mother. But I was badly shaken. What if I had missed?

Sixteen

◆

Devotion and
In Our Time

*T*he next movie I made in Hollywood for Warner Brothers, after *Casablanca*, was *Devotion*, the story of the Brontë sisters. It was made in 1943, but it wasn't released until 1946, and then the reviews were less than generous, most reviewers objecting to the merciless liberties taken with the lives of the Brontë sisters. A love interest was introduced, a curate, the part I played, and in the screenplay both Emily, played by Ida Lupino, and Charlotte, played by Olivia de Havilland, were supposed to be in love with him. Arthur Kennedy played Branwell Brontë, the girls' brother, and the script made no attempt to be factual.

For some reason, probably because I was so often cast as a foreign lover, I was always suspected of having affairs with my leading ladies. The truth is, I never did. I liked many of them tremendously, and others I disliked, but the type of woman who always appealed to me was one I had to take care of, someone who had a streak of vulnerability. Stars are not vulnerable women. To get to the top you must have an aggressive nature.

But of all the women I worked with, Ida Lupino seemed the most vulnerable. She was a soft person with a great sense of sweetness about her, but anything that might have developed between us was destroyed by Olivia's machinations. Olivia de Havilland, to me, seemed wrong in this film, and I had trouble believing any of her lines.

Of course, these were my impressions, and there may have been no truth behind them. I saw both young women engage in some distasteful tricks with the director, Curtis Bernhardt. Curtis, or Kurt, as he was called back in Germany, was a good director. I liked him, and liked working with him, but he had a touch of arrogance about him, a brusqueness that could be hurtful. I once asked him why he had directed a scene against a background of a wall of books instead of against a fireplace in the same room. "I want to know," I told him, "because directing interests me. I'd like to try it."

"Well, when you do, you can use a fireplace instead of books as a background," he snapped and walked off.

The two women, Ida and Olivia, decided to take him down a peg or two, and they made up a story between them that Lewis Milestone was going to take over the direction of the picture if the rushes did not improve. They hoped it would throw Curtis off-stride and make him less critical of them. It didn't work, however, and the only result was that he suspected Ida of being the ringleader in the affair. I have the feeling that Olivia encouraged him in this, and it seems to me that it was the reason he was party to a very dirty trick that Jack Warner played on Ida.

Jack wanted Ida to get top billing because she was a bigger star, and a bigger draw, then Olivia, but he thought Olivia had potential, and he wanted her for future films. It occurred to him that if Ida had her top billing, but Olivia got me in the end of the picture, they would both do well. It was very important, in those days, for a Hollywood actress to wind up with the male romantic lead, just as I always wanted to get the girl in my movies. It helped the audience to identify with you, and it upped your box-office drawing power.

In *Devotion*, the problem was, who would get Paul Henreid, the curate and the male lead? Since most of the movie was a scriptwriter's fantasy, it didn't matter what ending they wrote in. It didn't matter—except to Ida and Olivia. In the movie, they were both supposed to be in love with me, and both wanted to end up with me in the final embrace.

Jack Warner gave Ida a script that ended with her, Emily's, death, but he had another ending that he didn't show to Ida. It was a sort of epilogue in which I played a last love scene with Charlotte, Olivia. I didn't know what was going on because I assumed all the scripts were the same. Curtis knew, but he still suspected that Ida had instigated the story about another director taking over, so he kept quiet. After Ida had finished her part, they shot the second ending.

When Ida saw the final version, she was furious and came to me at once. "I've always been your friend, Paul. How could you do this to me?"

"What are you talking about?" I asked, genuinely puzzled.

"You knew they were shooting another ending," she answered furiously.

"But I didn't know," I protested. "My script always had that ending in it. I had no way of knowing that yours didn't."

Ida began to weep. "But Olivia said you did know!"

I realized that Olivia too was in on the trick and was trying to shift some blame onto me. "Ida," I said, "I swear to you that I didn't know, and if I had, I'd have told you. Olivia is a trouble-maker!"

"Oh, Paulie!" And Ida, still crying, came into my arms to be comforted.

I was grateful that she finally believed me, because we were both due to begin shooting another picture, *In Our Time*, playing opposite each other, and it would have been a terrible situation if we went into it with that kind of suspicion and distrust between us.

As much as Ida disliked what they did with *Devotion*, Jack Warner loved the picture, and in spite of some nasty reviews it did well.

At the end of each year, Warner Brothers always gave a big dinner party at the Palladium for just about everyone who worked for them—stars, crews, even business managers. Seats were arranged on three tiers, with the most important people at tables on the lowest tier, and others on successively higher tiers, the least important at tables set on the top floor. Importance, of course, was tied to money-making ability.

The highlight of the dinner was a showing of the "outtakes" from the year's shooting, usually situations where someone had blown his lines. In one scene Errol Flynn had to mount a horse and he couldn't get up. He tried two or three times, and finally, in exasperation, shouted, "Goddamn it, how does anyone expect me to get on a horse at six o'clock in the morning?"

In another outtake, Bette Davis began a speech and in the middle came out with, "Oh, fuck it, I forgot the goddamn line!" In still another, Ida Lupino had a speech and midway through it forgot her lines but without changing her tone said, "Goddamn if I know how the rest of the speech goes, but I'll look at you and talk as long as the camera turns . . ."

And to my chagrin, they showed one of me I had forgotten all about. It was from *Devotion*, where I'm supposed to make a gallant gesture and subdue two unruly horses pulling a coach with the Brontë sisters in it. In the scene, the horses rear and I grab their bridle, and I'm supposed to pull them down. To film it properly, the coach wheels were attached to the stage, and the horse was trained to rear on cue. But one horse had a wicked look in his eye, and as he reared, he turned toward me and bared his teeth. I saw that angry eye and the hooves coming for me, and I turned tail and ran, the camera following me with great delight across the stage.

It was about this time that Lisl got a phone call from Warner Brothers' publicity department. "We have had so many nice interviews with Mr. Henreid," they told her, "that we'd like to do one with you without him. Jimmy Fiddler, the gossip columnist, will use it in his column. Can you come to the Warner Brothers' commissary for lunch any day at your convenience?"

Lisl was flattered, thinking for a moment that they wanted to talk to her about her own work in Europe and New York. At the luncheon, the Warner representative introduced a redheaded young man who worked for *Movie Magazine*, and he immediately asked, "How do you feel about your husband being here in Hollywood?"

Lisl sighed. "We both love Hollywood. The air is very clean, and we go to the beach almost every day. It's a grand place."

"Yes, but how do you feel about all the beautiful girls here?" He looked around the commissary with a furtive sort of eagerness, pointing to some of the pretty young starlets.

Lisl shrugged. "To tell you the truth, I have trouble telling them apart. They all look alike to me."

"Oh no," the young reporter assured her. "They *are* different. It's so exciting for me to see them so close. But aren't you afraid you'll lose your husband to one? You know the girls are all after him. They all want him."

Poor Lisl had thought the interview would be about her, not about how she felt about me. "This is what Paul wanted," she explained patiently. "He wanted to be a star." Then, because the young man was so serious and intense, she couldn't resist teasing him. "He took the job so he could buy me what I wished. You mustn't worry about me. I'm not a bit afraid."

The young man persisted. "I talked to my wife and she told me she'd be scared if I were out here. I really think you should be scared."

"You think I should?" Lisl looked at him, realizing how naive he was, and she decided the only way to get through the interview was to kid around. "I'll tell you," she said with a show of confidence. "If any woman is interested in my husband, really interested, I invite her to my house as often as I can. I even let her live with us until Paul says, 'My God, I've had enough! I can't stand her living with us any longer!' and it's over. Understand?"

The little fellow looked at Lisl as if she had committed a terrible crime. He simply couldn't see the humor of what she was saying. The Warner Brothers representative made a few feeble attempts to change the subject, but Lisl, having a good time, went on in that teasing vein for the rest of the interview.

A week later the Fiddler column came out with a blazing headline: MRS. HENREID ENCOURAGES HUSBAND TO FLIRT. Warners was outraged, especially when Fiddler, who also had a radio program, said over the air, "I wish Mrs. Henreid, with her dirty ideas and dirty mind, would go back to where she came from."

Warner called me and said, "This is simply horrible. We can't sue Fiddler. You've no idea of the power of these gossip mongers. Would you ask for an interview with Mr. Fiddler and tell him your wife made a mistake?"

"But she didn't make a mistake," I said mildly, "she made a joke!" Later, I asked Lisl, "Do you want to talk to this Fiddler person and set the record straight?"

She shuddered. "Not at all. That boy he sent to interview me was an idiot. You can talk to him, Paul, but don't you dare apologize. Tell him under no condition will I do what he said I should and go back to where I came from. I'm staying right here with you, no matter what he thinks. I don't want to see him or talk to him. Let's leave it the way it is!"

We did just that in spite of Warner's pleas, and eventually the whole thing blew over. But while it lasted it opened up a very ugly seam in the bright and beautiful Hollywood fabric that seemed to be woven out of so much fun and fancy. The gossip columnists, who were very much like scavenger cockroaches living on the filth and garbage that spilled out of the stars' lives, were always an ugly part of the movie culture, not the only ugly part, but a very obvious one.

The next picture I made was *In Our Time,* Ida Lupino playing an English girl traveling in pre-war Poland who falls in love with me, a Polish count. We're married, and she teaches me "the Democratic Way." I try to change my family estate with all its serfs into a democratic enterprise, but one of my uncles, a Nazi sympathizer, forces me to give up the idea. The film ends with the Nazis taking over Poland and Ida and me staying on to fight with the peasants —another piece of pseudo-historical romance concocted by Howard Koch and another writer in the heat of World War II.

Another uncle, a sympathetic one who was supposed to like my progressive ideas, was played in the film by Michael Chekhov. Chekhov, a brilliant Russian character actor who had set up acting schools in Berlin, London, and New York, had written a fascinating book about the stage and his beliefs about acting. When my Nazi uncle tells me off in front of him and my mother, played by Alla Nazimova, then leaves, Chekhov makes an impassioned and moving speech about how he's suffered all his life under this domineering older brother. He's glad we're fighting him and wants us to go on.

Chekhov, then in his early fifties, delivered the speech at rehearsal superbly. He did it simply, with no tears, a matter-of-fact delivery, but incredibly moving just because it was so simple. When he finished, Ida, Nazimova, and I broke into spontaneous applause.

At that point Vincent Sherman, the director, went to work on Chekhov. "Can't you take a handkerchief out and show you're moved by sniffing while you're talking?" One by one he gave him bits of business that slowly turned the impassioned speech into a terribly sentimental delivery. By the time Sherman was finished and the speech was shot, it was god-awful!

I felt that it was a devastating experience. I could hardly believe that any director could destroy such a brilliant performance by such a talented actor. The next day Chekhov and I were being driven to our location, the Warner Ranch out in the valley, and I turned to him and asked, "Why did you let Vincent Sherman do that? Your performance was so moving in rehearsal, so splendid—how could you let him destroy it?"

Chekhov was silent for a while, staring out the window. Then he sighed and turned to me, his eyes dark with a sense of pain. "Paul," he said in a tired voice, "I've played Shakespeare, Ibsen, Shaw, Goethe —I've played everything good, and I've had my time. I played my parts as I saw them, and I've had a wonderful career. Now I'm in a foreign land. I don't understand much. I'm old. I don't want any more trouble. I don't feel it's important to argue about a piece of second-rate writing. One way or the other, what difference does it make in the overall scheme of things? This script is a piece of nothing. It isn't Goethe or Schiller, and your Mr. Sherman . . ."

He fell silent, and I couldn't answer. My throat was too full, and I think I would have cried if I'd said a word.

Seventeen

◆

My First
Pirate Role

The Conspirators, shot in 1944, was my first movie with Hedy Lamarr, and my first introduction to her brand of wooden acting was a scene in which, according to the script, Hedy was supposed to express "flustered embarrassment." She looked unbelievably beautiful; she had the kind of face you couldn't help staring at, and for this scene she wore a filmy white negligee, but she wasn't up to looking either flustered or embarrassed while she was looking at me. Jean Negulesco, the director, explained what he wanted again and again and again, and shot the scene over and over, but each time Hedy tilted her beautiful head and, looking as if she were carved out of exquisite ivory, said her lines, not to me, but up to the heavens.

Finally, in desperation, Negulesco said, "We'll do it one more time, and that's it, no matter how it comes out!"

Hedy prepared to step forward and emote, but before she did, I leaned over and whispered something in her ear. She reacted at once, and her perfect show of flustered embarrassment was caught by the camera. Negulesco was enraptured. "Pauli, cookie . . ." He pulled me aside. "What did you whisper to her? What magic word made her act?"

I grinned and said, "I told her that with the lights behind her I could see right through her negligee, as if she were naked!"

It's a strange thing about actresses, and actors, for that matter. I've never had the slightest trouble with the really tough ones like Bette Davis—never, as long as they were good. It was the bad actors and actresses who gave me problems, the ones lacking in talent.

Hedy Lamarr was ravishingly beautiful, but altogether lacking in talent. With a good director she was able to turn in an acceptable performance; with people who weren't experienced she'd get into trouble. Negulesco was a second-unit director who had been given *The Conspirators* as his first major motion picture. Why he got it, I don't know. Probably as a reward for some good work he had done. With a good leading lady there would have been no problem. Hedy had come from MGM on an exchange commitment, and she needed a strong, competent man to direct her. Negulesco was neither. Rumanian-born, his accent was atrocious and his command of English even worse. When we started shooting, he came to me with the script and said, "Cookie"—his favorite name for me—"Cookie, I need your advice."

"You have it, Jean," I told him. "How can I help?"

"I want to ask you something about the script. This crazy English language . . . ."

"What do you want to know?"

"What is ivy?"

"It's a plant, a vine. There's a lot of it out here."

"No, no—it can't be that. Look, in the script, all the time it's ivy, ivy, ivy—and I don't understand what it means."

Puzzled, I said, "But, Jean, I haven't seen it in the script at all."

"Well, I'll show you." And he called over the scriptgirl and took the screenplay from her. "See here: *I've* got to go. . . . And here: *I've* had too much. *I've, I've*—what does it mean?" and each time he pronounced *I've, Ivy*.

That was our director, and the one thing he seemed totally incapable of doing was directing Hedy. He simply didn't have the strength of character to order anyone to do something, let alone Hedy. He gave excellent direction to the cameraman and the crew. He had been an artist back in Rumania, and he had an artist's eye for excellent shots, but as far as people went he was hopeless. To get over it, he relied on Warner Brothers' stock company—Sidney Greenstreet, Peter Lorre, and the rest, and he let them all have their way, knowing they'd do good jobs.

But Hedy was another matter. Left alone, she was posing without a bit of motivation or thought-out character, and Negulesco realized he had to direct her. His solution, finally, was to come to me and ask my opinion of the way she had played the scene. I said,

"Please, Jean, leave me out of it." But he insisted, and finally I made a suggestion and he leaped at it. "But you tell her," he begged. "She'll listen to you."

I argued, but he was so miserable that finally I gave in. "But one thing," I cautioned him. "Don't ever let her know you asked me to do this. She'd be furious if she thought I was directing her."

"Of course not, Cookie," he promised. "She'll never know. I won't bring you into it at all."

So we'd work out her motivation and mine, and I'd suggest it to her. I'd stroll into her dressing room and say, "Do you mind running through our scene? I could use some polishing up."

"Of course, Paul," she'd agree, and we'd do the scene. Then, uncertainly, she would ask, "Do you think I'm doing it all right?"

"Well, as long as you ask me," I'd tell her, "I think you'd look better if you did it differently here and there, this way . . ."

She was very unsure of herself, and because of that I could count on her always asking my opinion. It worked well, even though I was treading on thin ice. No actor likes to be directed by another actor. Then one scene came up where we both sit at a café table, and she recites a poem from memory. When she did it at rehearsal, she looked off into the camera again instead of at me, and it seemed ridiculous. "Do you think that's right?" I asked her.

"But what's wrong?" she said anxiously.

"Nothing is exactly wrong, it's just that it's hard for me to react to the poem unless you look at me while you say it."

"But this is a great moment for me," Hedy protested, and it was one of the rare times she stood up to me. "I must say it to the camera."

"Well, that's only my opinion, Hedy," I told her. "You did ask me, and I feel that if you looked at me, it would be very natural. The other way is like an old-fashioned soliloquy, direct to the audience —the camera. But, of course, you do it the way you think best."

We came on the set and Hedy did the poem just as she wanted to, and Negulesco reacted automatically. I could understand why. It was a bad way to play the scene from anybody's point of view, and the two of us had discussed how it should be done. He called out,

"Hedy, I think you should say the poem to Paul, not to the camera. Am I right, Paul?"

I turned away in embarrassment, and that did it. Hedy, suddenly realizing what was going on, exploded. "Paul! You got him to say that. You went behind my back and talked to him; otherwise he would have liked it!"

I said, "Hedy, don't be ridiculous. I just gave you my opinion. I never spoke to Jean about it."

She started off the set in tears, crying and carrying on, and shooting was held up for two hours until the producer could calm her down. Then he appealed to me. "Paul, tell her how good she was."

I went to her and said, "Hedy, darling, I apologize because Jean said the same thing I did, but I was not in collusion with him. I promise I'll never again make a suggestion to you, even if you ask."

We went back to the set and shot it her way, and half the scene ended on the cutting-room floor. What was left was her voice and the camera on my listening face.

A week later Jean approached me again. "Please, Cookie, tell her how to play it, just this one scene?"

I shook my fist at him. "Get out, Jean! No more, no more! Do you hear me?"

Hedy was a strange woman. There was a story going around that she did her first movie, *Extase (Ecstasy),* when she was fifteen, then she married a European multimillionaire, Fritz Mandl, and was terribly unhappy in the marriage. She went to the opera with him one night, loaded down with a fortune in jewels. He kept these in his safe and only gave them to her to wear for important occasions. Halfway through the performance, she told him that she was sick. "I don't want to spoil your evening," she said. "I'll go home, but you stay and see the rest."

She convinced him, went home alone, took the suitcases she had packed and her jewels and took off. Eventually she ended up in Hollywood.

She was friendly with Lisl and me; we had known each other in Vienna. One afternoon she appeared at our house with a bagful of her laundry. "Your girl does such a beautiful job of ironing," she told Lisl. "Let's you and me chat over some coffee while she does these things."

Lisl was too stunned to protest, but the second time Hedy tried it, Lisl told her, "No, once and for all!" Hedy shrugged it off and still remained friendly. One evening, at a dinner party at our house, she took me aside and said, "I have this millionaire Texan who says he loves me and wants to marry me. What should I do, Paul?"

"Why ask me?" I laughed. "If you love him, Hedy, marry him."

"Oh yes, love—well, I thought I'd have my lawyer draw up a marriage contract."

"What do you mean by a marriage contract?" I asked in bewilderment.

"Why, a contract that stipulates exactly how much money I'll get if he divorces me."

I stared at her, not believing what I'd heard, then I said, "I've had no experience with marriage contracts, Hedy, so I can't give you any advice. I've heard that rich people make them here, but why they get married at all is more than I can understand."

"I think I'm right," she said after a moment's reflection. "I'll get him to sign it or tell him I won't marry him!"

I know she married her Texan and moved to Texas, but I never found out if she got the contract signed. I heard later that they were divorced, but I haven't seen Hedy since.

In spite of Hedy's bad acting and, in my opinion, rather peculiar outlook on life, I had a very warm feeling for her. Indeed, I had that same feeling for most of the women I played opposite. Acting love scenes with someone is an intimate experience, and you can't avoid a certain degree of emotional attachment even when you're extremely careful about any physical relationship.

And yet I, like many other actors, was continually linked to my leading ladies. One form of this was the anonymous letter. These letters were rampant in all of Hollywood. An unsigned letter would come to Lisl. One, for instance, said, "You are probably unaware that your husband is having an affair with Zsa Zsa Gabor."

Now we knew and liked the Gabor girls and found them very

amusing. This particular letter came when I was doing a picture, not with Zsa Zsa, but with Katharine Hepburn, *Song of Love*. It went on to say,

> When your husband isn't shooting, she picks him up at MGM's parking lot and they drive away, leaving his car there, and they return several hours later to pick up his car. I have documentary proof of this in photos. If you'll meet me at Sunset and La Cienega at nine tomorrow night, I'll turn this proof over to you—for one hundred dollars.

Not all the letters offered to sell documentation. Many were just crude slanders. Often they were well written, some printed in block letters, but many making no attempt to disguise the handwriting. One said, "Paul and Ida Lupino were together last Tuesday. They really finished work at two P.M. and they were in Paul's dressing room until six!"

One similar letter said, "I know Paul's dressing room very well, and although it's on the second story, I have a way of peeking in and I watched them . . ." The letter went on in vivid detail. ". . . they decided the floor was better, and they rolled around on it completely naked." The fantasies in the letters were often incredible.

Lisl received an enormous amount of these anonymous letters about every leading lady I worked with. I don't know if the wives of other actors received as many, but I assumed that they did, and the quantity of letters varied depending on my co-star. There was a huge number of them when I appeared with Michele Morgan— with other actresses there were fewer. At first I assumed they were written by people who could actually watch my coming and goings, perhaps someone working on the picture with me, but in spite of the odd hours I kept, there was no connection between the statements in the letters and my actual absences from the sets. In fact, I once took Eleanor Parker home from the studio to pick up some allergy pills, and we spent a few moments in her apartment while she searched for them. Now if an anonymous letter writer had been watching us, he or she would have reported this incident, but no mention was made of it. I realized then what complete fantasies the letters were. They did no real harm to me or to Lisl, but they left me feeling unclean.

After I finished shooting *The Conspirators,* Jack Warner wanted me to do *Watch on the Rhine.* They were making the play into a movie, and Bette Davis would be my co-star. However, I made a foolish mistake and turned it down, afraid of being typecast as a Nazi villain. I also felt that *Watch on the Rhine* was a contrived play, in no way up to Elmer Rice's *Flight to the West.* My original contract had stipulated that I would always get the girl, and I used that as an excuse to get out of the movie. Jack Warner gave in reluctantly and Paul Lukas did the part—and got an Oscar for it!

Jack offered me *Mr. Skeffington* next, again with Bette Davis, and though I wanted to play opposite her, I turned it down.

The character I was to play, Mr. Skeffington, loves his wife so much that when she tires of him and begins having affairs with younger men, he accepts it quite complacently, even going so far as to welcome the young men into his house. "I could never make it convincing," I assured Jack, and after a moment's thought he said, "All right. I'll go along with that, but this is my last offer." And he handed me the script of *Between Two Worlds,* a rewrite of *Outward Bound,* the 1923 play by Sutton Vale. It had been done in 1930 with Leslie Howard and Douglas Fairbanks, Jr., and this was to be an updated version. It was the story of a boat that shuttles between this world and the next filled with passengers who are dead, but unaware of it. One couple are suicides, hovering between life and death, and I played the man while a newcomer for whom Warner had great hopes, Eleanor Parker, played the woman. John Garfield was also in the picture and the director was Edward A. Blatt, a pleasant fellow but inexperienced.

Julius Garfinkle, renamed John Garfield for the screen because his real name was too "ethnic" for Hollywood, was an excellent actor who had been trained on the New York stage. I found him bright and pleasant, though somewhat naive, and we got along very well. John had to learn card tricks for the part, and he became tremendously excited about them. He practiced constantly, and bored all of us with them. But Lisl and I were fond of him and his wife, a very nice young woman. Neither of them were pretentious, and probably because of that didn't mix with Hollywood "society."

Between Two Worlds was received very well by the critics and public, although the attempt to update it in a prologue, which had all the other passengers on the boat killed by a bomb, took away from the eerie quality of the play. The play's slowly unfolding realization that these people are all dead didn't work in the version we did. The audience knew it, and the suspense was gone. The reviews picked this up, and though they praised our performances, they weren't happy about the script.

The search for challenging movies that would change my image as an actor finally made me decide to write out a quick treatment of an idea that had been simmering in my mind for a long time. I was getting tired of being cast as the suave ladies' man, and I had definitely decided no more Nazis, so I started to think in terms of something that would be more fun, a swashbuckling part in a pirate film. The idea I came up with was far from having any literary quality, but it would definitely change my image and give me a chance to play around with swords and pistols.

The main character in my treatment, a Dutchman, was a pirate who fought for freedom of the seas from both the English and the Spanish. He is commissioned to deliver a bride to the governor of Tortuga, and of course he falls in love with the girl on the way. When he gets her there, the governor confiscates his ship and jails him and his crew. He escapes with the girl, encourages a slave uprising, and at the climax the city is set on fire.

I took the story treatment to Jack Warner, and he tossed it back at me after leafing through it. "It's out of the question."

"But why? Jack, it would make an exciting picture," I argued. "And just think of it in color."

"Look, when I want a lover, I'll take you. When I want a pirate, I'll get Errol Flynn!"

Lew Wasserman shrugged when I told him about it. "What did you expect, Paul? You're successful in one type of role. No one is going to want you swinging from the yardarm with a bare chest. Now

RKO still has nothing for you. You'll have to do another picture for Warners."

"Then let's take this idea to RKO," I told him. "I'm convinced that it's great."

Over Lew's objections I took it to the head of production at RKO, Charles Koerner, and he thought it was a wonderful idea. They assigned a writer named George W. Yates to do a screenplay, and when the first hundred pages were done, they sent them to me for approval. "We'll discuss it at lunch at the Beverly Hills Hotel," they told me, and the producer, the associate producer, and Frank Borzage, who was to direct it, came along with Yates.

I had read the hundred pages they gave me, and I hated all of it. It was a completely different story from the one I had concocted, and I was furious. At the lunch I told them I refused to do the picture unless they rewrote the screenplay following my outline.

They calmed me down and promised to rewrite it and be faithful to my outline, but when they sent me forty pages of the so-called rewrite, I found that it was exactly the same as Yates' first draft.

They had already started work on the sets, the pirate ship, and "round horizons," one of Tortuga and one of the open sea. In short, they had already invested too much money to turn back. They had budgeted the movie at $2 million, and I was sure that they needed me. It gave me clout, and Lew Wasserman and I worked out a strategy of refusal and then gradual acceptance. "I refuse to do the script as it stands," I told them. "You can put me on suspension."

They gave in at once, and my demand, which was simply that they take Yates off the script and give me full power as producer, was met. At that time Herman Mankiewicz, a brilliant and witty man, was the top writer at RKO. I knew one of his weaknesses was good Scotch, and I bought a bottle of the best and took it to his office. Like most writers I have met, he was delighted at any interruption and immediately took out two glasses.

"Now what's the occasion? What are we celebrating?"

"My troubles, Herman."

"Well, let's drink to them, Paul. What are they?"

"They gave me one lousy writer for this film I'm doing, and I just got rid of him."

"I'll drink to that." Herman lifted his glass. "So far no trouble. Here's to your picture."

"*Our* picture, Herman," I said with a smile. "I want you to do the script for it."

"For a pirate picture? Forget it!" Herman scowled at me. "I don't do pirate pictures."

"Now take it easy," I reassured him, filling his glass again. "This is a different kind of story. Let me tell it to you." Another glass of whiskey calmed him down, and by the time I had finished the plot, emphasizing the fight for freedom of the seas, he was hooked—and most of the bottle of Scotch was finished.

"What I like," he told me unsteadily, "is that there's political color to it, a pirate as a freedom fighter. That's great!" Drunk and amiable, he agreed to do it, and as I left, I said, "Oh yes, and you start tomorrow."

He sobered up pretty quickly. "But my assignment . . ." He gestured at his desk and the heaps of manuscript.

"I'll tell the front office to take you off it."

"Can you?" he asked doubtfully, scowling at his desk. "Not that I'm fond of this crap . . ."

"Of course I can, Herman. They gave me the power to do it," I assured him.

The script Herman did, his first adventure story, was perfect, an exciting, thrilling story with everything I wanted in it. His final scene was the slave revolt and the burning of Tortuga. We shot the movie called *The Spanish Main,* in 1944, with beautiful Maureen O'Hara as my leading lady, and everything went well until close to the end, when the head of production took me aside. "Paul, the ending is fantastic, but it's going to add two hundred thousand dollars to the budget, and we simply can't afford it. We're budgeted at two million, and we won't go over that. The studio is in enough trouble as it is."

I wanted that ending so much! I felt it would make the picture perfect. I tried to argue with him, but he was firm. However, finally he said, "If you're willing to put up the two hundred thousand yourself, we'll build the sets and do the ending and give you fifty percent of the film."

I went to Lew with the idea. I could have raised the money, and the offer was tempting, but Lew was against it. "You're an actor, Paul. You're involved in the creative end of films. You shouldn't be concerned with money problems. My advice is to tell them no."

So we decided to rewrite the ending, and it broke my heart to leave the fire out. Herman was furious. "I gave you a terrific script, and you told me you had the power to do it, and now you want me to butcher the ending. I won't do it!"

Someone else rewrote it, and the film turned out to be a colossal success. Dore Schary, who became head of production at RKO in 1945, shortly after *The Spanish Main* was shot, told me that the film had grossed $14 million, and, for the time being, kept RKO alive.

Hugh Marlowe, the actor who had played with me in *Flight to the West* on Broadway, stayed a close friend until he died. Whenever he came to Hollywood, he would stay with us, and when he was doing *Meet Me in St. Louis,* I had to take off on a publicity tour. Hugh was still a bachelor, and he took me aside before I left. "Do you think I ought to move into a hotel while you're gone?" he asked.

I said, "Don't be foolish. You stay here with Lisl, and perhaps we can get a big, juicy scandal going. We'll leak the news to some Hollywood gossip writers."

After I left, Lisl received an invitation from Henry Blanke to a party at his house. "I'd love to go," Lisl told Hugh. "Will you take me?"

Hugh said, "Of course." And she called Blanke and said, "Paul is out of town. Do you mind if I bring Hugh Marlowe?"

He was delighted, and after she hung up Lisl told Hugh, "Now the talk is bound to start. Henry is an A-one gossip!" They went to the party in Lisl's car, and everything was in full swing by the time they arrived. Lisl took a drink and wandered around. "At one point," she told me later, "I saw Hugh sitting on a sofa, and Eva Gabor, that lovely blonde, was stretched out on the floor at his feet, positioned so that her cleavage was easily visible to Hugh."

I said, "But of course."

She shrugged. "Well, why not? Hugh is divorced and free—and eager. I circulated a bit, had something to eat and another drink. Much later, when the party was breaking up, Eva came up to me and asked, 'Lisl, I must ask you something. Does Hugh belong to you?'"

"What did you say?" I asked, laughing.

"I was very generous. I said, 'You can have him, sweetheart. I'll keep Paul. He may be dull, but what the hell, I'm used to him.' Then I looked around the room and asked her, 'I'm curious. Who did you come with?'

"She pointed to a dapper man in his eighties. 'That lovely old gentleman.' I was amused but kept a straight face and asked, 'But, Eva, isn't he a little old for you?' She shrugged. 'But he has such a lovely Rolls and chauffeur!' A little later, Hugh came up to me and said, 'I know you want to go home, Lisl. Tell me the truth: Do I have to go with you? Or can I stay a little longer?'

"I told him it was perfectly all right, and I didn't mind driving home alone, and I left. How do you like that?"

I laughed and said, "Well, obviously they're having an affair, and I like them both. Every time I see Hugh now he looks exhausted, but of course he does look happy."

And he was happy, no matter how tired. Then one afternoon the three of us, Hugh, Lisl, and I, were having a drink at our house when the phone rang. It was for Hugh. He hardly said a word after "Hello," but when he put it down he looked badly shaken. "What's wrong?" I asked.

"That was Eva. She just told me that she's getting married! I don't understand it. Yesterday we were . . . Well! It just doesn't make sense."

"To tell you the truth," I said cheerfully, "you look a bit relieved. Come on. Have another drink."

Eighteen

♦

I Become
Independent

*A*fter finishing *The Spanish Main* for RKO, I went back to
Warner Brothers to do *Of Human Bondage*, with Eleanor Parker as
my co-star. The script was very well written. Edmund Goulding was
the director and Henry Blanke the producer. Blanke's trouble was
that he couldn't ride herd on Goulding. He knew what should be
done, but hadn't the strength to insist on his own ideas, and Goulding, who fancied himself as a writer, rewrote the screenplay as we
went along.

The film became less and less like the original fine screenplay,
and more and more Goulding's work. I was upset at that and also
at Goulding's method of directing. He would gather the cast together every day before shooting and discuss motivation in what
struck me as a rather childish way. I tried unsuccessfully to hide my
feelings, but Goulding became aware of them, and we were at odds
most of the shooting. We fought about how each scene should be
played, and though I never acted like that with a director I respected, I insisted on playing it my way every time.

One of Goulding's techniques was to shoot five or six pages in
one setup. We'd rehearse for two days with the camera on a crane,
then shoot it in one day, and after the rushes were seen we'd invariably have to do it over. The cost of the picture began to mount up,
and the long takes, incredibly long without cover-cuts or close-ups,
began to affect the picture. Blanke asked me if I would talk to
Goulding. "I can't reach him," he said unhappily.

"What makes you think I can?" I asked. "We've been at odds
all along."

Now most directors who do what Goulding did—that is, work
with very long takes—will do additional close-ups and distance two-

shots, long shots, high setups and low setups, so that they can cut to them to relieve the monotony of a single point of view. Or they can eliminate gestures or parts of the scene. Goulding wouldn't consider this, and Blanke became increasingly agitated as the picture neared completion. "You must do something," he told me in desperation, and I finally agreed to fluff my lines whenever I thought the take was too long. This would force Goulding to stop the shot and go back to a point before my fluff and re-shoot. The camera angle was usually somewhat changed and it would force a cut at that point unless he was willing to reshoot the entire take. He had sense enough not to try that.

At about this time I had seen one of the new optical benches that allowed the technician to enlarge pieces of a take and achieve the equivalent of a zoom lens or close-up. I told Lew Wasserman about it and assured him that the film might eventually be salvaged if Blanke had the guts to redo the print. The screening of the first print depressed all of us, and that night, at Romanoff's, Lew, Blanke, and I sat around the table with our wives as if at a wake. Finally, with a sigh, Blanke said, "Lew, Paul, the picture is a complete disaster."

Lew, a funny light in his eyes, said, "Henry, I think there may be a way out. Let me mull it over."

Blanke stood up and looked down at his unfinished meal. "You can think about it all you like, but I don't think anything you can come up with will save our skin." Then he turned and walked out heavily with his wife.

After he had gone, I shook my head. "You don't think we can pull out of a disaster like this, Lew."

"Remember what you told me about that new optical bench, Paul, about redoing the print, and the pick-ups he had to do because of your voluntary fluffs?"

"But Blanke wouldn't have the guts."

"Go through the final shooting script and write down how we could cut the film with the help of the new optical bench. Describe where you'd put close-ups and cuts."

"I think I could," I told him. "It's all pretty fresh in my memory, but Blanke and Goulding aren't going to accept any idea of mine on how it should be fixed."

"But that's the point. We'll tell them it's my idea," Lew said. "I've already laid the groundwork with Blanke and he's desperate enough to try with or without Goulding's permission."

I went home and sat up all night working from the shooting script and my memory of the screening. The next morning I gave my notes to Lew, and he sat down with me and the script and to my amazement memorized all the changes in half an hour. "This way," he assured me, "Blanke is going to think the changes came from me, not you—and I believe he'll put them in, at least I hope to hell he will!"

After his meeting with Blanke, he called me, elated. "It worked, Paul. We sat down in his office, and he said, wasn't it a shame that such a beautiful script had been turned into such a horrible movie. Then I told him I thought there was a chance to repair the damage, and I gave him the changes you suggested and told him about the new optical bench—and, Paul, he bought it! He called his secretary in and had me dictate it all to her."

Indeed, he not only bought it, but, as often happens with producers and directors, became convinced it was his own original idea. He called me the next day and said, "Paul, I've slept on this disaster, and I have some excellent ideas on how to salvage it. Trust me, I'll save the picture. I've got a new cutter, fresh blood—you'll be pleased."

And the recutting worked. The extra-long scenes and repetitions that had made the print so boring were eliminated, and we ended up with a good film; in fact, except for Leslie Howard's brilliant performance, I felt it was better than the 1934 version.

Henry Blanke was the producer of the next Warner Brothers film I did, *Deception,* and again I was teamed with Bette Davis. Both of us were very happy about it. We had wanted to be together since we made *Now Voyager,* and finally we had made it. Unfortunately, we also had *Now Voyager's* director, Irving Rapper. I hadn't gotten along with him before, and this was no better. Finally a blow-up between Rapper and me led to Blanke's stepping in. Rapper was told to let me go my own way, and I was happy to do it. From then on we barely spoke to each other on the set.

During the filming of *Deception*, Bette, still married to William Sherry, became pregnant, and in her typical fashion started calling the picture *Conception*. The marriage was in great trouble by then, and Lisl and I thought the pregnancy was an attempt to hold it together; but if so, it was a futile attempt, and during the making of the movie I could see her marriage crumble. To make matters worse, the rumor on the set was that I was really the father of Bette's baby!

Bette, for reasons of her own and probably to spite her husband, encouraged the rumor. She would tell our friends, "I have such a crush on Paul, but he just won't give me the right time. I don't know how I can get an affair going with him." It started as a joke at first, and I took it as one, but eventually the humor, if any, began to wear thin, and it started to annoy Lisl and me, particularly since I never believed she really wanted an affair. It was simply a ploy to annoy her husband.

At the Warners' lot, we each had our own dressing room where we could relax, eat, smoke, or nap, a place to grab a little privacy from the constant parade of tourists who were shown around the studios. These mobile dressing rooms were quite elaborate affairs with sitting room, bedroom, shower, and even a kitchenette and air conditioning—in effect, each was a complete mobile home.

Bette, as a leading star at Warners, got one of the most elaborate of these, and we would often run through our lines in her trailer. Whenever we were there together and she saw her husband coming on the lot, she'd lock her door and, if he knocked, she would shout out, "Paul and I are busy! Leave us alone!" The implication was that being "busy" was more than just rehearsing lines. I began to think the "joke" had gone far enough, because Bette's husband was not only a very jealous man, but also a very strong one.

One day Bette and I were in her trailer going over a scene, when suddenly the trailer began to shake violently. "My God," I said, "it's a California earthquake! We'd better get out."

Bette put her script down and rolled her eyes up to the ceiling in disgust. "Earthquake my ass! It's that stupid bastard of a husband of mine."

I pulled the shade up and, sure enough, Sherry had picked one corner of the trailer up and was shaking it violently. When he saw my face at the window, he shouted, "Come on out of there! I know what's going on!"

Bette opened the door and stepped back, hands on her hips. "Oh, for Christ's sake, come on in! It's all over anyway." As Sherry hesitated, she added, "We've had our little affair and now we're having coffee. You might as well be civilized and join us."

His face darkened and he glared at her for a moment, then he turned and strode off furiously. "Now why did you do that?" I asked.

She smiled at me with that absolute charm of hers and said, "But we might as well have an affair, Paulie—everyone thinks we are."

"Thanks to you. Let's get back to work." And that was that. We did get back to work, with no monkey business, nor was there ever any between us.

Bette's baby was a girl, and she named her Barbara, but, characteristically, she called her BD, after her own initials. Lisl and I and our children would often drive out to Laguna where Bette had a house, and we'd spend the day with her, the children happy together and we adults relaxed and comfortable. Eventually Bette moved to Maine, claiming she couldn't stand Hollywood and the people there. When she had to do a film she'd come back and rent a penthouse at the grand old Marmont Hotel, or a beach house on the Pacific Coast Highway in Santa Monica or Malibu.

I used to be a good drinker and always prided myself on being able to hold my liquor, but Bette was much better at it than I was. "Well, it looks as if the sun is setting on the yardarm," she'd say, and take out the Scotch. She would start off being very funny and sweet, then, as she drank, she'd become more witty and sharp, and her comments about our Hollywood friends would be very biting— savage but true. "Let me give you another drink," she'd insist each time she replenished her own, then she'd look at me wickedly.

"Someday I'm going to get you good and drunk, Paul. I'd love to see what would happen once your guard is down. You're such a goddamn proper gentleman!"

Fortunately, she never did get me that drunk, though once or twice I was tipsy enough to feel uneasy about driving home, and she loved that!

The story on which *Deception* was based came from a French play. A husband and wife are separated, and the husband is believed dead. The woman has an affair with another man, and the husband returns. The three face the situation, and she goes back to her husband.

The screenwriter, John Collier, and my first producer-writer from Vienna, Joseph Than, turned out a good script, but the Breen Office, the censors who had to pass on every Hollywood picture, began to interfere. The woman, they insisted, had to be punished because she had committed adultery with another man. The solution they finally arrived at was to have her shoot and kill the other man and then go to jail, a thoroughly unbelievable situation, and the entire picture suffered from it. Bette played the woman; I was the husband, and Claude Rains was the other man. The three of us enjoyed acting together, and we got on well.

My contract with Warners had one more film to go when MGM offered me *Song of Love* with Katharine Hepburn as the female lead. Clarence Brown, a man I admired tremendously, was to direct, and Arthur Rubinstein to play the piano for Katy and me. I was to get $115,000 for making it, a top salary in those days. It was a fabulous deal because Warner Brothers was paying me $75,000 a picture. I realized that, although Warners had no current assignment for me, if I asked Jack to release me I would take a chance on his refusal. What I decided to do instead was buy back my contract for $75,000. What actually happened was that Warners simply did not pay me the last $75,000 they owed, and I did the picture for MGM instead.

The film, the life story of Robert Schumann, the composer, was a delight to make. Brown, the director, was thoroughly professional and exciting. Katharine Hepburn was lovely and radiant and, in those days, much less mannered as an actress than she is now. She was fun to work with, and working with her introduced me to Spencer Tracy, her intimate friend.

He would come to the set each morning, say hello, and then, with a half-smile, ask me, "Is she behaving herself?"

Without smiling, I'd say, "Oh yes, Spence. She's being marvelous."

"Good, good." He would turn to Hepburn. "Now, Kate, have you learned your lines?"

Rather demurely, she'd say, "Yes, dear."

He'd go on: "Now don't forget. Say the lines loud and clear. Don't grin and make faces—just say the words."

And, grinning at him like a child, she'd say, "Yes, Spence, I will."

Spence treated her like a child, and in some personal areas she did seem childish. There was the matter of smell. Before each scene we did together, she would disappear into her dressing room and come out smelling like lilacs. Finally, out of curiosity, I asked her, "What on earth do you do in your dressing room that gives you that smell?"

She fidgeted a bit, looking embarrassed, then, avoiding my eyes, said, "I have to make sure that my partner has a good feeling about me."

"But what do you do?" I persisted.

She looked around, but we were alone. Then, taking my hand, she pulled me toward her dressing room. "I'll show you." Inside she dipped a cotton-tipped applicator into perfume and dabbed a bit at each nostril and some around her mouth. "See?" She giggled. "Now in the close-ups you won't have to worry. I'll smell like lilacs!"

It was a typical Hepburn trick, sweet and silly and concerned about her leading man. During the shooting of the movie I began to realize that even with those rather silly tricks, and although Tracy treated her as if she were an adorable but backward little girl, she had a bright, incisive mind of her own and an intelligent, political view of things. At that time she had decided that the third-party candidate for President, Henry Wallace, Roosevelt's former Secretary of Agriculture, was a much better choice than either the Democratic or Republican candidate. It was a conclusion she reached independent of Tracy or anyone else, and she came out for Wallace openly and introduced him at a rally in Los Angeles.

Henry Wallace, considered by the American Legion and the Daughters of the American Revolution as a flaming red, was picketed by both organizations, and, through the then rampant policy of "guilt by association," our movie, when it opened, was also picketed in Los Angeles. The box office there was poor, but fortunately it did well in other towns. It was a good picture, but not a smash hit.

During the filming of *Song of Love*, Tracy and I came to know each other well. He, too, was a chess player, and we'd play a few games when I was free, and in the evenings we'd play at his house or mine. I felt that Tracy was a splendid actor with an earthy sense of power in his performances. He was an intelligent man, and any discussion or argument with him was bound to make good sense, no matter which side he took.

I had developed a circle of friends among the Hollywood actors who were not only good at their craft, but were also good company and intellectuals as well. Among them were Judy Garland, Edward G. Robinson, Paul Muni, Bette Davis, Lew Ayers, Paul Stewart, Hugh Marlowe, Franchot Tone, Frederic March, and Gary Cooper, an actor I thought highly underrated during his career, as successful as it was. Cooper was a magnificent actor and very intelligent in his performances. Off the screen he lost that laconic air and became talkative and sparkling in conversation. The same is true with my old friend Paul Stewart, with whom I lunch at least twice a month.

Nineteen

The Committee for the First Amendment

*N*ineteen forty-seven, the year *Song of Love* was released, was a troubling political time. In that year a subcommittee of the House Un-American Activities Committee (HUAC), headed by J. Parnell Thomas, was assigned to investigate the film industry. The committee contended that Hollywood was making films drenched with pro-Communist propaganda, and there was a behind-the-scenes plot to influence the minds of America and turn us all toward the Soviet Union.

In Hollywood, HUAC found a source of tremendous publicity, and the red-menace scenario proved effective in bringing the press to their side and terrifying the Hollywood studio heads. In 1943, Warners had released a film called *Mission to Moscow,* directed by Michael Curtiz with a script by Howard Koch. It was based on the book by Joseph Davies, who was ambassador to Russia in the late thirties. In 1943 the Soviet Union was our ally, and it seemed good sense to do the movie. Now, in 1947, the film was used as an example of Communist influence in Hollywood.

When the accusations were made, the studio heads caved in at once. They agreed that anyone asked by the committee should go to Washington to answer the committee's charges. Gary Cooper, John Wayne, and Irene Dunne were among those asked to appear, but there was considerable confusion about why they were there. The confusion was even greater among the American public who read the newspaper reports of the HUAC activities. Some readers even believed Cooper was a Communist. Why else, they asked, had he appeared before the committee? There was a tremendous effort to stigmatize people with the label "red."

Then the committee presented a list of people they claimed

were the real Communists in Hollywood. They subpoenaed nineteen, and called up eleven before HUAC. One of the eleven was my friend Bertolt Brecht. He appeared before the committee and said, "I'd like to cooperate with you to the fullest. Unfortunately, I never belonged to the Communist party. I believe in certain ideals, and I'm grateful to the United States for giving me a place to take refuge in from Germany. You ask me for the names of fellow Communists, and if I knew any I'd give them, but I don't, and I'm sorry to disappoint you."

They thanked him for his testimony, and he flew to New York and took the next boat to Europe, certain that if he stayed he'd be called back and re-interrogated.

Nine of the ten remaining men were very talented Hollywood writers; most of them had been, or still were, members of the Communist party. They were Alvah Bessie, Herbert Biberman, Lester Cole, Ring Lardner, Jr., John Howard Lawsen, Albert Maltz, Samuel Ornitz, Dalton Trumbo, Robert Adrian Scott, a producer as well as a writer, and Edward Dmytryk, a director. Called up before the committee, they all refused to answer questions about their Communist party membership, basing their stand on the First Amendment guarantee against incursions on free speech rather than the Fifth Amendment protection against self-incrimination. They told the committee, in some very moving statements, that to their knowledge there was no Communist conspiracy, and that no pro-Communist films had been made in Hollywood, and called on their constitutional right to be silent about their personal and political beliefs.

But after all the brave speeches of the Hollywood Ten, as they came to be known, their First Amendment rights were swept aside by the committee. They were found guilty of contempt of Congress for refusing to name others who might be Communists, and they were jailed.

It's an interesting comment on one of the men who jailed them that J. Parnell Thomas, the chairman of the committee, was convicted of taking kickbacks from his staff and, in 1948, a year later, was jailed at the Federal Correctional Institute in Danbury, Connecticut, along with Ring Lardner, Jr., and Lester Cole, two of the Hollywood Ten he had sent to prison.

The jailing of the Hollywood Ten sent shock waves through the community. Everyone was enraged at the breach of constitutional rights, and a group of people led by John Huston decided to do something about it. They gave a party at Lewis Milestone's house and invited people they felt were progressive—actors, writers and directors—with me among them.

John Huston explained what the plan was. "We intend to form a committee for the First Amendment to counteract HUAC and what they're trying to do. It's all perfectly legitimate and within our constitutional rights. In fact, it's the American Way."

Everyone agreed, and we all contributed some money to send out invitations to everybody with a prominent name to help us to write and produce a radio broadcast that would be carried all over America by one of the big networks.

Most of the people we contacted accepted, but there were one or two who didn't. One was John Ford. "I'm with you," he said, "but I won't participate in anything political. I might go to Washington on my own, but not with a committee, not publicly."

The broadcast we did included some of the brightest Hollywood stars, among them Judy Garland, Irene Dunne, and Claudette Colbert, and its theme was that no one should be robbed of the rights guaranteed in the Constitution by its First Amendment, such as the right to freedom of speech or freedom of religion. The broadcast was very successful and the newspapers applauded it.

In a meeting called after the broadcast, it was suggested that all of us, or at least a large group of us, take a trip to Washington to file a petition of grievances with Congress. "Citizens have a right to do this, according to the Constitution," Philip Dunne, the screenwriter, told us. "We'll go, file our petition, and return."

I raised my hand. "A trip like this should have some official sanction."

"What do you mean?" Huston asked me, "and how could we get it?"

"When a group of stars go to Washington for the March of Dimes or any other big charitable cause, the President invites them to tea or lunch or dinner. Why shouldn't Truman recognize us?"

Everyone thought it was a fine idea and would give a stamp of official approval to the venture. Someone in the group who was close to Truman called and, sure enough, Truman invited us all to lunch the day after we were to arrive. We needed a plane, and someone else close to Howard Hughes called and asked him to furnish one. Hughes was completely sympathetic to our plan and offered us a TWA plane to fly in. We made arrangements to stay at the Hays Adams Hotel, and the hotel reserved two floors for us. We were the white knights in shining armor riding to save the Constitution!

Lisl was asked to keep the books of the newly formed committee, since so many contributions were pouring in, particularly from the heads of studios: Selznick, Mayer, Warner, Hughes—people, oddly enough, we had always associated with the extreme right. Lisl guarded the book with all their names very carefully.

The group of us that finally went on the flight included Humphrey Bogart, Lauren Bacall, Richard Conte, Geraldine Brooks, Evelyn Keyes, Danny Kaye, Marsha Hunt, Gene Kelly, Jane Wyatt, Sterling Hayden, John Huston, Philip Dunne, and Joe Sistrom. Others joined us from New York among them my dear friends Frederic March and Hugh Marlowe.

At one of the meetings before we left, John Huston called for order and said, "I'm going to ask you all to do something that's against your First Amendment rights, but I think it's terribly important. We can't have anyone on the committee who is, or ever was, a member of the Communist party or of any front organization that advocates Marxist-Leninist principles."

We all agreed that that was essential, and we all shook hands on it and assured him we weren't. We were beyond reproach, and we were—almost. Only one didn't tell the truth. He had been a party member in college, and of course that came out later.

I took John Huston aside and said, "John, tell me the truth. Should I go on this trip?"

"You? Of course. Why not?"

"I'm a naturalized citizen, but a foreigner, John. I wasn't born here."

"All the more reason for you to go," he assured me. And my beloved Lisl agreed with Huston. "Go with your friends," she said.

Our group left Los Angeles and flew to Cincinnati, where we refueled. Someone tuned in a radio in the lounge and we heard Louella Parsons of *The Herald-Tribune,* one of the two most prominent and influential gossip mongers in Hollywood, announce that in her opinion Hollywood had come of age, and our trip to Washington showed we wouldn't be pushed around. She congratulated our entire committee for striving to protect the First Amendment.

It cheered us up considerably, and when we arrived in Washington we found that the motion-picture industry was also behind us. They had taken out full-page ads in the newspapers to declare themselves. The press interviewed us and gave us special coverage. The next morning we went to one of the hearings, and J. Parnell Thomas and his committee grew very nervous when we walked in, a group of Hollywood stars. They closed the meeting early, and we felt true heroes.

In the afternoon we filed our petition of grievances, and we were free for the rest of the day. I had a pleasant dinner with a dear friend, producer Joe Sistrom, and then went back to the hotel, where I found a note from Huston. There was an urgent meeting in his suite at eleven. At the meeting he announced, sadly, that Truman had canceled our luncheon the next day. "I think our mission here is finished," he told us. "You all have your return tickets, and you can get back any way you want."

We woke up the next morning to find that the press, which had praised us so fully, had done a complete about-face. We were no longer knights in shining armor. We were "dupes and fellow travelers," "pinkos," who were trying to undermine the country.

Our brave crusade had become a disaster, and from that moment on there was a campaign of innuendos launched in an attempt to frighten and discredit us—a very successful attempt. All of us were attacked by the very columnists who had been so proud of us, and any potential source of embarrassment was dug up and exposed.

Humphrey Bogart and Lauren Bacall flew back by way of Chicago and stopped there while Bogart gave an interview to the press in which he attempted to retract what he had said and done. "I didn't know the people I was with were fellow travelers," he told the reporters, acknowledging in his statement the validity of the false accusations against us.

I felt Bogart's statement was a form of betrayal, and it was also the end of our friendship—and the end of many of Bogart's other friendships. The rest of us stood firm, but we were all shattered by what was going on—and more than shattered. Frederic March, one of the most decent of men, was blacklisted for the next ten years. He spent a million dollars trying to fight his blacklisting legally, but to no avail.

An interesting sidelight of the whole affair is that the book in which Lisl kept the listing of all our contributors, studio heads among them, simply disappeared from our house. There was no sign of a break-in, and nothing else of value was missing.

Back in Hollywood, I had finished *Song of Love*, and I was free of any assignment. Now I could accept anything a major studio offered. But when I called Lew Wasserman to find out if any offers had come in, he told me, "I'm not happy about this trip to Washington, Paul. I don't think any good ever comes of politicking. You're an actor and should stick to acting."

I said, "That's funny, Lew. My father once gave me very similar advice."

"Well, your father was right, and you should have listened to him, Paul. Now look, you have an offer from MGM for a seven-year contract. They'll pay you one hundred fifty thousand a year. The contract says you can't be suspended for any reason except committing adultery, and it allows you to turn down any picture you don't like."

"But, Lew," I said, puzzled. "That's just what I wanted to get away from, a contract that ties me up and prevents me from doing any really good pictures if another studio offers them."

"Look, Paul, my advice is that you take this contract," Lew said tightly. "The terms are fantastic and they'll treat you ten times as well as Jack Warner did. I assure you of that."

"I gave Warners seventy-five thousand to be free to do what I want. We both thought it was right, and now you reverse everything you said and advise me to tie myself up with another major studio."

"You'll be treated well," he said stubbornly. "Louis B. Mayer loves you, and Clarence Brown is crazy about you. He's bought the rights to Grieg's music for *Peer Gynt* and wants you to do it. Paul —take the contract!"

"You still haven't given me a really good reason, Lew."

He was silent for a long time, then, bitterly, he said, "Maybe your trip to Washington was reason enough."

I went home and talked it over with Lisl, and she too said, "Take the contract, Paul. Lew is right, and I'm worried about that Washington trip now."

But I refused to listen to either of them. I was stubborn, and, in retrospect, stupid about it, and I wouldn't admit that my venture into politics might have harmed me. I turned down the contract, and Lew was so angry at me that when a new project came up he gave the contract to one of his associates to handle, with the excuse that as the new head of MCA he was too busy to devote the proper amount of time to it.

The new project was an offer to do a picture for a new independent outfit called Eagle Lion Pictures. It was financed by Robert Young, a railroad millionaire who had decided to dabble in pictures. I had optioned a novel, *Hollow Triumph*, which had been brought to my attention by Steve Sekely, a Hungarian director, with the understanding that if I bought it he would direct it, and he did.

It was a different role for me. I would play a gangster, and I was eager to try it because of the challenge it presented. I would also be the producer. Unfortunately, the contract that Lew Wasserman's associate had approved was a bad one. I hadn't read all the fine print, and Lew hadn't looked it over and warned me.

Hollow Triumph was part of a four-picture deal, the other three done by other star-producers, all four linked together financially. While *Hollow Triumph* did very well, the other three flopped, and I couldn't collect any profit until the producers got back the money spent for all four. As a result I collected very little on the deal.

Between Two Worlds had been written by Daniel Fuchs, and it was an excellent script. Now I heard that Danny was broke and down on his luck. I asked him to write the script for *Hollow Triumph*, but he was very doubtful. "I haven't done a script in a long time, Paul."

"Do this for me, Danny, please," I asked him, and he agreed, but a week later he called and said he had to see me.

He came to my house and said, "I'm grateful to you for offering me the script, Paul, and I need the money, but I'm afraid I can't do it justice."

"But why?"

"I just can't write about gangsters."

"Oh, come on, Danny. You wrote *Summer in Williamsburg*, a wonderful novel, and you're a Brooklyn boy. You grew up with gangsters." I coaxed and flattered him and talked till midnight, and finally he agreed to keep trying.

"All right, but if you're not pleased, if the script isn't acceptable, I'll do no rewriting on it," he warned me.

The script, when he handed it in, was perfect, a brilliant piece of work. I wanted Evelyn Keyes to do it, and I sent the script to Harry Cohn at Columbia, where she was under contract. "I'll give you Keyes," he told me, "if you come to Columbia with the whole package. Not only that, but I'll give you double your budget."

"I can't, Harry," I said. "I've already signed a contract with Robert Young."

"Contract? Hell, I'll get you out of that. Let me call my lawyer."

"No. I made a deal, Harry, and I'm going to honor it."

As a result, I didn't get Keyes, but I remembered Joan Bennett, a lovely actress and perfect for the part. She could handle a part sympathetically but without sentimentality, and she did a sensational job in the movie.

"There's one thing you must know, Paul," Danny Fuchs explained when we began to shoot the film.

"What's that?"

"I don't think much of your director, Sekely, so I've written down what every scene is supposed to convey, and what point to make."

I explained Danny's notes to Sekely, but he couldn't seem to absorb them, or perhaps he was just unwilling to accept advice or direction from a writer. After a number of retakes, Eagle Lion called me in. "Paul, you're the producer and we want your approval before we take Steve Sekely off the picture."

"Why take him off?" I asked.

"Because we're not satisfied with him, and you know you aren't either."

"Yes, but *can* you take him off?"

"We can do it by closing down the picture," they explained. "He'll be let go, and then, a week later, we'll change our mind and reopen it. It's a tactic that's worked before, and all we'll really be out is Joan's salary for an extra week."

I agreed somewhat reluctantly, but they assured me that Steve would get credit for the finished picture no matter who did the rest of it. They closed the picture down, and I waited to hear whom they would suggest for the next director. Since I was the producer, I had to agree to the choice, so when the week was almost up, I went to them and asked, "Now who's going to direct it? I have to talk over the script with him and explain Danny's notes. We don't want another problem like Sekely."

"You'll direct it," they told me, "and any problem will be yours."

"That's very funny." I smiled. "But I've never directed a film before."

"You'll do well," they assured me. "You know what the script is all about, and you've been directed often enough yourself."

So I took over, and I must confess I had the time of my life. I learned a great deal about filmmaking and was very pleased with the final print—pleased, too, that I had become a director.

Twenty

◆

The Blacklist Starts

$\mathcal{O}$nce *Hollow Triumph* (released later on television under the title *The Scar*) was finished, I was approached by two young brothers, Harry and Edward Danziger, who had inherited Luna Park, the giant amusement center, had sold it for a small fortune, and wanted to get into producing movies. They had a script by Jean Rouverol and Hugo Butler, a screenwriter who had been blacklisted in Hollywood and had moved to Mexico with his wife. The script was called *So Young So Bad.*

The Danziger brothers had never produced a film, but after the success of *Hollow Triumph* they came to me with the screenplay and asked me to play the lead. The story intrigued me. It was about juvenile delinquent girls in New York. The part they offered me was a small one, a psychiatrist who helps them, but they told me they'd enlarge the part. "We'll make the psychiatrist a bigger figure and give him a love interest, a social worker."

I discussed this approach with Butler and his wife, and they agreed that the changes the Danzigers wanted would make a better story. The brothers would finance the movie, and United Artists would release it. I would have the power of producer, although the brothers would get billing credit, but, most important to me, the deal would give me 50 percent of the profits.

After the trouble with the last contract, Lew Wasserman had assigned George Chasen, a top agent at MCA, to represent me, but Chasen advised me against the deal. "I don't like you tied up with independent producers. You can count on the big studios, but you take a chance with these fly-by-night outfits. Often they just don't fulfill their contracts, and you're out in the cold."

I ignored his advice, and for once I was right. The picture did well and I made more money out of it than out of anything I've ever been connected with. The Danziger brothers treated me with complete honesty. The picture was shot in New York, and I interviewed three hundred actresses before I found the three girls I wanted to play the leads. They were Rita Moreno, Anne Jackson, and Anne Francis, all of whom went on to grand careers after *So Young So Bad.*

When I finished *So Young So Bad,* I went to France to fulfill a picture commitment to an old friend, André Sarve, a French producer. He had a good script about a Frenchman who goes to live in a dilapidated château and an American woman, played by Merle Oberon, who is traveling through Provence with her children. She loses her way and ends up at the château. Result: romance.

It was a pleasant-enough love story called *Pardon My French,* and I was to be co-producer along with Sarve.

While shooting *So Young So Bad* in New York, Packard Motors approached me to pose for an ad for their cars; in exchange they would give me a station wagon. I agreed, and when we went to Europe on the *Îsle de France*—Lisl, our two girls, and Lutzi sailing with me—we shipped the Packard over too and arrived in style, an entire entourage in a badly bombed and ruined France.

My contract stipulated that I had to be paid when we arrived, $30,000 or 10 million francs. Our Paris representative from MCA met me at Le Havre, very nervous. "We have to pick up the money at the local bank," he told me.

"Is there anything wrong?" I asked, watching the furtive way he looked around.

"Well, yes. We have to pick it up in cash, in French francs, and I'm very nervous about gangsters."

"Here?" I laughed, and then I stopped laughing and looked at him closely. "You aren't serious?"

"But I am!" He held out a brown paper bag. "I brought this along just to fool anyone. Now who would expect us to carry money in a paper bag?"

"Certainly not gangsters," I agreed uneasily.

The sheer volume of the money, when we picked it up, was staggering. It came in ten big blocks like paving stones, each block tied with cord and sealed by the bank of France. We rushed it from the bank to the car and drove to the hotel anxiously, watching behind us for my friend's imaginary gangsters. At the hotel we demanded the largest safe they had and we put nine of the blocks in it, the MCA representative taking the tenth as his commission and hurrying off in a taxi.

During the shooting of *Pardon My French*, I used the cash in the safe to pay my expenses, and it was the only time I've felt rich in the sense of actually "feeling" every franc I paid out. Now I understood the motivation behind men who carry huge bankrolls with them. I had never paid for anything in cash. I had charge accounts, and I used a business manager who took care of all my bills. The sensation of paying people with actual money was different, and I enjoyed it.

While doing *So Young So Bad* and *Pardon My French*, I received absolutely no offers from any of the major studios, and I couldn't understand why. I began to suspect that Lou Wasserman's fears had come true, and I was on some blacklist because of the trip to Washington. But why was I singled out? The others who had gone on the trip—Frank Sinatra, Groucho Marx, Humphrey Bogart— none of them had been blacklisted. But they all had studio contracts, and none of the major studios were willing to have one of their stars blacklisted. They had enough clout to protect them. I had made the bad mistake of becoming independent—and obviously an example. Yet, when I asked around, no one seemed to know anything about my being blacklisted.

Then, while I was still uncertain, someone at MCA called and said, "Desi Arnaz asked if you'd be interested in doing a television series." When I hesitated, he added, "The money is very good."

"If it's a good script, and the money is good, why not?"

"Well, the script is up to you. He wants you to come up with an idea."

I mulled it over for a while, then remembered a story I had heard about a man inheriting a factory and having to run it without knowing anything about the business. I wrote a story outline for a comedy about two European brothers. One stays in Europe and becomes an actor; the other goes to America, becomes an industrialist, dies, and leaves his two children and his industry to his younger brother. The actor arrives in the States knowing nothing about the factory he must take over, but he keeps the secretary his brother had, and she runs it for him. I thought of Marie Windsor, a fine comedienne, for the secretary.

Desi Arnaz liked the idea very much, and while I was in his office he called the network and their reaction was excellent. "Paul," he told me delightedly, "There's no problem. We have a deal!" And we shook hands on it.

Chasen at MCA was delighted, and he and Arnaz worked out a contract giving me both a very good salary and a percentage. I felt good about it. After all, there had been a year of no offers. This was 1948, a year after my trip to Washington.

But then there was silence. Chasen didn't call me, and Arnaz didn't call. When I tried to reach either one, he was in a meeting. Finally I went down to Chasen's office without an appointment and simply waited until he had to talk to me, though I must admit I did it with a sense of foreboding.

Reluctantly, Chasen told me, "It's no deal, Paul. Everything has fallen through. I don't know why, and I can't seem to get together with Desi to find out."

I was sure that he did know why, and that was why he had made so many excuses about seeing me. I went to Dore Schary, who was then head of production at MGM and who had always been a good friend, and I said, "Dore, we've been friends a long time . . . you're the godfather of my daughter. For heaven's sake, tell me the truth so I can orient my life. Am I or am I not blacklisted?"

He wet his lips and sighed. "Yes, Paul, you are," he told me heavily. "But please, don't tell anyone I told you, or I could lose my job."

"Why, Dore?" I asked tightly. "Why did they do this to me?"

"I don't know, Paul."

"It's because of that trip to Washington, isn't it?"

"I honestly don't know, Paul. I'm sorry."

"And all the others who went," I asked helplessly. "Huston, Kelly, Bacall, Bogart—what about them? They're still working."

"They all had studio contracts." He shrugged. "The studios will protect their own, Paul. You've got no one behind you. I'm sorry. I can't hire you, and I don't think anyone connected with a major studio would dare to."

That was it. I had been blacklisted for a year, and I had only now received confirmation. I was never to receive any more confirmation than that. I stayed on the blacklist for four more years, and during that time I couldn't get a job with any major studio or work in TV for any major network. MCA let me go as a client, and I went to Ingo Preminger, a dear friend and Otto Preminger's brother, a decent man who, as an agent, had taken care of many blacklisted Hollywood writers by getting them deals under different names or by finding other men and women to front for them. He pulled a lot of them through this bad time.

"I'll handle you, Paul," he told me. "but first let's get some lawyers and try to fight this blacklist business. I know a fine man in New York, William Feitelson. He represents United States Steel, and he knows his way around. Let's fly to New York and talk to him."

Preminger made all the arrangements, and we flew to New York and I told Feitelson the story. "I've done nothing political except take that trip to Washington," I assured him. "I belong to no organizations on the attorney's list, and I am not a Communist, nor have I ever been one. My God, on that trip some of the most respected Hollywood actors and actresses were with me, and most of them are still working!"

"We'll go after it at once and clear it up," Feitelson assured me. "I work with a fine attorney in Hollywood, Martin Gang, and the two of us will work on it."

They did, but neither one could ever find out why I was blacklisted, or even get an admission that I was. Then, after five years, just as mysteriously, my blacklisting was lifted and I was free once more to work for the studios.

I did do one film for a major studio very early during the years I was blacklisted, and that was partly because the blacklist was not completely in force, and partly because a very good friend, William Dieterle, was directing the picture for Hal Wallis at Paramount. Dieterle, one of Wallis' favorite directors, had done some movie classics. He was not only a great director, but a respected one and had considerable clout.

We were good friends, and at the very beginning of the black-list years, 1948, Lisl, without telling me, called Dieterle's wife and asked if he could possibly intervene and get me a part in his film *Rope of Sand.* She knew then what I had been reluctant to admit even to myself, that I would not be hired by any major studio.

Dieterle was a liberal person who thought the blacklist was a shameful thing, and Hal Wallis knew my work and liked it. In defiance of the blacklist, the two of them hired me. The part I got, however, was a departure from my old suave lover roles, and even from the swashbuckling *Spanish Main* pirate. I was cast as a sadistic and brutal guard at a diamond mine. But it was a part that had the greatest lines in the script, and I had a lot of fun doing it and received good reviews from the film critics. Burt Lancaster played the hero in this. He had been in films since 1946, but hadn't yet developed the fine acting style he showed some years later in *Come Back, Little Sheba.*

In terms of fun, it was one of the best pictures I ever made. Besides Burt Lancaster, my co-stars were Claude Rains and Peter Lorre as well as a new French actress making her American screen debut, Corinne Calvet. In terms of location, it was one of the worst. We went out to Yuma, Arizona, to shoot the desert scenes. There was no sandstorm in the script, but there was an awful one going on in Yuma when we arrived. Dieterle and Wallis thought it would be great to incorporate it into the picture during some of the scenes between Burt and me. As a result of this decision, they shot many of the scenes in the sandstorm. It was ghastly work. Our eyes and mouths would fill with sand, and they had to stop shooting con-stantly to let us clean them out. They even flew in a doctor from Los Angeles to wash out our eyes for us.

But after all these heroics they got back to the studio and discovered that a sandstorm didn't photograph properly. The winds were too fast for the camera, and the sand too fine to register. To solve this, they trucked a mess of sand into the studio and reshot all the closeup scenes there, using a wind machine!

After *Rope of Sand* I did a film with two independent producers, Eddy and Bill Nasseur, who also asked me to produce and direct. The film was about hazing in college. In the screenplay a young man refuses to go through the hazing of a fraternity initiation, and tries to escape the fraternity boys. His car crashes and he's killed. I played the part of a professor at the school, a man who crusades to abolish hazing.

I wanted to call the picture *Hell Night,* but the Breen Office objected to the use of "Hell" in a title, so the distributors decided on *For Men Only,* the title of the original story. It symbolized a fraternity, they told me, but I thought it came closer to symbolizing a men's room! To prove I was wrong, the producers wrote letters to many movie houses asking them what they thought of the title *For Men Only.* They all liked it except two theatres in Boston, who objected to the name. Yet later, billed as *For Men Only* at both these theatres, it was a smash hit!

All in all, the picture did very well in the first run, but the second run was a disaster. It was teamed on a double bill with a poor picture called *The Crimson Pirate,* with Burt Lancaster as the star. The marquee read, *For Men Only—The Crimson Pirate.* Everyone thought it was one picture, *The Crimson Pirate,* a film for men only. At any rate, both pictures did miserably, and I withdrew it and changed the title to *The Tall Lie.* It limped along, never making more than a modest profit after the first run.

Even with work denied to me at the major studios during the early fifties, I was quite busy with independent productions here and abroad.

Another job all of us did for the studios was the radio adaptations of our movies, and we also substituted in radio adaptations of other movies. They would try to get as many of the stars from a picture as they could for the radio show, but if they couldn't get all, they'd substitute another well-known actor. I would pick up five thousand dollars a shot for these appearances on the Lux Radio Theatre, and the blacklist didn't affect my demand.

There were other radio shows constantly available, and at one point Elmer Rice wrote a play just for radio. It was broadcast from the NBC studios at Rockefeller Center in Radio City, and I flew into New York to do it.

Elmer picked Lisl and me up at the airport, and we drove to the studio, rehearsed, and then had dinner together. After dinner we did the broadcast, and as I left the studio, Elmer grabbed me, his face white.

"What's wrong?" I asked, alarmed at his look.

"We have to be careful, Paul," he told me. "I've heard that mobs of fans are converging on the building. The police have blocked off Rockefeller Plaza."

"What do we do?" I asked nervously. I knew how threatening fans could be in their enthusiasm.

"We'll take the elevator down to the garage in the basement," he said, rushing us into it. But when we got down to the garage and the doors opened, we saw what seemed to be thousands of fans waiting. They let out a roar and rushed forward as the elevator operator slammed the doors.

"Where to?" he asked uneasily.

"The first floor," I answered. "If the crowd is down in the garage, we should be able to slip away easily." How wrong I was! At the first floor a dozen burly police in uniform were trying to hold back a pushing, screaming mob. Rice said, "Oh my God!" and before I could do anything, four of the policemen converged on me and literally lifted me up and bulldozed their way through the crowd.

The fans rushed me, screaming my name and reaching out to pull at me. My tie was ripped off, almost strangling me, my jacket and shirt torn and hanging in shreds as the police bundled me into the limousine.

"Where's Lisl?" I shouted to Elmer, who had come out behind the police and was standing there looking dazed.

"Oh no!" He turned back to the building. "Lock the car doors,

Paul. I'll find her." And he dashed off as I rolled up the limo's windows and locked the doors. The car rocked as the fans climbed on it, and I was terrified that the glass would be smashed and the car rolled over. It seemed forever before Elmer came back, dragging a terrified Lisl behind him. They crowded into the car as the police pushed the crowd back, and we drove off.

"What happened to you? Are you all right?" I asked Lisl.

"I'm all right, but look at you! Oh Paul, are you hurt?"

"No, I'm fine," I reassured her.

"The guards wouldn't let me in the front door," Elmer explained, "and I had to go around the side and show all kinds of identification."

"And they wouldn't let me out after you, Paul!" Lisl laughed almost hysterically. "I told them I was your wife, and one of them said, 'Sure, lady, that's what they all say.' "

The wildness of the fans in those days was unbelievable. The only things I've seen to compare with some of the crowd scenes when we made personal appearances were some of the rock concerts in the sixties. We had to hide constantly and sneak about town for fear we'd be recognized. Some fans were always on duty at the more popular clubs and restaurants, and if a star went inside, an instant grapevine would alert everyone in the city, it seemed, and they'd all descend with autograph books and cameras.

I got a respite from my fans after I played the sadistic villain in *Rope of Sand*. The majority sent notes that they were dissolving their clubs. Their hero had become a villain and they wanted nothing more to do with him.

Twenty-One

◆

Pirates and
The Merry Widow

*I*n 1951, when the blacklist had been in operation for almost three years, I got a call from Ed Lester, who had founded the Los Angeles Civic Light Opera Company. "I managed to get your unlisted phone number, Paul, because I thought it was better to talk to you privately than through an agent."

"About what?" I asked.

"You know *The Merry Widow*, that Viennese operetta?"

"Of course. Why?"

"Well, I'm going to do it out here, and I want you to play Danilo."

I agreed with some pleasure. I was anxious to get back on the stage, and Danilo is a fine part. For the female lead Lester had Mary Pickens, a buxom lady with a lovely mezzo-soprano voice, and the soprano part had to be transposed.

I had a good time rehearsing with Pickens, but less than a good time with Lester. There's a ball in the operetta, and traditionally, the Merry Widow comes in wearing black. After all, she's a widow, and the audience is told that by her black gown, the only one at the ball. In the time the operetta took place, widows wore black for a year of mourning after their husbands died.

When I saw our costumes, I realized that Lester had put her in white for the opening scene. In the final scene she was to wear black.

"It's wrong, Ed," I told him. "Believe me, it's wrong. I've seen the operetta in Vienna and I know about it. This is so wrong. . . . Now all you have to do is change the costumes around. Open with black and close with white. Another thing, though . . . her white dress against my white uniform has no contrast."

"I'll think about it," he promised, but this thinking didn't change his mind. At the dress rehearsal she wore white, and to my dismay the scenery was dark green, white, and brown. I shuddered and went to Lester again.

"Ed, if there's one critic who knows anything about the period the operetta takes place in, he'll tell you the colors were pink and pale blue, never brown and green! This looks like the forties not 1905."

"Oh Paul, come on! No one's going to notice that. You're too much of a perfectionist, and anyway, the set looks beautiful."

I shook my head. "Not to me, Ed. It's a dreary color. No ballroom in Europe is done in dark green." But in spite of my protests he wouldn't give in.

We opened in San Francisco, and I had the "I told you so" pleasure, however mean, of having the critics all seize on the exact points I had tried to get him to change. I also had the justification of reading in the reviews, "The only performance true to the play was Paul Henreid's." But there is very little satisfaction in such justification. I wanted the play to succeed.

Ed called a rehearsal the next day, and when I arrived he had the cast lined up and was telling them, "Don't believe the critics. I'm right about the play and they're wrong."

"But they're right and you're wrong," I wanted to tell him, but I kept my mouth shut. We had a wonderful subscription to the play, and in spite of the bad reviews it had a long run. Then, ten days before the San Francisco run ended and we were to go on to Los Angeles, I was hit with more concrete evidence of the blacklist. Ed came to me and said, "I'll have to replace you, Paul. Of course we'll pay your salary for the run of the contract."

"But why?" I was startled and bewildered.

He hemmed and hawed a bit, and finally came out and told me that the American Legion and the D.A.R. (The Daughters of the American Revolution) had threatened to picket the show in Los Angeles if I played Danilo. "I'm afraid you're on their shit list, Paul I don't know why." But I'm sure he did know.

I shrugged. "Shit list, blacklist, it's pretty much the same thing."

During the blacklist years the scavengers that always want to make some sort of profit descended. In *Rope of Sand,* the decency of Dieterle and Wallis in hiring me was offset by the studio's paying me only half of my usual fee. Other independent producers also came around offering me very low salaries, but with some I was able to bargain and get a percentage of the profits as well.

One independent producer, Robert L. Lippert, offered me a film called *Stolen Face.* He had connections with a London outfit that paid for the production. Lippert paid the stars' expenses and salaries, usually offering them a percentage of the film to make up for driving a hard bargain. I played the part of a plastic surgeon in *Stolen Face,* and husky-voiced Lizabeth Scott played a prostitute whose face was badly scarred. I fall in love with her and I give her a new beautiful face in the hope that it will change her character, but the plan doesn't work.

The success of *Stolen Face* prompted the Lipperts, father and son, to come up with another script, *Man in Hiding,* a detective film. Rex Harrison's third wife, Kay Kendall, played a small role in this film. Again my salary was small, and the percentage excellent, but the film was grade B; still, as Ingo Preminger pointed out, it was the only game in town.

A few weeks later he called to tell me that Columbia had formed an independent company called SK Pictures and would like me to do a pirate film for them. Columbia wouldn't hire me because of the blacklist, but SK was able to. I was offered the usual smaller salary, but a large percentage of the profits—if there were any.

I took the deal and co-starred with Jack Oakie in *Last of the Buccaneers.* The percentage deal got the independent company off the hook. If the picture was a flop, all they'd lose was my small salary. If it succeeded, they still had their percentage. It was a gamble for both of us, and with this picture the gamble paid off for me. *Last of the Buccaneers,* like *The Spanish Main,* was a huge success, and my percentage brought in an enormous amount of money.

With the success of the picture, Harry Cohn, the president of Columbia Pictures, called Ingo and asked if I was prepared to settle for a straight-out payment instead of my percentage. Ingo and I said absolutely not. After failing to buy me out, Columbia had SK hire me for another picture, *Pirates of Tripoli*, again with a percentage deal, and this too did extremely well.

After the second pirate picture, I was asked by a European producer to come to Munich and do a movie to be called *Cabaret*, the life story of a popular German composer.

In Munich, the Geisel-Gasteig Studios had been put together again, and they were now the largest studio in West Germany. Ufa was gone, and in its place was the New German Film Company in Munich. A former captain of the German Navy, Günther von Stapenhorst, who had been active in film productions before the war, directed the company. He had invited me to make *Cabaret*, and the original plan was that I would go to Munich to do the film, and Lisl and the children would follow. We would spend Christmas together in Munich.

Once there, we'd look around and see if we could be happy living in Germany. The blacklist was making it impossible for me to do any decent films in Hollywood, and I thought things might be different in Germany now. However, our plans collapsed when both children came down with influenza, and Lisl phoned that she just couldn't leave them with Lutzi. "And I don't feel so well myself, Paul. I think I'm coming down with it too. It's better if I stay here."

In the meantime Maria Schell, my co-star in *Cabaret*, had canceled out of the film because she felt her part wasn't big enough. I had mixed emotions about her leaving. I was unhappy because she was Germany's top star, and her playing opposite me would have been good for me, but on the other hand I wasn't impressed with her acting ability, and the woman who took her part, a newcomer from the stage, was supposed to be very talented.

The director of the picture, Willie Forst, had a reputation for being very modern in his approach. Unfortunately, he had made this reputation back in the thirties, and now I found his "modern" attitudes very old-fashioned. He was slow and ponderous and had a Prussian military streak of stubbornness. I didn't go along with this, but played my part my own way, and this forced others in the scene to play it my way too. Willie didn't like this, but I was the star and I stuck to my guns.

Willie would tell us, "We shoot tomorrow at nine. Everyone must be ready then." And he wouldn't appear until eleven o'clock. When this happened a second time, I went to him and said, "You were late filming and you kept us all waiting two hours. I think that's a childish thing to do. If you do it again, Willie, I too will be late."

"Oh no, it won't happen," he assured me and apologized profusely, but the next day he repeated the same trick, making the whole cast wait two hours.

That's enough of that, I decided, and the day after that I didn't show up until two in the afternoon. That settled things, and from then on he was on time, which was fine for me. I had to get back to the States to do still another pirate picture.

Cabaret, when it was finished, was a good job, and Günther von Stapenhorst liked it tremendously and offered me a fantastic deal. I could make three pictures a year at a fixed salary and 22 percent of the profit in Germany. I could be either the star, the producer, or the director, or I could do all three of the jobs or just two. My salary would increase in proportion. I could have my choice and total freedom to find my material, to decide what to do. He had seen *For Men Only* and was very impressed with it.

They had one story bought already, and they offered it to me, hoping I'd direct and star in it. However, the male lead was weak, and I said if I accepted it, I'd direct it, not play in it. I told Günther I'd let him know what I decided when I got back to Hollywood. "After all, it's a decision my wife and I must make together. Relocation is a serious business."

I thought about the offer all the way home, and when I arrived I talked it over with Lisl. "In a way it's a fantastic opportunity, and I must remember that here I'm crippled by the blacklist. On the other hand I'm sure that eventually the blacklist will be lifted and I'll be vindicated. I'll be a leading man again."

"But maybe it won't be lifted," Lisl said.

I was silent for a while, then I said, "The real reason that I'm holding back is that Germany is such a desolation after the war. Those bombed-out cities, the rubble—I sincerely doubt that they can ever build it up again. I think it's a doomed country, and I'd rather take my chances here."

Was it a wrong decision? Certainly I was dead wrong about Germany's ability to rebuild itself. I was also wrong about becoming a leading man again after the blacklist. I never came close to the heights of popularity I had reached before. In 1942 my fan mail at Warner Brothers topped all other stars on the lot, including Bette Davis and Humphrey Bogart. After the blacklist I was never again a box-office star. I might have made a new career as a star or producer-director in Germany, but I don't regret my decision. The United States had become my home, and I was still doing well here —I loved my home.

I arrived in Los Angeles on the flight from Munich at nine in the evening and found a regular welcoming committee at the airport. Lisl was there and with her were the wardrobe man and his assistant. The director was there too, and so was the producer of my new pirate picture, Sam Katzman.

"You'll have to excuse us," Sam explained as the wardrobe man hurried beside me. "We start shooting tomorrow, and we must fit you." And they dragged me off to the lot to be measured for my costumes, which had already been made, but needed some final adjustments. It was a good three hours before I could get home with Lisl and kiss my daughters.

Patricia Medina was the leading lady in *Siren of Bagdad*, the new pirate picture, and the director was Richard Quine. He wanted to do the film as a satire, a Chaplinesque burlesque of pirate films in general, and he succeeded. I was a little fed up with the swash-buckling life, and I went along and had a great deal of fun making it. All of us at the studio thought it would be great.

The preview at the Pickwick Theatre seemed to justify our expectations. Every situation joke worked, and the audience howled. I came out of the theatre beaming, and Katzman, Quine, and I congratulated one another on the very funny picture. The only one who looked unhappy was Sam Katzman's wife.

"What's the matter?" I asked her. "Didn't you like it?"

"Oh, I liked it. It was very funny," she said slowly, "but I just don't think you have a hit on your hands."

"But you heard them all laugh," her husband said.

"Yes, but that's the preview audience."

"All the audience cards are positive," Richard Quine said. "We've checked them through, and they really loved it."

Stubbornly, Mrs. Katzman said, "I just don't think it will be a success."

Annoyed, her husband brushed aside her predictions, but I was uneasy. Mrs. Katzman was no fool, and I took her aside later and asked her, "Why are you so sure it won't be a hit?"

"Why? Because people who go to pirate pictures want just that, a pirate picture. They aren't as sophisticated as this preview audience. They want their pictures to follow a strict formula. You can't kid around with them. They want it played straight. This picture pokes fun at the sacred formula—and I don't think they'll accept that."

As it turned out, she was absolutely right, and the rest of us were wrong. The picture was a flop!

The other pirate pictures, however, the ones we had treated seriously, were still running successfully, and my share of the percentage was making me wealthy. And then Ingo Preminger got a very threatening call from Harry Cohn, the head of Columbia Pictures.

"I want you to sell me all of Paul's interest in the pirate pictures," he told Ingo. "Columbia is going to buy those pictures from SK productions, and we don't want Paul in the deal as a shareholder. It would disturb our bookkeeping. We must have his percentages."

Once again Ingo said no, I didn't want to sell. In a flat voice, Cohn told him, "Then you'll please tell Paul that if he won't go along with this deal I personally will see to it that he never makes another picture in Hollywood as long as he lives, even after the blacklist stops. And believe me, I can do it, and I will!"

"Can he really do it?" I asked Ingo when he told me of Cohn's ultimatum.

"He can, Paul. This is dangerous stuff. When it comes to business, all these studio heads stick together. There's no doubt that if Cohn gives the word, they'll blacklist you forever." He shook his head and sighed. "I must advise you to take Cohn's offer."

I shrugged. "If you say I have no choice, Ingo, I'd better give in to his blackmail. You've done well for me during the blacklist, and I know you have my interests at heart. It makes my blood boil, but go ahead, make the deal."

A session of haggling started, and eventually I wound up with a very handsome price for my percentages. I asked that it be spread out over the years to avoid a heavy tax.

Columbia, after the flop of the last pirate picture, decided that since I had made four, and the last had been less than successful, there was no longer a market for them, but I was inclined to favor Mrs. Katzman's view—the audience didn't want a favorite formula tampered with.

It was around that time, 1954, that I was offered the lead in a Broadway play by Sam and Bella Spewack. They had turned out several scripts for Hollywood, but basically considered themselves playwrights. I read their play, *Festival,* and thought it was a pretty bad job, but I was eager to try the stage again, and I let my better judgment be persuaded by that desire. I told the Spewacks that if they rewrote certain parts of the play, I'd do it, and they agreed. But at the first rehearsal I discovered that they had done no substantial rewriting at all. I was angry, but legally committed. They had "discovered" an untalented leading lady for me, and it took a week to have her fired, and another week to persuade Betty Field to do the part.

We opened in Boston, and, as they say, we bombed. Still, I received some notices that at least boosted my ego. The Boston *Herald* called me "an actor of undeniable ability and poise," and the Boston *Post* decided I was "suave and handsome," those tired old clichés again! But as for the play, it was best forgotten. It limped into New York, and again the reviews praised me and damned the play.

I didn't like the play, and I didn't like the Spewacks. Sam had an annoying habit of waiting just inside the theatre lobby until I hailed a cab and then popping out and asking brightly, "Oh Paul, are you going my way?" then bumming a free ride.

The night before we opened he did this, and as we rode uptown he asked brightly, "Don't you think the play is going to be an absolute triumph tomorrow?"

I stared at him as if he were mad, then I said, "I'd think so—if we had a play." But it didn't faze him. He laughed, thinking I had made a very funny joke.

The failure of *Festival* deepened my conviction that the Broadway stage was not for me, and I returned to Hollywood and the search for independent producers not affected by the blacklist. I did several films in London for expenses; little pay but ownership of the United States and Canadian rights. Later, television bought them for a substantial amount.

I don't know whether it was fear of our income going down, or the fact that our children were now older and Lisl had more time, but in 1955 she decided that she would start a cotillion for young people, a school that could also function as a social club.

"It's hard to believe that a place like Hollywood has nowhere that boys and girls can meet each other and learn some social graces," she told me as she explained her idea.

"If it's money you're worried about," I said, "we're managing very well."

"Maybe, but the house is getting more and more expensive to run, and with taxes going up—no, let me try this, Paul."

Lisl found a beautiful studio in Santa Monica and started her dance club, but it didn't work out. With all the money in Hollywood, parents were still reluctant to send their children to a dancing school. "It's not only old-fashioned," they told Lisl, "but we have such beautiful backyards. The kids can get enough social activity by having their friends over to play."

Finally Lisl decided that instead of a school she would approach a hotel and rent a ballroom. "I'll have balls and dances for children."

"That's a good idea," I agreed. "The parents who bring their kids can go to the bar and booze up. That's Hollywood's great activity. They can even take rooms at the hotel and have a quick fling while the children dance."

"Paul, you're too cynical."

I said, "Maybe," but I reminded her that only a little while ago at a friend's party one of Hollywood's leading ladies had suggested that I go off with her for an hour's "quickie." "No one would miss us," she assured me. I had apologized and explained that I couldn't make love "on demand."

But in spite of my poking fun at Lisl's idea, it caught on. The mothers were very interested, and the hotel we picked, the Beverly Wilshire, was interested too. The woman who owned it and ran it then, Mrs. Sharp, cooperated fully because it gave the hotel some good publicity. The dances, called cotillions, were held once a month from three P.M. to midnight, in three divisions—first, small children, then pre-teens, and finally teenagers. In between the cotillions there were dancing lessons at the hotel to prepare and practice for the big night. Cookies and punch were served at these sessions.

I was surprised and delighted at Lisl's success, though with her "track record" in business ventures I should have been prepared for it. One afternoon, watching the dancing class, I asked one young boy, "Do you enjoy the lessons?"

He looked at me as if I were crazy. "Nah, I only come for the cookies and punch—and because my mother makes me!"

At the cotillions, trophies were given out to the best dancers, and of course the parents were drawn in to dance with their sons and daughters. The stars whose children attended the cotillions were among the top in the industry. They included June Allyson, Dick Powell, Lloyd Bridges, Carol Burnett, Jackie Coogan, Robert Cummings, Bette Davis, Jimmy Durante, Bonita Granville, Charlton Heston, Bob Hope, Burt Lancaster, Jerry Lewis, Art Linkletter, James Mason, and on and on.

The cotillions went on for fifteen years, from 1960 until 1975; they had been started five years after the dancing school failed. In all that time, say what you will about juvenile delinquents and modern kids, we never had the slightest trouble with the children.

Some parents were a different matter. One Hollywood matron brought her young son and took Lisl aside before she registered him.

"Do you have any Jewish children here?"

"What are you talking about?" Lisl asked, freezing up instantly. "I don't ask the kids their religion. They're here to learn how to dance, not pray!"

The woman looked around uneasily and spotted one dark-haired, olive-skinned child with a thoughtful expression. "I do see Jewish faces," she said. "I can always recognize them."

"You have quite a gift," Lisl told her and called over the child. He was a Doheny, a youngster from one of Los Angeles' oldest families. "This is the mother of one of the boys who won't be attending our school," Lisl said as she introduced him. That ended the interview, but a few weeks later Lisl was shopping in a Jewish delicatessen in Beverly Hills, and there at one of the tables she saw this woman with a friend.

"How nice to see you," Lisl said, stopping at the table.

The woman introduced Lisl to her friend. "Won't you sit down?"

"Thanks, no. I'm in a hurry, but you know, you shouldn't eat here."

"Why not?" the woman asked, startled.

Lisl looked around, then bent down and in a stage whisper said, "Don't you realize this is a Jewish restaurant? You'd better pay and go!"

When the cotillions stopped after fifteen years, it was not because they had lost popularity, but because the hotel had changed management, and the new manager raised the rentals to the point where there was no profit to be made from the affairs.

◆

Twenty-Two

The Blacklist Ends

*O*ne of the movies I directed during the blacklist period was called *Acapulco*. It was a good script, the story of a man shell-shocked in World War II who gets married and comes to Acapulco with his bride on their honeymoon. Once there, the shell shock recurs.

I had been asked to direct by the producer, a man who had never produced a film before. Republic Pictures Corporation was to distribute it, a fact that I didn't know when I signed the contract. Republic had always done "B" pictures, and Herbert J. Yates, the studio's head, had agreed to back the picture provided I directed and co-starred in it as the police inspector.

It was a good character role, but I had to find a male and female lead. I had seen an exciting picture done by Ralph Meeker, one of MGM's upcoming stars, and I managed to get him for *Acapulco*, then I signed up Janice Rule for his wife. What I didn't know was that they had done a play together in New York and had scrapped all the way through it. My friends, when they heard what I had done, told me I was crazy. "They'll fight all over the set!" But as it turned out, they got along famously.

The picture went well, and I was very pleased with the final cut. In my enthusiasm I asked a friend, Franz Waxman, to do the score for the picture. He said if it was as good as I seemed to think, he'd do it for royalties alone, with no down payment. I showed him the print and he liked it very much and agreed.

Since the husband and wife in the film were Americans, I felt that the main score should be modern American music. When the locale shifted to Mexico, the bar or the street, then the music should be Mexican. Waxman agreed, and I was excited when I went in to see Yates, the head of Republic. "I have some very good news," I announced. "I showed the film to Mr. Waxman and he's willing to score it for a royalty and no advance."

I had always gotten along with Herbert Yates, and I felt that he respected my work and judgment, but now, to my astonishment, he asked, "Who gave you permission to show the film to Waxman?"

"My producer, Mr. Bach," I answered, puzzled at his tone.

"But Mr. Bach has no right to give you that permission. I'm head of this studio. This film is my property!"

"I'm sorry," I said slowly. "I didn't realize you felt that way."

"I certainly do," he said tightly, "and what's more, Waxman won't do this film. I want a completely Mexican score."

And that was that! He got Les Brown to do a score I felt was all wrong, and I believed it ruined the picture. An incident like that can break a director's heart.

Lisl and the two girls came down to Mexico City and Acapulco when we went on location to film the picture. Monika was twelve and Mimi was ten, two lovely children. Mimi was thrilled with Acapulco, particularly with the water skiing. A natural-born athlete, she took to any sport with an instinctive ability. She was a born tennis player and at fifteen, in the "15 years old or under" class, she became the number-one woman player in America on a hard court, and the number-two player on a clay court!

But then, at ten, water-skiing was her great love, and I had some fine footage taken of her skiing across the water at Acapulco, and then we used the footage in the movie *Acapulco* under the titles. I gave Monika equal time; at twelve she was beautiful and had a lovely little figure. I had her running into the water with one of the local boys for another title sequence. It set the atmosphere for the beginning of the picture.

Then one day in 1955, I got an unusual phone call. A hoarse, asthmatic voice said, "I saw a film you directed, Mr. Henreid, and you did a fine job of it. You should be working for me."

I recognized Alfred Hitchcock's distinctive rumble, and I asked, "What picture, Mr. Hitchcock?"

"*For Men Only.* I talked to Louis B. Mayer and he loved it too, and he wants you to come to work for him, to be a stock director at MGM."

"But—but the blacklist . . ." I stammered.

Hitchcock chuckled. "I think that's over, Mr. Henreid, and high time. But I advised your agent against Mr. Mayer's offer. I want you to work for me instead, and I'd like you to do my next television film."

I was overwhelmed. After five years the major studios were beginning to want me again—not as an actor, but as a director. "I've never directed television," I protested weakly. "I don't know if I can work that fast."

"If I can do it, you can do it," he breathed huskily. And that was that. I decided to take him up on his offer and go into television work. But was the blacklist really over, or was Hitchcock just saying that?

I got in touch with Ingo and he called William Feitelson, the lawyer who had been fighting the blacklist for me, and Feitelson said to him, "I think Paul is all right now."

I believed him when Dore Schary called me shortly after that and asked me to do a guest-star appearance as Flo Ziegfeld in a film at MGM about Sigmund Romberg.

Lisl and I had our own celebration, then I wrote both Feitelson and Gang, thanking them for what they had done and asking them what their fee was. Amazingly, both wrote back, each in his own way, saying that it had been an honor to represent me in this type of fight, and they both felt my case was important in terms of freedom in America and they would not dream of accepting any payment for their work.

I was very touched by the letters, and now when I reread them I can't help but think of what Frederic March went through in his fight and the money it eventually cost him—and still he failed to clear his name.

As Hitchcock had predicted, Louis B. Mayer sent me an offer, but I turned it down. The salary he suggested wasn't very good, and I would have had no choice of pictures. The blacklist was over, and I was sure that other offers would come my way. I felt that I would have a new career now—and I did, but not in the direction I thought it would take.

My five years of being blacklisted from all the major studios had cut off much of my box-office value as a star. The public forgets very quickly, and today's star can be tomorrow's has-been. Besides, I realized that I was almost fifty years old, a little long in the tooth for the suave, romantic lover. But, most important of all, I had had a taste of directing, and I loved it. The new career I was to make had to lie in that field.

I became a director for Hitchcock, and also for Review, the company MCA founded to produce television features. The first ten major directorial assignments I got were for *Alfred Hitchcock Presents, The General Electric Theatre,* and *The Schlitz Playhouse of Stars.* Review very quickly mushroomed into a monstrous outfit, until the government stepped in a year or two later and forced them to divorce themselves from the agency business.

Give up one or the other, the government directed. You've become a monopoly. They gave up the agency, and Review then bought Universal Studios.

To me, the basic difference between directing a movie and directing a television show is time and the quality of the writing. It was the reason I hesitated when Hitchcock first approached me. When you direct an "A" picture in Hollywood and do three pages of script in a day, you're a hero to the front office. To be a hero in television, you must do at least twelve pages a day. It goes so fast that you rarely have time for careful work.

There is also the matter of material. Television is a fearful gobbler-up of material. It's a monster that eats up scripts. When I started with Hitchcock, the material available was all first-class, good short stories in the suspense genre, the cream of the literature. In the second year there were fewer stories available because we had used all the good ones up, and in the third year we were reaching for the dregs. Then we were forced to use original scripts, never as good as the classics. In the fourth year, the scripts were all original, the calibre at its lowest.

Television uses so much that it devours all that is good very quickly, and there just isn't enough talent available to fill its gigantic maw. Thousands and thousands of feet of film must be produced each year, and even with reruns to eat up some time, there just is not enough talent around to produce what the box needs.

Fortunately we had access to the best actors and actresses, and as I directed them I began to believe whether true or not, that the best actors and actresses were American, the next-best Austrian; after them came the French, and fourth in line were the English. At least that was how it seemed to me in the mid-fifties. Things have changed now, and English actors are looser and fresher and less stylized.

While working for Hitchcock I got one script that I thought was excellent. It was based on a *New Yorker* short story, and was called *The Crooked Road*. Reading it, I thought of a yet unknown actor I had seen in New York, and I realized he'd be perfect for the part of the sheriff. His name was Walter Matthau. The entire film, I thought excitedly, could be shot from the point of view of two people in a car who are stopped by the sheriff. It would require plates for back projection and point-of-view shots, and I'd have to bring my New York discovery, Matthau, out to the coast—altogether an expensive deal.

I told Joan Harrison, the producer of the Hitchcock show, what I wanted, and she was doubtful. "That means a lot of money. I'll have to talk it over with Hitch."

That same evening Hitch called me. "Let me understand this. You want to shoot the whole show from the point of view of the couple in the car, the couple stopped by the police?"

I said, "Right. I don't want to show anything else but what they see, except for some establishing shots. You see, in the story they're FBI, investigating the town, and the chief crook is the sheriff. I want to show what the report they make to the authorities will be, and this young actor Matthau is going to be great in the part."

"And expensive," Hitch added drily.

"And expensive," I agreed.

He chuckled, then said, "An excellent idea. If it works it should be fabulous. I'll tell Joan to go ahead."

"You won't be sorry," I assured him.

"The only thing I'm sorry about is that I didn't come up with the idea first," he said thoughtfully. "You know, I've a good mind to take it away from you and do it myself. It's such a good idea."

"You wouldn't do that!"

"No, I guess I wouldn't."

The next day I told Joan, and she asked Matthau to come out. He was delighted with the offer, and he did a superb job. It was a joy to watch and direct him. In discussing his role, I said, "You should never push anyone around physically. Just show your meanness by the way you lie, by the edge in your voice and eye. Do you know what I mean?"

"Absolutely," he agreed, and he played it just that way, with a supressed violence that never surfaced. The final show turned out to be a classic of its kind, and it's still listed as one of the best TV scripts ever done.

Hitchcock and I had different views about directing. I have heard him say that actors are like cattle. "Prod them in the right direction and they'll go that way."

Hitch never came on the set when I was directing, but at a dinner party at Joan Harrison's one evening, he told me that to his way of thinking, acting was the third element in order of importance in any show.

"What are the first two?" I asked.

He pursed up his lips and in that deep, throaty voice of his, said, "Script first, directing second."

"But what can the best director do with bad actors?" When he didn't answer, I pushed it. "If a good actor has a good script, he can do something with it no matter how bad the director. If the director is good and the script is bad, you're in trouble. But if the actor is bad, even with a good script and a good director your film at best is mediocre."

"No, no, Paul! Without a proper directorial approach and point of view, a first-class job is impossible."

I shrugged at that. "Hitch, you know you never get just one point of view. Maybe someone with your clout could do it—you'd have approval of the final cut, possibly—though I don't think it's likely. In this TV industry, it's a question of who comes after the director and what he does to the final print."

When he shook his head in disagreement, I said, "I was in a movie theatre where they showed *Song of Love,* a film I was in, and the projectionist got the reels out of order. That disordered showing was the final product, and who, director, scriptwriter, or actors, had control over that? It's the people who take over after you finish—even a projectionist—who can change your point of view and your approach."

I thought I had a good argument there, but Hitchcock was unconvinced, and perhaps at his level, and at the level of directors like Stanley Kubrick, Billy Wilder, and John Ford, a point of view that no one could damage was possible. For those of us lower down in the directorial ranks there was no guarantee that someone would not step in at the last minute and change our point of view and approach. It had happened to me often enough.

As television expanded, I was asked to do other programs. The Goodyear Theatre asked me to do several episodes, one with Maximilian Schell that established him as a solid actor and gave him a crack at a part in *Judgment at Nuremberg.*

Warner Brothers eventually decided to make hour-long films for TV, and the first series they chose was something called *Maverick,* a Western with two engaging young actors, James Garner and Paul Kelly. Roy Huggins, who had thought up the series and produced it, hired me as the director. Huggins was a good writer and a fast one. I've seen him take a bad script and rewrite it overnight.

In 1959, in addition to *Maverick,* I was directing a series called *Cheyenne* and two or three other series at Warners. In between these directing jobs, Ingo Preminger called to ask if I would like to do a movie again.

I took time off my directorial chores to do a picture with Frank Sinatra and Gina Lollobrigida called *Never So Few.* The filming went well, with absolutely no hitches, and Sinatra and I got along beautifully. Then, one night after the filming was over, Lisl and I went out. All the servants had driven home, and Lutzi was left alone in the house.

Suddenly the doorbell rang, and Lutzi went to the door but wouldn't open it. "Who's there?" she asked distrustfully.

"It's Frank Sinatra. Can I see Mr. Henreid?"

"No, you can't," she snapped, then, softening a bit, she added,

"They're all out, and I'm not opening the door to anyone I don't know."

In a mild voice, Frank said, "That's very wise of you. I have a book for Mr. Henreid, and I'll leave it on the doorstep. I'll walk away and when I'm gone you can open the door and pick it up."

He walked off and left a beautifully boxed, leather-bound copy of the screenplay for *Never So Few.*

Almost all of the roles I was offered in the years that followed the blacklist only strengthened my determination to stick to directing. Most were forgettable parts in very ordinary, if not downright awful, films. I did *Holiday for Lovers* in 1959, and *Ten Thousand Bedrooms* in 1960, but my real interest lay in my directing assignments in television.

And then, at the height of my television directing career, when I was doing more work than any other director in Hollywood, my entire career suddenly collapsed. It happened when we were doing a segment of *Wagon Train* out in the Valley in winter. The mornings were ice-cold and the days stifling hot. I had been working hard, too hard, driving myself to meet the ever-growing payments on our enormous house. I had taken job after job, regardless of how good or bad the script was. I needed the money, but I also found a security in so much work after so many lean years.

I began to have trouble sleeping during the filming, and one morning I woke up with a raging fever and a full-blown case of influenza. The episode was almost finished, and I stubbornly refused to turn it over to anyone else but stayed with it until it was completed. My doctor had given me shots of antibiotics to protect me against pneumonia, but afterward, when I went to see him, he shook his head uneasily. "I don't know what's going on, Paul. Your fever is down. You should be better."

"I should be, but I'm not," I told him. "I'm still wheezing and coughing, and I'm up half the night. I don't want to become dependent on drugs to sleep."

He shrugged. "What more can I tell you? Your flu is cured, and I think you're just tired."

I was tired, but even after I had rested, the wheezing and

congestion continued, and I couldn't draw a breath of air without a struggle. That, plus a general lassitude, made me turn down assignment after assignment, and I began to worry.

Lisl suggested a psychiatrist, a friend of hers. "You have been under a lot of tension these past years, Paul. If the doctor says you're cured, perhaps this is all psychosomatic."

I couldn't believe that, but in desperation I tried the psychiatrist. After three visits he dismissed me. "Whatever is wrong with you, Mr. Henreid, I can't cure. Your mental health seems fine. You might benefit from analysis—anybody would, but that's not the answer to your problem. It strikes me that your symptoms are more like an allergy. Let me recommend a good allergist I know."

The allergist decided I was allergic to everything—dust, pollen, mold, cotton, feathers, hair, wool. . . . "How can I live, and where?" I asked him desperately. "In a tent?"

Very seriously, he shook his head. "That wouldn't do it. You're allergic to linen too."

What he finally prescribed was an iodine preparation to be taken orally. I took it religiously until I, my clothes, and everything I came in contact with reeked of iodine—but my difficulty in breathing remained as bad as ever.

At that time Lisl asked me to one of her cotillions to take some pictures for her brochure. I've always had a flair for photography, and one of Lisl's students, a twelve-year-old girl, was a delight to photograph and watch. She was very fond of me, and when she heard about my illness she said, "You must go to my father. He's a wonderful doctor and can cure anything."

Why not, I thought, grasping at any straw, and I paid her father a visit. He was a German refugee who had fled Hitler to come to America, and he shook his head when I told him about my problem. "I'd like to help you, Mr. Henreid, because, like my daughter, I'm a great fan of yours, but alas, I'm a urologist. If your prostrate gives you trouble, I'm your man, but allergies . . ."

I was about to leave, very depressed, when he stopped me at his office door. "You know, allergies may be your problem, but I think age has something to do with it too. I've found that at your age overwork often damages the immune system. I've had a lot of older patients who've had difficulty breathing, and I've found that very small doses of cortisone will help. If you would like to try it . . ."

"I'll try anything," I told him, and he gave me a prescription. To my amazement, the cortisone worked a miracle. I was suddenly able to breathe, and my entire outlook on life altered. I was no longer half dead and dragging my feet. I felt spry and ready to return to work at once.

When I went back to the urologist, he nodded with pleasure. "Your chest is clear and you look perfect. I think we can stop the drug now."

Alarmed, I said, "I don't think so. I have a feeling the cortisone has saved me, and I should continue."

"Well," he said doubtfully, "some people react to the steroid badly. I'll put you on a minimal dosage, but we'll have to watch you for any side effects."

I watched and he watched, but as long as I took the drug there were no side effects and my breathing was normal. I've stayed on the cortisone to this day, and expect to be on it for the rest of my life.

Twenty-Three

I Direct
<u>Dead Ringer</u>

In 1960 I had a part in *The Four Horsemen of the Apocalypse,* a remake of the picture that had introduced Rudolph Valentino as a star. Vincent Minnelli directed it, and it was done for MGM. Most of the picture was shot in Paris, my favorite city, and I thoroughly enjoyed it. There were some excellent actors in the film. Lee J. Cobb played the grandfather of a wealthy Argentine family. Charles Boyer was one of the sons, and Robert Wagner was another. I was the husband of Ingrid Thulin, who played the daughter. In the film I go to war and come back a beaten prisoner of the Nazis to find that my wife has fallen in love with Glenn Ford.

Minnelli was the most meticulous director I ever worked with. Everything he shot had to be important. There was one brief scene where I leave for war and Ingrid takes me to the train. She stays there until it pulls out and we kiss, then she's left alone in tears. End of scene.

The scene starts with everyone boarding the train, and Minnelli prepared everything with exacting care. Each extra was given a scenario and motivation. One heartbroken mother had to hold her baby up for her husband to kiss. Nuns with small children were boarding the train to be evacuated from Paris, and Minnelli went into all the justifications for their departure. There were Senegalese troops, and he explained their attitude toward the French. Each extra was rehearsed for a full day, and everyone had his own little story worked out.

But when the scene was finally shot, the camera panned and dollied to Ingrid and me walking to my compartment, and the dialogue was played on the walk and in front of my coach, all done relatively close. All the little scenarios around us were lost; the rehearsed, beautiful little bits never noticed, and what little was seen didn't register because the focus was on Ingrid and me!

But that was how Minnelli worked. He never took chances. He wanted every part perfect, but in spite of his perfectionist attitude he was a very pleasant man to work with. The best part of the picture, for me at least, was the long period of time we spent on location in Paris, all of us put up at very good hotels.

The main faults with the picture were the two stars, Glenn Ford and Ingrid Thulin. Both were good actors, but totally wrong for their parts. Valentino, in the original, had a lusty quality of mad desire that made it all believable. The audience felt that he could not help himself. Alice Terry, who played opposite him, had the same vitality. In that early version of the story the two were drawn to each other in joy and passion. They couldn't stop, and their destruction was all the more shocking.

Ingrid Thulin, however, had a wonderful quality of vulnerability and uncertainty. She was magnificent in the films she did with Bergman, but in this she was all wrong. Ford, too, played his part with reticence and with out passion; he was a "pebble kicker."

I don't think Minnelli understood what these two watered-down performances did to the picture because I am sure he could have directed them differently. But he was so enchanted with their acting—and they were good, just not right for the parts—that he lost sight of the overall film. Minnelli had always been at his best in those wonderful MGM musicals. This picture was just not his métier.

As for me, I left after the picture was finished and started in on a television project. They called me back for some final shots that they wanted to add, but I couldn't leave my TV commitment. I was pretty unhappy about that because the call-back would have paid me as much as the TV job.

My TV work, which had mushroomed so in the late fifties, continued during the sixties, but somehow we did manage to get away for an occasional vacation. Sometimes it was combined with the shooting of a film, and sometimes it was on our own.

In 1961, Lisl and I decided that we would take the two girls, Monika, a lovely eighteen-year-old, and Mimi, an equally lovely sixteen, on a tour of Europe. In the course of it we dropped in to visit Oona and Charles Chaplin. Oona had written us a very sweet letter inviting us to stay a week with them in Switzerland. "And of course bring the girls. We would love to see them. Charlie says to be sure to tell you he can't wait to see you."

Such generosity from Charles was a surprise. We had always been close friends of Charles and Oona, and we were familiar with and tolerant of the two sides of Charles' nature. On the one hand he was an extremely generous man, especially to his friends and his servants; on the other hand he had a peculiarly stingy streak. When he married Oona O'Neill, Eugene O'Neill's daughter, he didn't change. He still held on to possessions until they fell apart. He was an extremely rich man, but rather than replace a worn carpet he would put an ashtray over the hole to warn people and keep them from stumbling. He hated redecorating or remodeling because of the money it cost, and he was not exactly generous about inviting people to his home or treating them when he went out.

We suspected that when he left America, Oona put her foot down and said, "I'll go to Europe with you if you promise to lead a different sort of life. You certainly have enough money to afford it!"

And so he did. He gave her the freedom to buy the house she wanted and furnish it as she pleased. She bought a beautiful estate on Lake Geneva with tennis courts and swimming pool, greenhouses and garages—an enormous place, and Charles would drive you around it proudly in his new Bentley instead of his old Ford convertible. We were stunned when we saw the estate and realized the luxury old Charles was living in.

He met us at the door and shook my hand and kissed Lisl. "Well, what do you think of it?" He waved his hand expansively to include the vast estate and all the buildings. "Now I'm really rich, Paul. Do you know what I made last year? Seven million dollars! And all tax-free. Those stupid Americans could have had at least seventy percent of that money if they hadn't thrown me out for being a red! Here I can earn as much as I want. My re-runs alone bring in a constant supply of money."

In the afternoon, when we were sitting out on the lawn with Oona and the girls, he said to Mimi, my professional tennis player, "We might have a little game. Will you beat me again?"

She grinned and said, "Yes, Mr. Chaplin. You know I will." And she did.

We stayed with them for a week, and we couldn't get over the incredible change in Charles. He had finally overcome his poverty-stricken childhood and was learning to live in a style that measured up to his fortune. The furnishings in the house were exquisite, the carpets the best, the linen the finest, the silver, crystal, chairs, servants—everything was first-rate.

The little Chaplin girls had settled into their new life very comfortably. They all spoke French fluently, and little Victoria played the guitar and sang French songs with a lovely voice. Charles, admiring her, would pretend to be upset. "Goddamn it, Paul, here I am, an Englishman, and I don't understand my children at all. They speak nothing but French!"

The second day of our visit, after Mimi had beaten Charles unmercifully in two love sets of tennis, he came to us beaming with a brilliant idea. "This is the day the tennis pro who teaches us comes. I hate that man. He never lets me win a game, but I have a great plan. We'll play doubles, you and I, Mimi, against Paul and the pro!"

He was so excited about the idea that he could hardly wait until the pro arrived, and when he did I understood his resentment. The man was an arrogant, Prussian type of professional tennis coach who always went by the book, fair or unfair.

"We'll have a set of doubles," Charles told him eagerly. "You can play with Paul, he's very good, and I'll play with—let's see—oh yes, little Mimi." He emphasized the "little" because although Mimi was sixteen, she looked fourteen.

The coach agreed, rather smugly, smiling at me in anticipation of a real killing. Charles, in great excitement, rang a bell he kept on the grounds, a signal for everyone to assemble. The entire household —servants, children, and Oona—came running. "You've all got to watch the game," Charles announced. "Paul and the pro are playing me and the child."

And the game started—and was a complete massacre. Mimi and a gleeful Charles won every set, and the pro became more and more bewildered. I play a fair game, but we were no match for Mimi, and finally, utterly chastened, the coach left in a silent huff, and Charles was almost hysterical with laughter.

One evening in 1962, some time after we had all returned from our European tour, I was invited to dinner at the home of Emmet Lavery, the author of *The First Legion,* a film about the Jesuits. It had been a play originally, and I had been slated to play in it back in Vienna before Reinhardt let me go, and at the dinner Emmet and I were comparing notes about the Viennese stage. There was a Jesuit priest at dinner that night, Father Gerald E. Lucy, and we hit it off very well and had a long, pleasant discussion. We became good friends after that, and whenever Emmet invited us to his home, he'd invite Father Lucy too.

One evening Father Lucy said, "I hesitate to ask you, Paul, and if you haven't got the time to do it I'll understand, but we're giving a religious play at Loyola at Easter. . . ."

"What play?" I asked.

"What would you like to stage for us?"

"What about *Everyman?* In the von Hofmannsthal version, of course. That's the same version as the one done in Salzburg."

Father Lucy was delighted. "Could you really do that?" he asked. "I've seen the Salzburg production and it has an enormous cast."

"Let me try to put together a first-class cast with superb music. I'd like to renew and restage the Salzburg version. It's a long time since Rinehardt did it, and a lot of poor directors have changed things around. I saw it two years ago, and it was rather bad." I thought a moment or two and then said, "I'll ask my stock company."

"Stock company? Do you really have one?" he asked in surprise.

"I call my favorite actors that, the ones I work with in TV. I know them and they're all very good. They'd have to give me extra time after work, of course. I assume this would all be free of charge?"

Father Lucy nodded. "What about musicians to write the score and play it? Would they be free of charge too? And what about costumes?" He smiled. "You know, MGM likes Loyola. We've often let them shoot on our grounds. I'm sure they'd lend us costumes."

I wasn't that sure, but he was right. When I called the studio head, he said, "Of course. All you have to do is pay the man who supervises costumes."

"Can't you do that?" I suggested, "and make it a deductible donation?"

"A good idea," he agreed. "I'll have the legal department work it out with Father Lucy."

That worked, and we got the costumes at no cost to Loyola. The actors who agreed to do the play were all excited about it because it was such a radical departure from what they were doing. Vic Morrow, who had worked in many of the TV series I directed, was the one I chose to play Everyman, but he was scared at the idea, even though he wanted to do it.

"Hey, Paul, I started as a delinquent in *The Blackboard Jungle,* but I've never done a classic, never."

I said, "Vic, did you ever want to play Hamlet?"

"Of course, every actor does."

"Then just think of Everyman as Hamlet," I told him, "and then play it as Hamlet."

"Can I do that?" he asked, surprised.

"If you trust me."

"Well, why not? I've trusted you in every show we did together."

I said, "Fine, but you have to give me a definite answer now. I won't be able to replace you if halfway through you decide that you can't play the part."

"I won't let you down," he promised, and he didn't. He struggled over the part for the first week, and then he got even and easy. We cut scenes he felt uncomfortable with, and we worked over his lines till they were smooth.

Then, a few days after rehearsals started, Father Lucy wrote me a brief note. "Please don't allow smoking or coffee drinking in the chapel proper even though the blessed sacrament is removed."

I simply couldn't believe the letter, but I got in touch with him and said, "Let's call the play off!"

"But Paul, no! Why on earth do that?" he asked anxiously.

"Because I cannot and will not ask these actors not to smoke or drink coffee. I'm a Catholic too, Father, and I don't consider those practices sinful. These actors work at the TV studio until six, grab a bite to eat, and hurry here to donate their time, and they work until midnight! You want me to ask them not to take coffee or cigarette breaks? No. I won't do it, so you make up your mind. Do you or don't you want a play?"

"Give me a few moments, Paul," he said anxiously, "and don't, please don't do anything rash!"

I realized then that the letter had been dictated by someone higher up, and I felt better about that. Father Lucy called me back in a few minutes and said, "It's all right, Paul. I've straightened everything out." He laughed a bit. "All the wicked coffee drinking and smoking you want!"

I had assembled an excellent cast. My daughter, Monika, had developed into a most promising actress. I asked her to play the part of Good Deeds, and she did a fine, moving job.

When the play began to shape up I was immensely pleased. Reinhardt had done it in Salzburg in an open-air theatre. Here, in the church, there was a different atmosphere, almost an air of mystery. I had a record of the bells of St. Florian, a town famous for its bells. When all the churches in town ring their bells together, the effect is magnificent. I had placed loudspeakers all over the church, and I had put the record on tape. Once the audience was seated, the lights dimmed and the bells started to ring, softly at first, then louder and louder until the sound was tremendous.

When the church was completely dark, and the sound was at its loudest, a light picked out a crucifix onstage. Then the bells faded away and there was a knocking at the church door. The voice of God said, "Come in," and a costumed figure came down the aisle, climbed the stage and spoke the prologue. With his words the music, brilliantly composed and conducted by Gerald Fried, started, delicate and dainty, the light faded and the voice of God started the play.

The play was a smash even though we gave only five performances. Vic Morrow, who had been so unsure of his participation, received fantastic notices from the top Los Angeles critics.

While I was still directing Hitchcock material, Bette Davis did a show for him. Joan Harrison assigned me to the picture, and it was the first time I directed Bette. She was remarkably easy to work with, intelligent and very quick to grasp what you had in mind.

In the early sixties, neglected by the studios, Bette had dropped out of popularity, but then she made a comeback in a picture with Joan Crawford called *What Ever Happened to Baby Jane?* It was extremely successful, and suddenly Bette became "hot" again.

Jack Warner wanted to repeat the success of *Baby Jane,* and he asked me to direct her in an old script they had, *Dead Ringer,* provided Bette liked it. She did, and was delighted that I was going to direct it. "You're as good as Willie Wyler," she told me, but I knew that was her usual extravagance.

In *Baby Jane* there is a scene where Bette brings Joan Crawford a special dish on a silver salver with a silver cover. Crawford is excited and happy and lifts the lid, expecting a delicacy, only to find a dead rat! The rat became the hit of the film. It was so shocking that everyone talked about it, and people saw the movie just to be horrified by that scene.

Jack Warner wanted me to do something similar in *Dead Ringer,* something that would make everybody remember the film, and I agreed. It was a fine idea, but what to do? I kept trying to come up with something, and suddenly a great idea hit me. The story revolves about two twins, a good one and a bad one, both played by Bette. The bad one has stolen the good one's lover by pretending to be pregnant.

Eventually, the good twin murders the bad one and takes her identity, and in the end is unmasked. There was a scene, after she kills her twin, where Bette changes into the dead woman's clothes. This, I decided, could be our "dead rat." I shot the scene with cuts between the dead twin's face and the other twin stripping her and putting on her clothes piece by piece. It was a gruesome sequence, but terribly effective.

When I showed the rough cut, Jack Warner turned to me. "I think you've done an excellent job on this, and it should do as well as *Baby Jane.*" He turned to his ever-present entourage, the heads of music, production, publicity, and cutting. "Don't you think so?"

Rudi Fehr, the head of post production, was a cutter when I joined Warners. Now he supervised everything done to the films after Warner okayed the director's first cut. He said, "I like the picture very much, but I think the undressing scene is very shocking, and it should be shortened as much as possible."

Jack said, "What? I loved it. I thought it was marvelous."

Rudi shook his head and started criticizing the scene. I, in turn, defended it, explaining that it was the "dead rat" we wanted, and of course it was shocking. It was meant to be. "It's deliberately sensational," I said. "This is our chance to get the crowd that loved *Baby Jane.*"

"I think Paul is right," Jack agreed.

Then, with great sweetness, Rudi said, "Do you trust me, Mr. Warner?"

"Why?" Jack asked him.

"Because if you do, let me handle it. I'll just cut a bit." And he won, and naturally cut far more than a bit. Ninety percent of the scene went out on the cutting-room floor, and the shocking impact was lost. The man in charge of the budget, when he saw the finished print, said, "I think Paul's version should be restored. He brought this "A" picture in for one and a quarter million dollars, which no director on this lot has done in the past five or six years. I vote to go with his version."

But his opinion, like mine, was ignored. I think the picture might have done much better than it did if that sequence had been left in. I still considered the picture a directorial success. I liked the way I had done it, and I particularly liked one trick I used. Bette

Davis had a scene where one of the sisters she plays talks to the other. To do it, we'd shoot her while her double was with her back to the camera.

It was easy enough to shoot her talking to herself when the audience sees both faces, but why not, I thought, have her cross in front of herself while talking? No one had ever tried that. I let her cross the set while the camera followed her. Then I had her, as the other twin, sit and follow the route she had taken with her eyes. It was simple, but very effective, and it took a lot of careful planning. Both shots were printed with back projection on each other.

I've heard a good deal of talk about the difference between directors who plan carefully and directors who rely heavily on extemporaneous action. Whenever I hear that, I remember a visit I once paid to William Wyler. It was before I became a director, and Willie and I loved to play chess. I'd go to his home and his wife would prepare coffee and cake, and we'd set the board up in his studio where no one would disturb us.

One afternoon, when I arrived, I found that Willie was delayed. "Make yourself comfortable," his wife told me. "There are books and magazines to read. Willie will be home in a few minutes."

I looked around the room and saw a long table covered with plans. My curiosity got the better of me, and staring at them I saw they were for a movie he was working on, *The Heiress.* They were such detailed and comprehensive plans with notes for every camera position and shot, that I realized that Willie believed in total preparation. Yet, on the set, he used a finder, an instrument like the sighter on a camera, and he would walk about and discover various angles. In fact, I realized, he simply gave a performance in front of the actors. He pretended that he was creating a picture as he went along, using any idea that came his way, extemporizing like crazy.

When Wyler came back, I confronted him with what I had found, and he laughed. "Of course, I plan it all in detail, Paul. Improvisation on a set is only possible if you have a firm concept of what you want to do. If I know what I want, and an actor says, 'Mr. Wyler, how would it be if I did so-and-so?' and it strikes me as worth being added to what I had planned . . . okay. But otherwise, no."

Later, when I met Federico Fellini at a film festival in Cannes and asked him about his improvisation, he said, "You can improvise on something that stands, like adding a window to a room because you think it will help, but the room must be there, preconceived and ready. That's how I think of improvisation in films. I would never leave the basic story line." And I feel that way too. It was exactly how I directed my own films.

◆

Twenty-Four

European Interlude

*W*hile critics in America weren't very kind to *Dead Ringer*, it was a solid success in Europe. Miguel Salkind, a very elegant and smooth French producer, approached me after he had seen *Dead Ringer* and asked if I would consider doing a picture with Ray Charles, the blind black composer and pianist. Salkind was a brilliant manipulator who always managed to make a profit while all his associates came out of a picture broke. He would automatically try to cheat me in any business deal, but he would try with so much charm that I couldn't help but like him.

He had talked Ray Charles into a picture deal with no script, just some scribbled notes from Charles that stipulated the picture must avoid racial themes and picture Charles as a "good man." He was also to sing ten songs with his group, the Rayettes, six girls who backed him up.

Charles was an extraordinary man. Blind, he had flown his own plane with a co-pilot, and I was told he could even drive if his manager drove a car directly in front of him. He claimed he did it all by the reflection of sound, and I could almost believe him. I saw him do some remarkable things. The first time he came to visit me, he said, "Show me the room first."

I led him around it, indicating chairs, tables, doors, and windows. He would touch things—once a glass of brandy, and later he picked it up as if he could see it. From then on he moved around with complete self-confidence as if, in that momentary "showing," he had memorized the entire room.

There was a story Charles told me about what happened to him one night in London after a concert. "I was shown over the hotel suite," he said, "but very quickly because I was tired and wanted to get to bed. The main room had three doors: one to the bedroom, one to the bathroom, and, close to that, a third to the hall. I sleep in the nude, and that morning I woke up and had to go to the bathroom, but once the bathroom door closed behind me I realized I wasn't in the bathroom, but by mischance had taken the door to the hall! I tried to get back into my room, but the door had locked behind me.

"There I was in the corridor of one of London's swankiest hotels, a black man completely naked! I heard a vacuum cleaner going, and I walked toward it. If it was a hotel employee, he or she could help me. The noise of the vacuum stopped suddenly and a woman screamed, and then I heard frantic footsteps running from me. Poor soul! What a sight to see that early in the morning. What could I do but wait there, hearing occasional gasps as hotel guests hurried by.

"It seemed forever before a man came out of the elevator, the manager, and said, 'My God, Mr. Charles. Do you realize you're naked?'

" 'Of course I do,' I snapped at him. 'Just open my door and I'll explain inside!' "

The one sad thing about Ray Charles was that he took drugs, and this, of course, interfered with his performance. I understood that his blindness was accompanied by a great deal of pain, and the drugs relieved the pain.

"What we need," Salkind told me, "is a story that will include his blindness and his music. Can you come up with something?"

"I can try," I said. "I have a TV scriptwriter I have a lot of confidence in. I'll give the problem to him." The writer, Burton Wohl, and I wrote the original story, and Wohl wrote the screen play. In the script, Ray Charles would give a benefit in London at a school for blind children and meet a young blind boy with a widowed mother. He discovers that the boy, like Charles, lost his sight at the age of five and wants to be a musician. The mother is about to be married and Charles takes the boy to a doctor he knows to see if a new surgical procedure can cure him. The operation doesn't work, but the friendship with Charles gives the kid a reason to live. If Charles could become a musician, he can do it too.

The picture was to be shot on location in London, Ireland, and Paris. The final script was good, and I assembled an excellent cast and crew and even found a delightful young boy to play Charles' protégé. I took my oldest daughter, Monika, along with me on the trip as a secretary and paid her a salary of $60 a week plus expenses.

Monika had been having an affair with a young man, Paul Veglia, and both Lisl and I thought she should put a little distance between them and see a few other men before they became too involved with each other. Paul was older, but had never settled down to one job. He wanted to be a singer, but I doubted that he had the voice for it.

Monika, on the other hand, sang well and was very talented as an actress, but she rarely gave her talent a chance to work. Just as she seemed to be on the verge of a career, she would give it up and try something else. She had a small part in *Dead Ringer*, and she did a good job, so I wrote another small part for her in the Ray Charles picture. That, too, she did well, and I realized that with a little struggle she could become a successful actress. She certainly had the talent; but to our disappointment she didn't have the drive!

Our shooting in Ireland went well, but our one problem was Ray Charles himself. From time to time he would be "incapacitated," and production would have to halt. Then, one evening, he called my room. "I can't shoot tomorrow."

"Why?" I asked. "What's wrong?"

"Well . . ." He hemmed and hawed and finally said, "I broke my dental bridge and it's going to be a while before they fix it."

"Broke your bridge? What were you eating?"

"Mashed potatoes," he said sheepishly. "But it can happen. I'm sorry, Paul."

What could I do except shoot around him? But one of his bodyguards—two were always with him—told me what he called the true story of his broken bridge. His mistress had arrived unexpectedly from New York. Charles had an incredible ability to attract women, and he hardly ever locked his door for fear of losing the key if there were a fire. His New York girl had walked in on Charles making love to an Irish colleen. All hell exploded. She swung her handbag at him, back and forth across his face, and that did it. She broke his dentures!

Charles was only one of the problems I ran into in making the film. Salkind was even more of a problem. The checks he was supposed to send wouldn't appear, and the union would threaten to shut down the picture. The Irish who worked with us seemed to live on whiskey, and invariably they'd be plastered by noon each day. I remember walking into the *pissoir* of an Irish pub one day at the noon lunch break to see a line of men from our crew swaying back and forth over the trough, too drunk to stand straight.

I breathed a sigh of relief when the shooting in Ireland was finished and we were to move on to London. Mimi was away on a tennis tour. Lisl and Monika had joined me in Ireland and would fly to London with me. Lisl had smuggled our toy poodle into Dublin in her handbag. When the dog gave a feeble *woof* at the customs, Monika began singing to cover up the noise and drown it out. The slightly drunken Irish customs officer was delighted at the spontaneity of Americans who burst into song on any occasion.

There was no problem bringing the dog from Ireland to London, but the little poodle was not well-trained, and in London, a policeman stopped Lisl outside our hotel. "Madam, in London," he told her severely, "we require dogs to relieve themselves in the gutter, not on the sidewalk!"

Lisl sighed. "Yes, I know, and I've been telling him that for years, but he won't listen. Will you talk to him?"

Fortunately the policeman had a sense of humor and just laughed and walked away.

In London, I had Monika sing for the main coach of the Covent Garden Opera, the friend of a friend. She was impressed and said, "If you leave her with me I'll train her, and in two years she'll have a good contract with Covent Gardens as a soubrette. When she's older and her voice has developed, she'll be a fine soprano."

However, Monika was doubtful. "I'm not sure I want to be a singer," she told us. "Let me think about it."

We finished our shooting in London and went off to Paris. What neither Lisl nor I knew was that Monika had been saving her salary each week, and her boyfriend, Paul, had flown to Paris and joined her. "We want to go to Naples," Monika told me defensively. "Paul is going to see a singing teacher there and study for the opera."

I had never heard of a teacher in Naples. Florence or Rome, yes. Milano, yes, but Naples? I was really surprised and I protested, but Monika was determined to have her way. It was typical of Paul that he had the name of the teacher—he had gotten it from a friend —nothing else. No address. "Didn't you write to him?" I asked when he and Monika were about to leave Paris.

"No," Paul answered in an offhanded way. "This friend of mine said, just go and he'll be there."

"But without his address . . ."

"Hey, no problem! We'll find it in the phone book."

It seemed to me total insanity, but Monika was old enough to do as she wanted. She had drawn out some of her own money before she left for Ireland, and I realized that even then she had planned this trip. They went off, and of course never found the teacher, but they stayed on in Naples till their money ran out. Monika, through my agent in Paris, turned in her return ticket and bought two third-class passages on a Greek ship so that they could eventually come home.

Lisl's birthday came around while we were shooting in Paris, and I had decided on my birthday present to her, her favorite car —at that time, the XKE Jaguar, a two-seater convertible with red leather upholstery and a gun-metal-gray body—a dream of a car. I had bought the Jaguar earlier and told them to Americanize it, change the speedometer to miles and fix the lights to American standards. I made them promise to have it ready on Sunday, July 31, her birthday, and stay open. A few extra dollars did that.

On the morning of her birthday, I said, "Forgive me, but I must get your present, Lisl."

"Now?" she asked, surprised. "How silly! We're in this comfortable hotel room on a Sunday, and you want to rush out? What is it? Flowers? Candy? It can wait, Paul."

"This can't wait," I assured her, and I took off for the Jaguar shop. The car was ready, and I drove it back to the hotel, then went up to our room. We had a balcony overlooking the street, and I said, "The present was too big to carry up, so I left it on the street. Come and look."

"Paul, you're crazy," she said, following me out onto the balcony. "What kind of present . . ." And then she saw the car. "Oh no! My dream car!" And I got a very warm return for my efforts.

We drove from Paris to Austria to visit friends and relatives, and then went back to London, where I cut the Ray Charles picture, titled *Ballad in Blue*. I had contracted to co-star in another movie in Europe, *Operation Crossbow*, produced by Carlo Ponti for MGM. Michael Anderson was the director, and he decided to use a technique that had worked very well in *The Longest Day*. Like that movie, *Operation Crossbow* was a war story and had a magnificent cast—Sophia Loren, George Peppard, Trevor Howard, John Mills, Tom Courtenay, and Anthony Quayle.

Anderson decided that the Germans, in their section of the picture, would speak German, the Italians Italian, and the French French, and, of course, the English English. The picture would translate with subtitles. I was a German general in charge of development of the Buzz Bomb, a good part with some meat to it, and I was pleased with it, but I thought that playing it in German was a big mistake. I went to Anderson and said, "I know it's none of my business, but I hate the idea of doing this part in German. I think my scenes will end up on the cutting-room floor."

"They would never do that to one of my films," Anderson assured me.

"It's not that they'd have anything against your film," I said. "It's just that there's still a strong feeling against Germans and the German language, and Americans in general hate subtitles. I'm sure that the German scenes with subtitles will be cut. Mike, I'm willing to relearn my part in English. I'll even thicken my German accent for you."

"No, Paul," he said firmly. "It's been decided, and MGM agrees."

"Well, I can't say any more." I shrugged. "I hope you're right."

But as it turned out, he was wrong, and my part of the story was cut to pieces. The picture was recognized by reviewers as an attempt to be different, but it wasn't the hit it could have been. However, making the movie paid well, and I still had time when I returned to Los Angeles to do a good bit of television work. Financially, that year, 1964, was the best I'd had since the blacklist.

Twenty-Five

◆

The Madwoman of Chaillot
and Don Juan in Hell

I hadn't heard anything from John Huston since our memorable trip to Washington that put me on the studio's blacklist, but in 1969 I answered the phone to hear an enthusiastic "Goddammit, Paul, it's wonderful to hear your voice again."

"Who is this?" But I recognized the voice even as I asked.

"It's John. Don't you know me? John!"

"Huston?"

"Yes, goddammit. Now listen, I'm doing *The Madwoman of Chaillot,* the Giraudoux play, with an all-star cast, and I want you to do the part of the French general, a De Gaulle type. It's a superb script by Anhalt. I want you to play him as if you were De Gaulle —stiff and stupid!"

I laughed. It was a typical Huston bluster. "What's the problem, John? Of course I'll play it."

"I knew you would. I just wanted to call and hear it myself. Now I need the first two weeks free of charge."

"You want me to work for two weeks without pay? Why?"

For the first time I heard some of the bluster go out of Huston's voice, and he almost sounded embarrassed. "They won't let me do it otherwise. Look, Paul, I've got Boyer and Danny Kaye and Yul Brynner, and of course Katharine Hepburn will do the Madwoman."

"You've got all of them?" I asked, impressed.

"Well, Kate said yes, and now you've said yes. And I'm going to call Charles, and when he hears about you and Kate, he's going to come along, and once I've got you three the others will agree."

"Two weeks without pay." I hesitated. "When you do pay me, how much will it be?"

"For those six weeks we'll give you seven hundred fifty a week for expenses, then after two weeks your regular salary. It's going to be great. You'll see."

I agreed without too much coaxing. The promise of shooting in Nice was enough of an argument to make me sign up, and I respected John as a director.

What I didn't find out until I arrived in Nice was that Huston had had a fight with the producer, who wanted to rewrite the script, and Huston had walked out on the picture. They had then hired Bryan Forbes, an English director, who had been an actor and a scriptwriter. He did a good deal of rewriting on what had been a very fine original script, and to make matters worse, when he directed the film he gave Katharine Hepburn her head. When you let Hepburn do what she wants to do, you are in trouble. All during the picture I kept remembering what Spencer Tracy was always telling her: "Say your lines clearly and don't make any silly faces."

But I liked Kate, and after all, we had worked together in *Song of Love,* so I bought her a large box of very fine chocolates, her weakness as I remembered. She was delighted with the gift and kissed me and thanked me profusely. Then she opened the box and started eating them without even offering me one—and I love chocolates too!

A few days later she called me into her dressing room. "Those chocolates you gave me were so delicious that I went into town to buy some more, but they were terribly expensive. You shouldn't have paid so much. Now someone told me about this little shop out of town where chocolates are half the price. I bought these there. Try one."

She waited expectantly while I tasted her chocolate. "Aren't they wonderful?"

I swallowed and nodded, but they were much too sweet, really not comparable to the ones I had bought, or was I just annoyed about the whole situation? What could I say? "They're fine, Kate," I lied to her. "You must give me the name of the place."

She was delighted and we sat there talking while she went through the rest of the box. I never saw anyone who could eat as much as she did and never put on weight. Of course she was always in motion, busy at the studio, running around the city—she probably burned it all up!

She had changed tremendously from the time she lived with Spence. He had constantly put her down, telling her what to do, and, as he put it, he had "kept her in her place." Without him she seemed much freer, much more her own person, but unfortunately she had kept many of the mannerisms he had nagged her about.

In my first scene in the movie, I'm seen addressing a group of cadets, and I had memorized the speech, a very good one. Forbes, however, had rewritten the speech, and he handed me the rewritten version. I looked at it and then, remembering what Huston had suggested about the De Gaulle nature of the character I was playing, I told Forbes, "Bryan, I'm sorry but I can't do it this way. I'll use the original speech."

He was too dumbfounded to object, and the scene was very effective, but I lost a bit of my respect for him as a director. I would never have allowed myself to be bullied like that by an actor. From then on he never bothered me with his changes, but he did change everyone else's lines, and I feel that in doing that to the graceful Giraudoux-Anhalt script he spoiled the movie, in particular the performance of a brilliant British character actor, Donald Pleasance.

There was a scene in the script where the group of conspirators —Yul Brynner, Charles Boyer, Oscar Homolka, John Gavin, and I —meet at a café and discuss our plans for getting at the oil we have found under the streets of Paris.

A man at another table, Donald Pleasance, approaches us and says, "I'm concerned with a problem and I'd like to tell you about it." One of us invites him to sit down, and he does and gives another brilliant Giraudoux speech. At the first take, after he had finished and the director said, "Cut," all of us broke into spontaneous applause. It was quite a compliment coming from as distinguished a group of actors as this, and Pleasance flushed with embarrassment.

Bryan Forbes, however, said, "Well, Donald, your colleagues are overwhelmed, but I'm not."

One of us said, "That's too bad, Bryan. He was really good."

"He can do much better," Forbes said tightly, and he proceeded to redo the scene again and again till all the spontaneity and freshness was gone.

I lost most of my respect for Forbes then, and the rest later when I invited him and his wife to dinner. He said, "You know, Paul, John Huston is a strange director. He had all the sets built facing north, and he can't get any sun at all in that direction."

"Are you serious, Bryan?" I asked in surprise.

"Of course. Don't you think it's a ridiculous thing to do? You've directed a lot, Paul, and you know how you need the sun."

"On the contrary, Bryan. If a producer will pay for the electricity, building your sets to face north will give you perfect control of the lighting without having to depend on the sun. But only a top director like Huston has the clout to get the sets built that way. Do you know who the cameraman is on this picture?"

"Yes. Jean Renoir's nephew, Claude."

"That's right. He's one of the greatest cameramen in France, and you'd never have gotten him without Huston!"

Lisl and I lived in the "Fonda" house until 1970. I'm amused at the fact that as long as we lived there it was called the "Fonda" house, but now that Norman Lear owns it, it's called the "Paul Henreid" house. I suppose when Lear sells it, it will be known as the "Norman Lear" house.

When we bought the house from the Fondas, it was an excellent buy. In those days I received a star's salary, and I was able to run the house and pay the servants and the enormous bills for taxes and upkeep. During the blacklist period it was very difficult, and we often talked of selling it and finding a more modest place, one that wouldn't take every extra dollar to run, but the house was comfortable and roomy enough when the children came home or guests came to visit.

During my TV-directing career I took almost every show that was offered to me, and I often used the upkeep of the house as an excuse. But the truth is that it was more than that. The blacklist years had done something to me, shown me how insecure anyone's footing in Hollywood could be, how easy it was to be in and out of favor as an actor or director. Unconsciously, I think I felt the need to take every job I could get, and a great many came my way.

I directed 80 Hitchcock shows and I don't know how many *Schlitz Playhouse of Stars* programs, at least 12 shows for General Electric, and 12 *Maverick* episodes. The *Maverick* series did so well that they hired me for a new series called *Bourbon Street,* and raised my salary—and so it went, show after show.

I met James Garner while directing the Maverick series and I enjoyed working with him. He had a great deal of energy and charm, both of which qualities came through on film, and he was willing to do anything I asked him to. Nothing seemed too much work.

I've heard many stories about the irresponsibility of many TV actors, but I must admit I never found this true. The great majority of them were serious and hardworking. Certainly Jim Garner was, and so was Steve McQueen. I did one show with McQueen, and when my friends discovered that I was going to direct him, they were all sadly sympathetic.

"The man is impossible," they warned me. "He gets on his motorcycle and takes off in the middle of shooting, and he's a big-enough star so that everyone has to wait until he gets back!"

I approached the show apprehensively, but to my delight found absolutely no problem with him. He was prompt, always available, showed great respect for his craft and for me as the director, and was gratified with whatever I told him—and I didn't have to tell him much. He was a very talented actor.

I had liked working with Walter Matthau in that early Hitchcock show, and I was pleased when another story came up with a part just suited for him. He was married to a young woman who, under the name of Carol Grace, had done some work on the Broadway stage. There was a part in the TV script that fitted Carol perfectly, and Walter asked me if she could try out for it.

She did, and I hired her and ran into one of the most common problems in acting—a wife and husband on the same set! It took me back to Kate Hepburn and Tracy. Like Tracy, Matthau was after his wife constantly to "Do this," or "Do that." "Speak louder, Carol," or "Stand to that side."

Finally, in desperation, I told him, "Look, Walter. You direct your wife at home and let me direct her on the set!"

It worked. Matthau, rather shamefacedly, left her alone, and she turned in an excellent performance.

But with all the TV work and my increased income, the cost of the Fonda house and its lavish grounds kept mounting up, and finally, in 1970, when I was sixty-two and our two girls had married and gone off to live their own lives, Lisl and I decided to sell the house.

It wasn't an easy decision. It was not only a comfortable place, but its extravagant spaciousness was a great boost to my ego. In the Hollywood milieu, where you are judged by your possessions and credits, it made a statement about me and my work. It said, very plainly, "Henreid is a success. He's able to manage this enormous estate and live like one of the old-fashioned movie stars. He's someone to respect and reckon with."

But at the same time the house was draining us financially and physically. Live-in help was scarce, and we were alone in the evenings and on weekends, and often after entertaining on a Saturday night we would spend the entire Sunday putting the house in order.

Once we decided to sell the house, Lisl set out looking for another place. We almost bought a smaller house in Brentwood, but the deal fell through, and finally we settled for a place in Pacific Palisades, just the size we wanted. It had a guest house behind it that would be just right for Mimi during her frequent visits home. It had the state forest in back, an assurance of privacy, and from the edge of our lawn we had a fine view of the untroubled Pacific.

There were a lot of changes to be made, and I was glad that for a while at least there was no TV work. I had decided to retire and take my pensions, one from the Directors' Guild and one from the Screen Actors'. These, plus social security and some investments I had made over the years, would keep us very comfortable.

"But if a film comes along, I'll take it," I told Lisl.

"Providing you like it," she said sternly. "No more of this grabbing at every job. That was why we got rid of the house."

I agreed with her meekly, feeling that I deserved a rest of sorts. Besides, I had a few projects I wanted to work on. I had told my lawyer to option a short novel that I thought would make a splendid film, and I had an idea for a television series based on de Maupassant's short stories. I was working on that when an offer came to do *Don Juan in Hell* as a reading on a six-month tour.

It had been done once before with Charles Laughton directing it and acting in it, and I had seen it and had been impressed. Laughton was a magnificent director and actor. In this present version I would play the commander, Agnes Moorehead would repeat her original role as Donna Anna, though she was a bit along in years for the part—two years older than I, her father! Edward Mulhare would be the devil, and Ricardo Montalban would be Don Juan. John Houseman was to direct.

I thought at first that I would turn the offer down because I was so in love with my new house. "I hate to leave it for six months," I told Lisl.

"I think you should," she said seriously. "Look at it this way. You started with Goethe's *Faust*, and the last thing you did on stage was that horror *Festival* of Sam and Bella Spewack. What a terrible way to end your theatrical career."

I smiled. "And you think this would be better?"

"Of course. Start with Goethe in Vienna and Salzburg and end with Shaw in every great city in America. You'll finish at the Palace on Broadway in New York. That makes sense. Anyway, if I know you, you'll enjoy the house for another month and then get so restless that you'll go back to that TV stuff! Besides, you knew Shaw. You liked him, and he's one of the greatest writers of our time."

I said, "You're right," and I picked up the phone and called the producer. "You have a deal," I told him.

However, this was one time Lisl was wrong. I went on tour with *Don Juan* and was completely miserable, and Lisl stayed home and was miserable too. That was a time when she was very depressed and started drinking too much vodka. Mimi, our younger daughter, who had come to stay in our guest house, made her aware of what she was doing and she abruptly stopped all alcohol except for some occasional wine.

We had both been puzzled during our early days in Los Angeles by the fact that almost no one drank wine. When we were invited to homes like Jack Benny's or Claudette Colbert's, no wine was served, although there was always an abundance of strong liquor. Guests would bring their Scotch or other liquor to the table when dinner was served. We started drinking to keep up with our friends, and found that Americans drank much more than Europeans. It seems to me that wine, as a popular drink, has only been discovered in the past twenty years.

The original reading of *Don Juan in Hell*, from Shaw's play *Man and Superman*, had been arranged by Charles Laughton and George Bernard Shaw himself, with Laughton directing. It was a splendid production with Charles Boyer, Sir Cedric Hardwicke, and Agnes Moorehead, as well as Laughton. When I saw the original production, I felt it was one of the most exciting theatrical evenings I had ever spent. The success of that reading depended very much on the actors' understanding of the characters and the material.

In our production, Montalban, though physically a splendid Don Juan, was incapable of reaching the heights of Charles Boyer. I found it painful to listen to him. Houseman, directing us, was overly concerned with diction and pronunciation and neglected the sense and meaning of the play.

In one of our early performances, Montalban, in the middle of the play, turned pale and interrupted his lines to say to the audience, "Please excuse me. I don't feel well!" and hurried off the stage. The rest of us stood there silent and nonplussed.

The atmosphere was unbearable. Nothing like this had ever happened to me before. Finally I said to the audience, "Please excuse Ricardo, but it seems more comfortable for all of us if we wait offstage for his return." I made a bow, and we all went offstage after receiving a round of applause from the audience.

"What on earth happened?" we asked him afterward.

"An attack of diarrhea," he explained sheepishly.

A proper diet, his doctor told him, would avoid it, but Montalban was reluctant to follow the doctor's advice, and the same thing happened a month later: an excuse to the audience, and the cast, leaving the stage and, after a while, returning with him. It was simply awful!

Mulhare, as the devil, was excellent, and Agnes Moorehead, as always, gave a polished performance. There were rumors that she had been hired by Laughton in the original production because he was very much in love with her. There may have been nothing physical in their love affair, but she did come into possession of Laughton's director's book for the production, and Houseman, who didn't know how Laughton had directed the original, desperately wanted this book! Again, rumor had it that this was why Moorehead, in her sixties, was hired to play a woman who is twenty-five during most of the play.

The play was done on a simple stage with a black backdrop and stools for the actors and stands for the scripts we were supposed to read. I'd walk in leading the group. We would put our scripts on the stands in front of us. The devil would remain onstage, and the three of us, the commander, Don Juan, and Donna Anna would go to stage rear and sit down. Then Mulhare would start the performance. The actors wore dinner jackets, Agnes an evening gown.

The directorial touch of Laughton, approved by Shaw, was that the stage be lit with cold, blue-white light that gave an eerie quality to the players. When the time came, Don Juan would move forward, then Donna Anna and I would assume our places. At the end of the play the commander decides that heaven is too dull, and the devil says, "Come along, old chap," and they go back a few steps and the spots on them fade out. That was the way Laughton did it.

Houseman, however, decided to put a red spot on us to signify hell. It was corny and unsuitable, and I told him so. Perhaps it was my age showing, but I was rather rude to Houseman during the rehearsals, and I was surprised after the play when he gave me a copy of a book he had written.

My rudeness, which of course was unforgivable, was because I felt he was a bad director. I took him aside at one point and complained that Montalban did not understand the play. "Why don't you, as the director, tell him what the play means," I suggested, "and for heaven's sakes, forget about his accent. You can't change that!"

Rather patiently, he said, "Paul, I know my job."

In a way he was right to tell me, in effect, to mind my own

business. No director wants an actor to tell him how to direct, but on the other hand, I, as a director, had often taken advice from actors. I knew I was rubbing him the wrong way during rehearsals, but I couldn't seem to stop myself. I was dreadfully afraid the play would flop, and this, my last appearance on the stage, just had to be very good!

To my immense relief the play was a great success in spite of all the flaws I seemed to see in it. Evidently the critics were not as sensitive as I, or I was making mountains out of molehills. The play's success, however, didn't improve my relationship with Houseman. He continued to call rehearsals after we had played it for weeks and weeks. At the rehearsals he would say, "I have a few notes here . . ." And he would read off some trivial changes. "Project a little more at this point. . . . Start a beat later here. . . . Pronounce this line in such and such a way. . . ."

I felt the notes were so much bullshit, and what he should really do was rehearse Montalban. I must say that in spite of my feelings about Montalban he was always polite to me and to Mulhare and thanked us for any suggestions we made—but also proceeded to ignore them!

Eventually I just avoided the rehearsals, and finally John Houseman stopped me after a performance and asked, "Why didn't you come to rehearsal?"

"John, forgive me," I told him. "I just couldn't chatter away about unimportant things and leave out the truly important one."

"No actor ever told me my rehearsals were superficial," he said in a rather hurt tone.

"Well, it's high time someone did!" I snapped and walked away, somewhat surprised at my own contentiousness.

Lisl, when I told her about it, shook her head. "You're growing old and irritable. I suppose the next thing I know you'll be ordering me around!"

"Oh, no," I protested, but there was a funny look in her eye, and I wondered if I hadn't been doing just that.

◆

Twenty-Six

My Last Movie

$\mathscr{I}$ accepted the fact that *Don Juan in Hell* would be my last stage appearance, and a few years later, in 1975, I did my last television acting job. I appeared as a villain in *Murderers Among Us*, a two-hour film for TV. Kate Reid played a lady detective in what they hoped would become a series. I had a fat, juicy, villainous role, and I thoroughly enjoyed it, especially playing with Kate and Martin Balsam as the other stars.

In 1976 my grandson Mario, Monika's son, came to live with Lisl and me. Monika and her husband Paul Veglia, had three children, two girls, Mimi and Mireille, and a boy, Mario, and then the marriage broke up. For a while she drifted about, at one point living in a terrible wreck of a house on the beach in a strange communal arrangement with some other couples. She was struggling to "find herself," she told us.

It was about that time that a close friend from Vienna came to visit us. An advertising executive, he was a serious member of what Monika referred to as "the establishment," but a close family friend. He had a wife and three children and was altogether "proper" in the old-fashioned, Viennese way. The last time he had seen Monika was when she was a young girl, and now he very much wanted to visit her.

I hemmed and hawed, a bit ashamed to tell him of the way Monika lived. But finally Lisl told me I was being foolish. "Stiff and stubborn," as she put it succinctly. So I gave our friend Monika's address.

He went to see her and came back slightly bemused. "I must say," he told us carefully, "It's an interesting life-style. I wish I had the courage to live that way."

"Interesting" I felt was a kind word for Monika's crazy ménage at the beach. And yet, a year later, I heard from Vienna that this young man had left his wife and children and moved in with a much younger woman in a life-style that was very close to Monika's!

Shortly after her beach commune, Monika took off with a baseball player who got a job in Mexico for three months. She took the two girls out of public school, but we had put the boy, Mario, in a private school, a very excellent one, and we thought it would be foolish to interrupt his education. Monika agreed, and so Mario came to live with us and travel with us. The three months became seven and a half years. We took him to New York twice and to Europe five times. He learned to speak and write German fluently and he is quite good in French.

When we took Mario to Europe for his first summer trip he loved every minute of it. It was all a "treat," he decided. When we drove from Zürich to Galtür in Austria, we took the famous Silvretta Road. As we came close to the pass, we stopped for the incredible view. Mario looked around, stared at the tops of the Silvretta Glaciers, and in an awestruck voice said, "And to think, all of this is real!" Up to then, the only glaciers he had seen were the wooden ones at Disneyland.

Two years ago, on another European trip, we spent an afternoon and night in the lovely medieval town of Kitzbühel in Austria. After lunch Lisl and I took a little rest while Mario explored the town and church. At the church he found a group of English women, tourists, and he chatted with them. He was quite helpful because of his fluent German, and he translated inscriptions for them.

"And what's your name, young man?" one lady finally asked him.

"Mario Henreid," he told her.

"And are you related to one of my favorite movie stars, Paul Henreid?"

"That's my grandfather," Mario said proudly.

"What a coincidence," the lady said. "About a month ago we had a memorial week for him in our most modern motion-picture theatre. We saw seven of his best films. The theatre was full, and all of us talked about him. What a pity he had to die so young!"

"Die?" Mario stared at her. "But you're all wrong. He and my grandmother are very much alive, just taking a little nap at the Hotel Maria Theresia!"

To both of us, Mario's coming was a wonderful experience. A bond grew up between us that is, in many ways, stronger than the bond between me and Monika. The skipping of a generation can make a remarkable difference. There is none of the tension between grandparent and grandchild that there is between a parent and child. We were able to become true friends and companions, and seeing Mario grow up has been a delightful experience. Of course I was also able to devote much more attention, because of my retirement, to him than I had to either Mimi or Monika. When they were children I was working long hours six days a week.

Lisl and I have come to love Mario and depend on him more and more as the years go by. I could not bear the thought of his leaving us to go back to Monika, and fortunately she seems to understand this. Back in California now, she still sees Mario frequently, but she has her two girls and another baby now, and her life, too, is very complete.

Mimi, our younger daughter, has made a career for herself in tennis. When we bought the Fonda house, Lisl, who was delighted with Mimi's early love for tennis, made a deal with a popular tennis pro we knew. She gave him the apartment behind the garage and use of the tennis court when we weren't using it in return for lessons for Mimi and Monika. They both were good, but Mimi was superb, and by fifteen she was a champion player.

At UCLA Mimi won the intercollegiate trophy for the school twice, but tennis, she thought then, had no future. That was before the enormous popularity of the game. To make a living she went into social work, but eventually left it to return to her first love, tennis. She took a job as the head-pro at a tennis club in Aspen and taught skiing in the winter. She fell in love with Aspen and after two years there, she was invited to tour with the Virginia Slims team.

After Aspen and the tour, Mimi had a short, unhappy marriage, before she went to Scottsdale to become a pro at a tennis ranch. She stayed there for over eight years. The first year she became head-pro at the Racquet Club in nearby Phoenix she bought a beautiful house and later came back to California and accepted a job she could not turn down, as the head coach at the Coronado Racquet Club. She still works there, close enough to come home for frequent visits. She rented a lovely house and furnished it with an apartment for our visits. She also has her tennis shop at the club and is doing very well, is very popular and well-loved by all her new friends and clients. We love her very much.

My life in the 1970s seemed very quiet and relaxed. My directing work had tapered off because of the poor quality of the scripts I was offered. I did direct Anthony Quinn, a very talented star, in a TV series, *The Man and the City,* and in 1975 played the ruthless killer in *Murderers Among Us* for NBC. But after that I stopped working completely and decided I was officially retired.

Then, in 1977, my agent called me with an offer to do the role of the cardinal in *Exorcist II.* Richard Burton was the star, and I knew him slightly and respected his work, but I was almost seventy and wondered if I could stand the pace of movie making.

"But it's only three days' work," my agent reassured me, "and it pays sixty-five thousand dollars. Your only scenes are with Richard and you are co-starred."

That put a different complexion on it, and I accepted the offer. When I met Richard Burton on the set, he was pleasant and very warm. The two of us got along famously, and I liked the new young lady he had with him. He married her soon afterward, but the marriage didn't last.

I had heard a lot about Richard's drinking and was a little apprehensive, but he never seemed even slightly out of control. He was constantly being handed what he told me were tall glasses of "lemonade." But once, when I was very thirsty and took the glass as it was handed to him, he grabbed it from me quickly. "Oh no, they'll pour one for you." Then, apologizing at grabbing it away: "It'll be fresher." But the truth, as I found out, was that his were half vodka.

I hadn't learned any long speeches since I did *Don Juan in Hell.*

The TV movie, *Murderers Among Us,* had consisted of short lines and a lot of action. Now I was suddenly faced with an eight-page scene, and almost all of it was a long speech by me, with Burton answering with one- or two-word replies.

I was very uneasy, and I called my understudy and asked him if he would come up to my house and practice with me if I paid him for his time. He was delighted to make the extra money, and we worked hard at it for the entire week before the shooting. There were two scenes to my part. In the first, which was only three pages of script, I leave a meeting of cardinals and go down a corridor toward my office. The camera follows me as I pass Burton in the waiting room. In my office I am divested of my hat and robe—an elaborate change—and my male secretary tells me that Burton has arrived and is waiting outside. The second scene is my long discussion with Burton.

The camera recorded the divesting of my clothes but did not, I hoped, record the terror I felt as each garment came off, leaving me, in my fancy, more vulnerable. For every line I had learned so carefully had passed out of my head completely. I couldn't even remember the beginning of the speech, and once the divesture was finished I had to go into it. This had never happened to me before, and I could feel the sweat stand out on my forehead.

This is a nightmare, I told myself. A horror and a catastrophe! It will end up with idiot cards on a Teleprompter. But worst of all was the blow to my professional pride. How could I ever look anyone in the face again?

To my overwhelming relief, we never got beyond the disrobing scene. At five P.M. Burton said, "Wouldn't it be better if we started the next scene tomorrow, when we're all fresh? We're tired now and I think we could use a good rest."

I agreed eagerly. One more night to study my part!

The next day, driving to the studio, I suddenly realized that I knew the entire speech, and knew it perfectly. I was fascinated that just one night's sleep had given me time to recover and remember.

The dialogue between Burton and me—or rather, my long speech to Burton—went very well at rehearsal. I was pleased, and so was our director and Burton. The shooting, too, worked out perfectly—it was just a shame that the picture got such terrible reviews!

There have been some very wonderful moments in my life, and the one of which I'm proudest was when the Austrian Cross of Honor for Sciences and Arts, First Class, was awarded to me by the President of Austria on July 9, 1980. It was presented two months later, on September 26, at a reception in the residence of the Austrian Consul-General, Dr. Peter Moser, and his charming wife, in Los Angeles. The fact that this was the highest medal of the country I came from made me particularly happy. CBS-TV covered the ceremony.

In 1960 the City of Los Angeles honored me with two stars on the Walk of Fame, one on Hollywood Boulevard and one on Vine Street. On June 29, 1942, I received a citation from the United States Treasury Department. More recently, on October 26, 1980, the National Film Society awarded me the American Classic Screen award, and in 1983 the Texas Film Society gave me the Yellow Rose Achievement award.

These honors from my native country and my adopted country have meant a great deal to me. I am proud of my Austrian heritage and of my citizenship in the United States.

I am very happy these days with Lisl and Mario in our lovely house overlooking the Pacific on one side and the mountains on the other. Looking back on my life, I seem to see it as a series of good luck in bad luck. The loss of my father when I was so young and the loss of our family fortune was bad luck, but my decision to become an actor and my success on the Vienna stage were good luck. Hitler's coming into power and my refusal to become a Ufa star and my subsequent blacklisting in Germany were bad luck, but my new career in London was good luck. The war breaking out and my becoming an enemy alien in England was bad luck. On arriving in America, it was good luck that Lisl was well known and could get immediate work; it was bad luck that the play I came here for was canceled.

It goes on like that. It was good luck that I got a new play and an offer from Hollywood; it was bad luck that the blacklist came and ended my career, a career that could have lasted five or six years longer, and bad luck that I was forced to accept secondary roles. But it was good luck that I became one of the most-sought-after television directors in Hollywood.

So, my life has been filled with good luck and bad luck, but isn't that what life is really about? How can we possibly appreciate the good without the bad for contrast? I have my regrets along with my overwhelming satisfactions, and my chief regret is that I never got to perform the classics I've always wanted to do, never got to play *Peer Gynt* and all the other pearls of European and American literature. But there is the continuing wonder of my life with Lisl and now with Mario, of watching him grow to manhood under our doting eyes. Indeed, the good outweighs the bad!

Theatre Chronology

Europe

1933   *Esther*, by Grillparzer, as Hauptman, at Neues Wiener Konservatorium; Director: Jacob Feldhammer.

Faust, by Goethe, as Schüler, at Theater in der Josefstadt, in Vienna; Director: Max Reinhardt. It was also performed at the Salzburger Festspiele at Salzburg.

Eine Frau, die weiss, was sie will, by Alfred Grünwald and Oscar Straus, as the Young Lover, at Scala, Vienna; Director: Rudolf Beer.

Immer die Liebe, by Karl Farkas, as Der Bonvivant, at Casino Theater, Vienna; Director: Karl Farkas.

1934   *Ball in Savoy,* by Alfred Grünwald and Fritz Löhner-Beda, musik by Paul Abraham, as Marquis Aristidé de Faublas, at Scala, Vienna: Director; Karl Heinz Martin.

Erdgeist (Lulu), by Wedekind, as Der Kutscher, at Scala, Vienna; Director: Max Reinhardt.

Herr über Millionen, by Wilhelm Lichtenberg, as Pieter Tersteog, at Scala, Vienna; Director: Rudolf Beer.

Die Verliebte Königin, by Alfred Grünwald and Beda, musik by Nikolaus Brodszky, as Trémoulin, at Scala, Vienna; Director: André Charlot.

1935   *Da stimmt was nicht,* by Franz Arnold, as Erbprinz Leopold Wilhelm, at Scala, Vienna; Director: Rudolf Beer.

Das Walzerparadies, by Alfred Grünwald, musik by Oscar Straus, as Wiesinger, at Scala, Vienna; Director: Rudolf Beer.

Das Unbekannte Mädchen, by Franz Molnar, as Rudolf, at D. Volkstheater, Vienna; Director: Heinrich Schnitzler.

Geburtstag, by Ladislaus Bus-Fekete, as Cargatti, at Deutsches Volkstheater, Vienna; Director: Rolf Jahn.

Wo die Liebe blüht, by Emil and Arnold Golz, musik by Bernard Grün, as Hans, at Die Komödie, Vienna; Director: Stefan Hock.

Der Mustergatte, by Avery Hopwood, as Hausfreund, at Scala, Vienna; Director: Erich Wenter.

1935 *Mizzi,* by Friedrich Moll, as Fritz Hofeneder, at D. Volkstheater, Vienna; Director: Heinrich Schnitzler.

1936 *Der Etappenhas,* by Karl Bunje, as Hans Feldmann, at Raimundtheater, Vienna and Stattheater, Salzburg; Director: Adi Berger.

1937 *Die Herrin von La Paz,* by Edith Ellis, as Clay van Rennen, at Scala, Vienna; Director: Rudolf Beer.

London

1936 *Cafe Chantant,* by Henry Sherek, as Count Egon von Kreutzbruck, at His Majesties Theatre, London; Director: Henry Sherek. I also repeated the Viennesse songs of the play every night at the Midnight Supershow at the Ritz Hotel, London.

1937–38 *Victoria Regina,* by Laurence Housman, as Prince Albert; Pamela Stanley as Victoria, at the Lyric Theatre, Shaftesbury Avenue, London; Producer: Gilbert Miller; Director: Norman Marshall.

1940 *The Jersey Lily,* by Sir Basil Bartlett, as Prince Battenberg; Hermione Hannen as Lily Langtry and Leo Genn as The Prince of Wales, at the Gate Theatre; Director: Norman Marshall.

United States

1940–41 *Flight to the West,* by Elmer Rice. Starring: Betty Field, Paul von Hernried, Hugh Marlowe, Arnold Moss. Played at McCarter Theater, Princeton, N.J.; National Theater, Washington, D.C.; Wilbur Theater, Boston; The Guild Theater, New York. Produced by the Playwrights Company; Director: Elmer Rice.

1951 *The Merry Widow,* by Franz Lehar. Starring: Paul Henreid and Jane Pickens, at the Curran Theater, San Francisco; Producer: Edwin Lester; Director: Vladimir Rosing.

1955 *Festival,* by Sam and Bella Spewack. Starring: Paul Henreid and Betty Field, at the Longacre Theater, New York; Producer: Walter Fried; Director: Albert Marre.

1957 *One Coat of White,* by Allen Smith. Starring: Claudette Colbert and Paul Henreid, as CBS *Playhouse Ninety;* Produced in Los Angeles.

1962 *Everyman,* by Hugo van Hoffmansthal. Starring: Vic Morrow, Ruth Hussey, Gail Kobe, Henry Beckman, at the Chapel of the Sacred Heart at Loyola University of Los Angeles; music by Gerald Fried; choreography by Mme. Lachine; Produced and directed by Paul Henreid.

1964 *King David,* a symphonic psalm by Honegger. Conductor: Zubin Mehta; Narrator: Paul Henreid; Performed by the Los Angeles Philharmonic Orchestra at the Pavillion, Music Center, Los Angeles.

1972 *Don Juan in Hell,* by George Bernard Shaw. Starring: Paul Henreid, Ricardo Montalban, Edward Mulhare, Agnes Moorehead. National Tour: Music Center Almanson Theater, Los Angeles; Civic Theater, San Diego; Shubert Theater, Chicago; Shubert Theater, Boston; National Theater, Washington, D.C.; Shubert Theater, Cincinnati; Forrest, Philadelphia; Nixon Theater, Pittsburgh; The Playhouse, Wilmington; the O'Keefe Centre, Toronto; The Palace Theatre, New York. Producers: Lee Orgell and William J. Griffiths; Director: John Houseman.

Filmography

Title	Stars	Company, City	Director	Year
Baroud-Spahi	Rex Ingram Alice Terry	Nice	Rex Ingram	1932
High School	Rudolf Forster	Joseph Than, prod. Vienna	Erich Engel	1935
Only a Comedian	Rudolf Forster	Joseph Than, prod. Vienna	Erich Engel	1936
Goodbye Mr. Chips	Robert Donat	M.G.M. London	Sam Wood	1938
Under Your Hat	Edmund Gwenn	Elstree Studios London	Maurice Elvey	1939
An Englishman's Home	Edmund Gwenn	Elstree Studios London	Albert de Courville	1939
Night Train to Munich (in U.S., *Night Train*)	Margaret Lockwood Rex Harrison Paul von Hernried	20th-Century Fox London	Carol Reed	1939
Joan of Paris	Michele Morgan Paul Henreid	R.K.O. Hollywood	Robert Stevenson	1941

Now Voyager	Bette Davis Paul Henreid	Warner Brothers Hollywood	Irving Rapper	1942
Casablanca	Humphrey Bogart Ingrid Bergman Paul Henreid	Warner Brothers Hollywood	Michael Curtiz	1942
Rope of Sand	Burt Lancaster Paul Henreid	Paramount Hollywood	Wilhelm Dieterle	1949
Last of the Buccaneers	Paul Henreid Jack Oakie	S.K.-Columbia Hollywood	Lew Landers	1950
For Men Only	Paul Henreid	Paul Henreid, prod. Lippert-U.A. Hollywood	Paul Henreid	1951
Man in Hiding	Paul Henreid	U.A. London	Terence Fisher	1951
Stolen Face	Paul Henreid Lizabeth Scott	Lippert-U.A. London	Terence Fisher	1951
Thief of Damascus	Paul Henreid	S.K.-Columbia Hollywood	Will Jason	1951
Siren of Bagdad	Paul Henreid Patricia Medina	S.K.-Columbia Hollywood	Richard Quine	1952
There Is No Escape	Paul Henreid	U.A. London	Terence Fisher	1952

Title	Stars	Company, City	Director	Year
Deep in My Heart	Jose Ferrer Merle Oberon Paul Henreid	M.G.M. Hollywood	Stanley Donen	1954
Pirates of Tripoli	Paul Henreid Patricia Medina	S.K.-Columbia Hollywood	Felix Feist	1955
Cabaret	Paul Henreid	Carlton Films Munich	Willi Forst	1955
Battleshock	Ralph Meeker Janice Rule Paul Henreid	Republic Hollywood	Paul Henreid	1955
Meet Me in Las Vegas	Dan Dailey Cyd Charisse Paul Henreid	M.G.M. Hollywood	Roy Rowland	1956
Live Fast, Die Young	Mara Corday	Universal Hollywood	Paul Henreid	1957
Girls on the Loose	Mary Murphy	Universal Hollywood	Paul Henreid	1957
Never So Few	Frank Sinatra Paul Henreid	M.G.M. Hollywood	John Sturges	1959

Holiday for Lovers	Clifton Webb Jane Wyman Paul Henreid	20th-Century Fox Hollywood	Henry Levin	1959
Ten Thousand Bedrooms	Dean Martin Anna Maria Alberghetti, Paul Henreid	M.G.M. Rome, Hollywood	Richard Thorpe	1960
The Four Horsemen of the *Apocalypse*	Glenn Ford Ingrid Thulin Paul Henreid	M.G.M. Paris, Hollywood	Vincente Minnelli	1960
Dead Ringer	Bette Davis Karl Malden Peter Lawford	Warner Brothers Hollywood	Paul Henreid	1963
Blues for Lovers	Ray Charles Tom Bell	20th-Century Fox Dublin, London, Paris	Paul Henreid	1964
Operation Crossbow	Sophia Loren George Peppard Trevor Howard Paul Henreid	M.G.M. London	Michael Anderson	1964
The Madwoman of Chaillot	Katharine Hepburn Charles Boyer Yul Brynner Paul Henreid Danny Kaye	Warner Brothers Commonwealth United Nice	Bryan Forbes	1969

Title	Stars	Company, City	Director	Year
The Failing of Raymond	Jane Wyman Paul Henreid	Warner Brothers TV Movie Hollywood	Boris Sagal	1975
Death Among Friends	Martin Balsam	Warner Brothers TV Movie Hollywood	Paul Wendkos	1975
Exorcist II: The Heretic	Richard Burton Louise Fletcher Paul Henreid	Warner Brothers Hollywood	John Boorman	1977
One Coat of White	Claudette Colbert Paul Henreid	CBS—Playhouse 90 Hollywood	Ralph Nelson	1957

It seems to me that I directed well over 300 television pictures (or segments), some a half hour long, many one hour long, and a few one and a half hours long. I don't remember all of them today, but some I do, and will mention them: about 80 *Alfred Hitchcock Presents*, 20 *Schlitz Playhouse of Stars*, 12 *General Electric*, 5 *Alcoa-Goodyear*, 12 *Maverick*, 15 *Bourbon Street*, 3 *Wagon Train*, 4 *Cheyenne*. About 6 *Johnny Staccato*, 4 *Sam Benedict*, 15 *The Big Valley*, 14 *Bracken's World* for one of my very favorite producers, Stanley Rubin; 5 *Bonanza*, 20 *The Iron Horse*, 5 *Thriller*, 14 *Man and the City*, starring my friend and the excellent actor, Anthony Quinn, and produced, again, by my dear friend, Stanley Rubin.

INDEX